THE GARDENS OF VERSAILLES

Raphaël Masson
Chief heritage curator, Musée National
des Châteaux de Versailles et de Trianon.

With the participation of, for the texts on trees, Gabriela Lamy, researcher,
Service des Jardins de Trianon, Direction du Patrimoine et des Jardins.

CHÂTEAU DE VERSAILLES

Views, parterres, fountains, cascades, groves, surprises – there are not enough words to describe the gardens of Versailles and Trianon. Louis XIV wanted them to be as important – if not more important – than the château, which they momentarily, through André Le Nôtre's brilliant witticism, erase from view when one goes up the Tapis-Vert. Sketched out by Louis XIII, designed throughout the reign of Louis XIV, they acquired incomparable strength because they combine the pleasure of the stroll with that of the eyes, all the while bearing witness to the prestige of power. Louis XIV walked there every day, sustaining his interest in them with the – rare – friendship he had for their creator, Le Nôtre.

He was the first guide to the gardens, precise, loving, concerned about the visitor who would linger in one of the most beautiful and largest open-air museums in the world. Raphaël Masson, chief heritage curator at the Château de Versailles, now follows in the monarch's footsteps. Without saying, he follows the instructions, as of the sequencing of the visit – which the king revised several times – was in the end immutable by the very coherence given to it by its designer. Even with this help, Masson imposes nothing. He suggests an itinerary to today's visitors, gives them the keys to understanding these extraordinary gardens, guides their gazes when they get lost, prepares them for the extraordinary dimensions of the estate and trains them in the genealogy of the gods that inhabit it.

Whether visitors are strolling through the falsely strict alleys of Versailles or getting lost among the falsely disorderly flowers of Trianon, emotion very quickly immerses geometry.

This guide is a framework from which our minds escape because every hour of the day the gardens meet the sky, which changes them, revealing new beauties and illusions. Although he approaches them as an expert, Masson is not immune to the magic of the place. For those, like him, who have the chance of frequenting them often, the points of interest follow each other and can change one's mood. And then the groves that reveal themselves in turn seem inseparable like an archipelago. One reveals the other over the seasons, enchanting them with infinite colours. However, behind the words, sometimes a preference appears: the Colonnade Grove, which "spectacularly celebrates the triumph of architecture in the gardens of Versailles"; the Temple of Love, one of the edifices commissioned by Marie-Antoinette to decorate the Trianon gardens, "masterpieces of equilibrium and elegance". A few stops discretely privileged by the author, like an extra, personal invitation to read this guide, which thus becomes – better than a guide – a way of telling the story of Versailles to his friends.

Catherine Pégard
President, Établissement Public
du Château, du Musée et du Domaine National de Versailles

CONTENTS

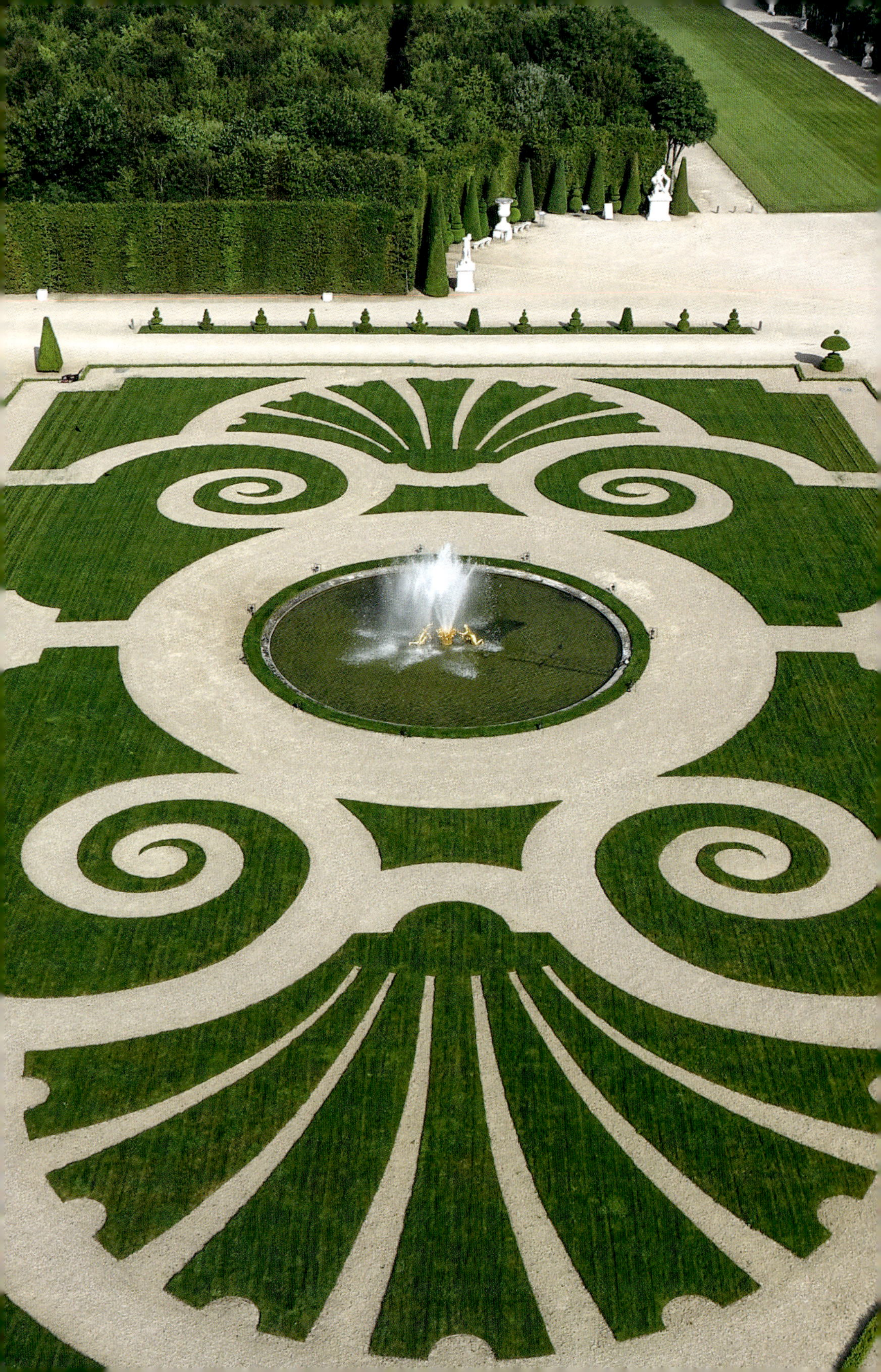

Foreword

The guidebook is a genuine literary genre to which a certain number of inspired writers-cum-travellers have lent prestige. In this family, the books dedicated to remarkable gardens have a particular savour and there is no shortage of prestigious examples. In the case of Versailles, the bar was immediately placed at the highest because it was Louis XIV himself who wrote the first one. His *Manière de montrer les jardins de Versailles* was particularly concise but, on principle, unsurpassable. We will, however, lean more in the present volume while finding a spirit faithful to the soberly metaphysical reflections of the Sun King. Although these gardens have been in existence for nearly four centuries, it is surprising to observe to what extent they correspond to a great project of Louis XIV and were only modified on an ad hoc basis during later periods. It's almost as though this Herculean achievement, once implemented – not to say completed, for this word does not exist at Versailles – could thereafter undergo only minor alterations. With the exception of the Petit Trianon, first dedicated to the botanical passion of Louis XV, then to the country and Anglo-Chinese fantasy of Marie-Antoinette, most of the gardens and grounds refer to the seventeenth century. The eighteenth-century modifications, such as the Queen's Grove and the Romantic landscape designed by Hubert Robert in the Apollo Grove, were far fewer in number than the incessant rewriting of the space and the upheavals of the iconographical programme that troubled the estate from the 1660s to the death of Louis XIV. It is now as difficult to read this landscape as it is to comprehend the château interior, with its strata of decoration and furnishings, scars and superpositions. In the garden, generations of trees followed each other, trellises suddenly sprang up to slowly disintegrate, statues strolled around and, more than once, putti escaped from one basin to another. This book, clear and precise, gives us the knowledge required for our enjoyment, to guide our steps while respecting the pleasure of wandering, to strengthen the sensations that may only be found in the alleys of Versailles.

Laurent Salomé
Director, Musée National des Châteaux
de Versailles et de Trianon

Aerial view of the Latona Parterre, on the south side.

INTRODUCTION

A few historical observations by way of an introduction

It was in August 1607 that the future Louis XIII, then six years old, came to Versailles for the first time to hunt in the company of his father, Henri IV. After he had become king, he frequented the place with his hunting parties and, from 1623, decided to build a modest hunting lodge there, which was completed the following year. Between 1631 and 1634, he had the building profoundly modified and extended, while gradually enlarging the estate. The future Louis XIV visited Versailles for the first time in 1641, when he was three years old. The garden developed very slowly, with a first parterre laid out under the west façade of the château. In the distance, heading westward, the park was made up of *carrés*, large wooded compartments crossed by orthogonal alleys. This plan definitively set the overall organisation of the gardens and laid out its alleys like a skeleton, which would not be modified. A few years later, the acquisition of land to the north and south of the château allowed the surroundings to be landscaped, especially on the south side where a vegetable garden, an orchard, and a small grove planted with holly – the future "Bois-Vert", that the enlargement of the South Parterre would latter make disappear – were created. When he died, in 1643, Louis XIII left an estate that occupied the present surface area of the garden, ending to the west with an ornamental lake, the future Apollo Basin.

Under the supervision of André Le Nôtre (1613–1700), the original garden underwent the most significant and spectacular transformations in its history. The *carrés* were kept but, traversed by new alleys, they henceforth housed groves enlivened by a variety of water effects, which became genuine *salons de verdure*. Major earthworks reduced the difference in level of the Royal Alley and contributed to the clearer structuring of the new spaces, such as the parterres and the Latona Amphitheatre. Over the years, increasingly sophisticated groves saw the light of day: the Dauphin's Grove and the Girandole Grove (1663); the Star Grove (1666); the Labyrinth Grove, the Feasting Chamber Grove, the Marsh Grove and the Water Theatre Grove (1674); the Grove of Fame (1675); the Triumphal Arch Grove and the Three Fountains Grove (1677); the Springs Grove and the Ancients Grove (1678); and the Ballroom Grove (1685). The alleys were also punctuated with fountains, such as the four basins of the seasons, whose exuberant decoration was completed in 1677. At the same time, the large ornamental lakes contributed their size, marking the horizon while opening it up to infinity towards the sky reflected in it: the Grand Canal (1668–73), the Neptune Basin (1678–82) and the Lake of the Swiss Guards (1679–86).

Louis XIV's first garden was the setting for lavish festivities, whose main vocation was to highlight the embellishments the king constantly added. It was also characterised by the imaginativeness of its fountains and the joyous, colourful profusion of its decoration. It was a triumph of gilded or naturalistically painted lead, and sandstone structures and trellises with complex and original architecture.

At the turn of the eighteenth century, at the instigation of Jules Hardouin-Mansart (1646–1708), who had been appointed superintendent of the King's Buildings in 1699, the gardens became simpler. New alleys profoundly transformed the stroller's perception: groves accessible only by winding paths that contributed to the surprise caused by their sudden discovery, were henceforth traversed from end to end and became the ornaments of a more orderly stroll. It was a time of

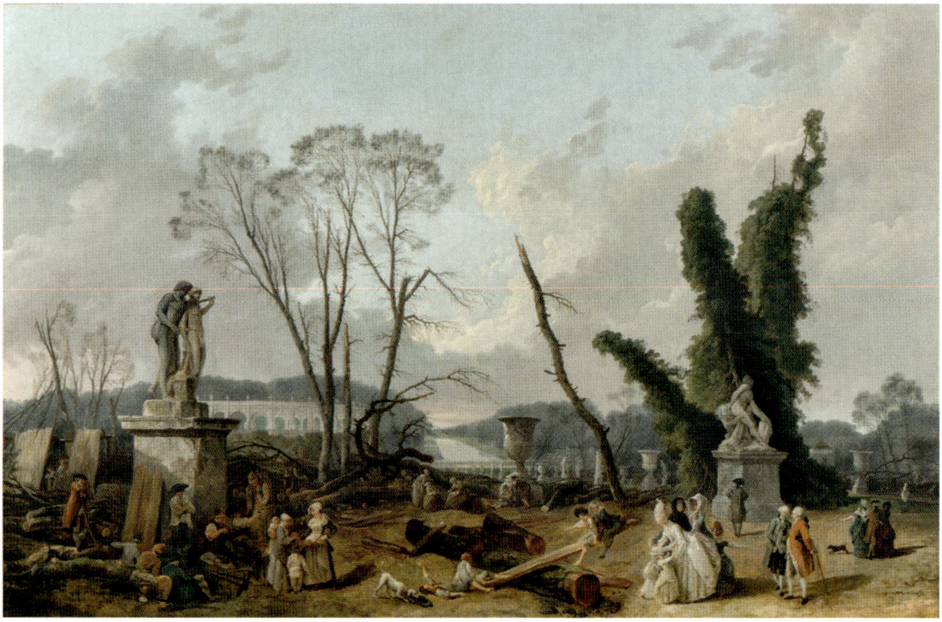

The replanting of the park in 1777 as seen by the painter Hubert Robert. In the distance, one can make out the Colonnade and the Grand Canal, and, on the right, one of the no longer extant pavilions of the Domes Grove.

simplification and a certain ennoblement: marble replaced stone, bronze replaced lead. The basins of the Seasons were made simpler, Mansart built his majestic Colonnade (1688), the Water Parterre was adorned by the Keller brothers' cast iron, the Enceladus Grove lost its trelliswork gallery, the Star Grove its labyrinthine character and the Feasting Chamber Grove gave way to the Obelisk Grove It was a change in style that, inside the château, was conveyed by the king's new apartments, completed in 1701.

After his death on 1 September 1715, Louis XIV left behind a finished garden (except for the Neptune Basin) that his successor Louis XV maintained with respect, only making minor modifications to it. When he acceded the throne in 1774, Louis XVI had to, on the other hand, make the difficult decision to replant the entire park, whose trees had reached maturity. This took place from 1775 to 1778 and was immortalized by the painter Hubert Robert. The king ordered that the gardens be replanted according to the plan by Le Nôtre but had to reconcile himself to getting rid of the most highly altered groves (and the most out of fashion), including the Labyrinth Grove replaced by the Venus Grove or Queen's Grove. The Grove of Apollo's Baths was entirely redesigned in the style of the day.

In the nineteenth century, the garden was maintained and the arrival of the railway to Versailles in 1839 popularised the Grandes Eaux, performed certain Sundays and which attracted crowds of Parisians. The park was replanted again during the Second Empire. More recently, the violent storms of the late twentieth century (those of 1990 and 1999 especially) caused great damage to hundred-year-old trees and led to another overall replantation, which was completed in 2010. The replanting was accompanied by the renovation of some of the disappeared groves, such as the Three Fountains Grove, the Dauphin's Grove and the Girandole Grove; the restoration of the

Enceladus Grove, the Orangery Parterre and the Latona Parterre; the restoration of the Fountain of France Triumphant, the last vestige of the Triumphal Arch Grove; and the creation of a contemporary garden on the site of the former Water Theatre.

By way of advice to visitors

The gardens of Versailles are beautiful at any time of day, in all seasons, and in all kinds of weather. Every stroll allows new beauties to be discovered: a vantage point, the detail of a sculpture, lighting – you should not be afraid of getting lost during a walk guided by chance: let yourself be surprised by the incomparable harmony of the place.

Long scorned for its regularity, synonymous with being boring, the *jardin régulier* (French formal garden, which became known as the *jardin à la française* during the triumph of the *jardin à l'anglaise*, or landscaped garden) is on the contrary a source of wonder and easily perceptible surprises that you soon make a game of discovering and appreciating. One example among many: watching the château shrink, lose a floor, and gradually disappear as you go up the Royal Alley. At the foot of the Latona Staircase, it has completely disappeared. A few steps higher, it surges theatrically, set in the jewel box of its parterres, revealing, from the North Wing to the South Wing the incomparable majesty of its façades.

The present guide, which will also accompany visitors to Trianon and Marly, whose history will be briefly recounted, aims to provide them with the most important information and enable them to make the most complete visit possible. At the back, it contains a deliberately short bibliography featuring easily accessible references that will allow readers to pursue their discovery of one of the most beautiful gardens in the world.

THE GARDENS AND GROUNDS OF THE CHÂTEAU

Aerial view of the Latona Amphitheatre.

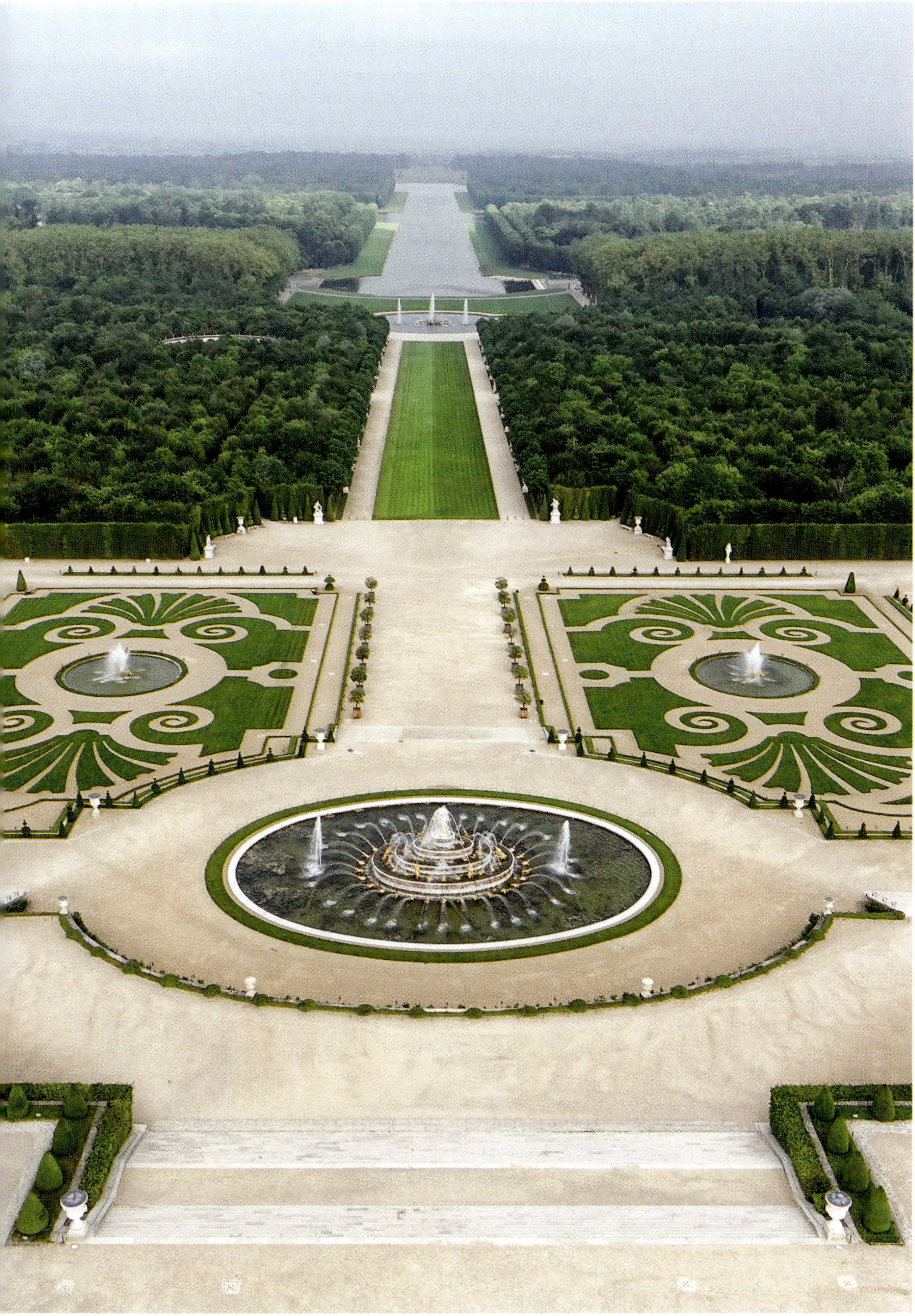

THE PARTERRES

The Water Parterre

At the foot of the central section of the château, the Water Parterre marks the starting point of the vista that extends to the Grand Canal and beyond. Meant to highlight the garden façade, the parterre, whose surface area is close to 2 hectares, has had various layouts. In 1672, after the construction of Le Vau's envelope, Charles Le Brun – to replace the older parterre inherited from Louis XIII – proposed a very elaborate plan in which the statues of the Great Commission were placed around a basin with a complex design. In around 1685, the parterre was once again entirely transformed, taking on its present configuration. The basin was destroyed to make way for two vast rectangular reflecting pools whose marble edge was punctuated by twenty-four bronze groups, made between 1688 and 1691, representing river deities, nymphs and children. To begin with, the centres of the pools were supposed to contain a sculpted group, one dedicated to Tethys, the other to Venus, but these groups were never executed. As in the rest of the garden, the successive modifications tended towards greater simplicity, marking the triumph of purity of line over complex layouts and decorations.

The shorter sides of each of the basins are occupied by allegories of the rivers of France. Each river, symbolised by a bearded man, is accompanied by one of its tributaries, represented by a female figure. The north basin thus contains *The Garonne* and *The Dordogne* by Coysevox (to the east of the château), a well as *The Seine* and *The Marne* by Le Hongre (to the west). On the edge of the south basin are *The Loire* and *The Loiret* by Regnaudin (to the east), and *The Rhône* and *The Saône* by Tuby (to the west). Along the longer sides, nymphs and water deities alternate with groups of children. Most of these remarkable bronzes were cast under the supervision of Balthasar Keller. Keller also cast the four bronzes after classical models placed at the foot of the château façade in around 1700:

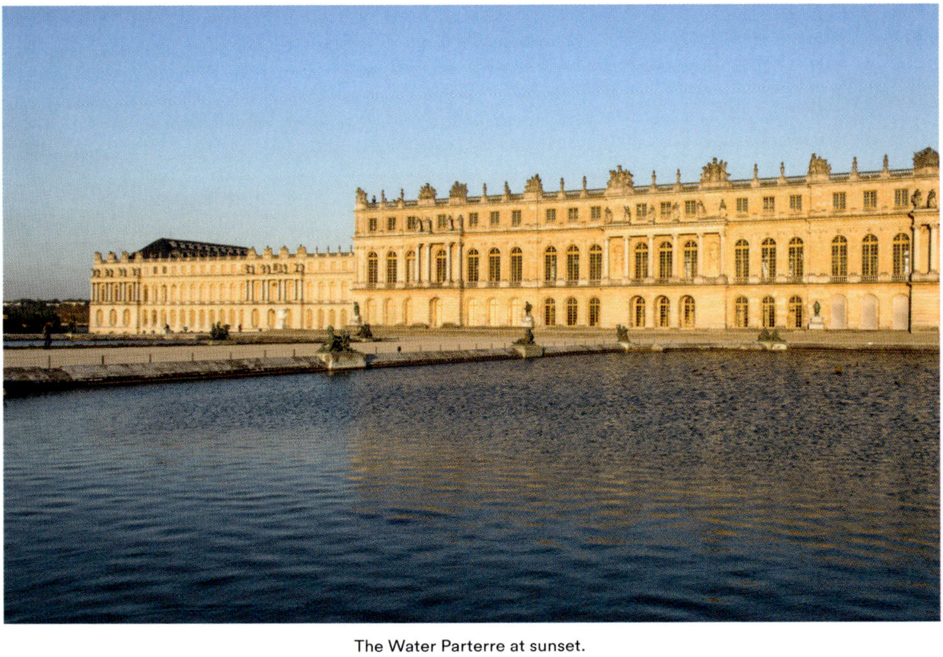

The Water Parterre at sunset.

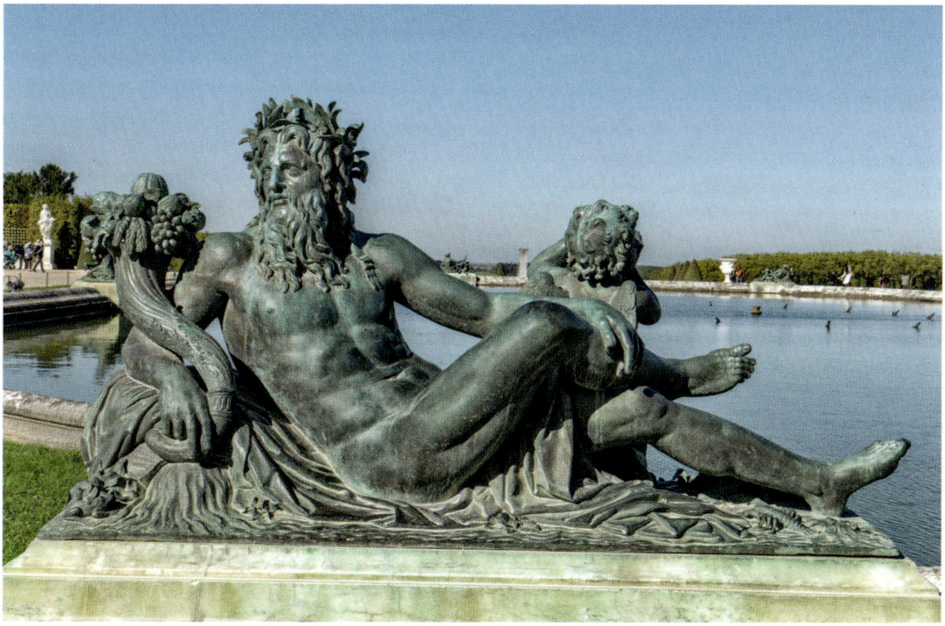

The Loire by Regnaudin (1685), edge of the south basin of the Water Parterre.

Bacchus at Rest, known as *the Versailles Bacchus*; *Belvedere Apollo*; *Belvedere Antinous*; and *Silenus Carrying Bacchus*, also known as the *Large Borghese Faun*.

Two gigantic marble vases, installed in 1686, complete the terrace decoration: the *War Vase* by Coysevox (to the north) and the *Peace Vase* by Tuby (to the south). Weakened, they were removed in 2013, put somewhere sheltered, and replaced by copies.

In the eighteenth century, the Water Parterre was often used for illuminations or fireworks, which the king and the court could admire from the windows of the Hall of Mirrors located on the first floor of the château. At the time, the perspective was often closed by painted canvas decorations representing architecture featuring colonnades and pavilions to which multitudes of light sources gave a magical aspect. In 1773, on the occasion of the marriage of the Comte d'Artois, a large fireworks performance was given on the basins themselves, on which had been build settings evocative of Vulcan's forges.

The North Parterre

The North Parterre was laid out from 1663. Originally, it only occupied half its present surface area and spread out exactly under the north façade of the central section of the château. From 1666, its surface area was doubled to the west, the alley that used to be beside it in this direction becoming the present central alley, which was extended by the Water Alley to the Neptune Basin. This substantial increase in size now makes it one of the largest parterres in the garden (more than 2.3 hectares). It is surrounded by marble bases that, to the east and to the west, follow the incline of the terrain by forming a ramp. The south base is adorned with fourteen bronze vases in seven different versions cast after models given by the goldsmith to the king, Claude Ballin. They are accompanied by marble vases. The staircase descending from the parterre is flanked by two bronze statues made in the seventeenth century after classical models: *The Knife Grinder*

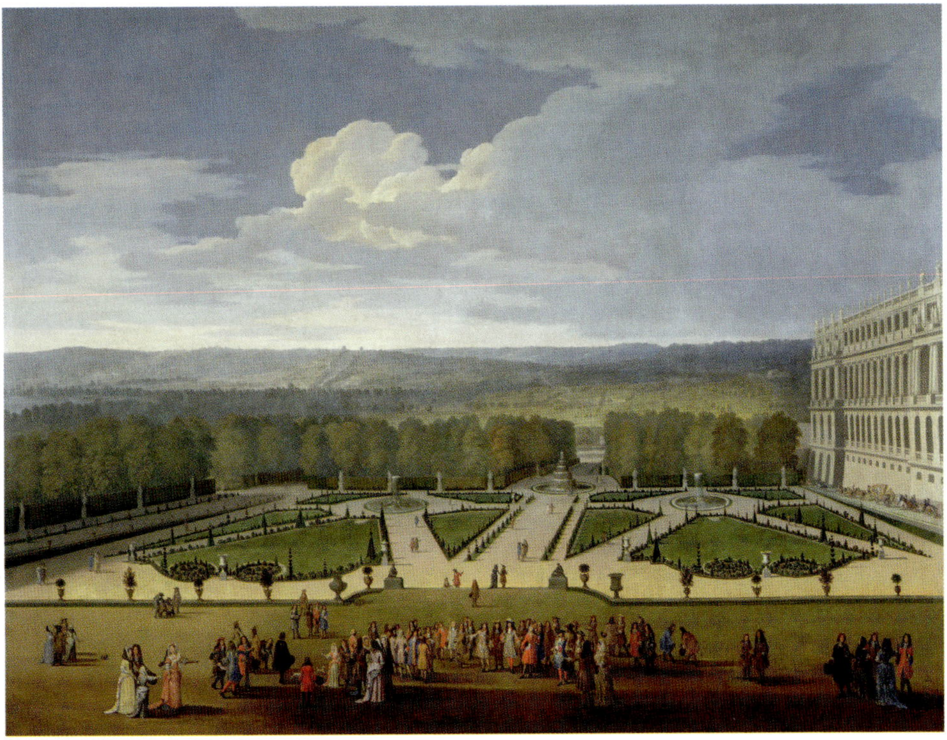

Étienne Allegrain, *Louis XIV Walks on the North Parterre*, c. 1688.

(François Girardon) and *Modest Venus* (Antoine Coysevox). At Venus' feet is a turtle, an animal that then symbolised reserve and modesty.

Divided into two groups of five compartments each adorned with a basin in which tritons and sirens swim, the parterre is a fine example of large sections of lawn divided by alleys and lined by a double box hedge outlining the flowerbeds. To the north and the west, along the hedges, some of the statues from the Great Commission were arranged when they left the Water Parterre. To the west, immediately after the Evening Fountain, are *Europe* (Mazeline), *Africa* (Cornu), *Night* (Raon), *Earth* (Massou) and *The Pastoral Poem* (Granier).

Beside the Three Fountains Grove, we can make out *Autumn* (Regnaudin), *America* (Guérin), *Summer* (Hutinot), *Winter* (Girardon) and, a little lower at the entrance to the Water Alley, *The Sanguine* (Jouvenet), and opposite, *The Choleric* (Houzeau). Beside the Triumphal Arch Grove are *The Satirical Poem* (Buyster), *Asia* (Roger), *The Phlegmatic* (Lespagnandelle) and *The Heroic Poem* (Houzeau).

The South Parterre

Located under the windows of the Queen's Apartment, a first parterre was laid out in 1663. In 1667 a basin, adorned with a cupid shooting an arrow by Lerambert (which may have been found and acquired by the château in 2009), gave it its first name, the Parterre d'Amour. In 1682, when the orangery was being completely rebuilt by Jules Hardouin-Mansart and its length doubled to the west, the surface area of the parterre was doubled to nearly 20,000 square metres. It is a parterre de broderie whose complex design, the result of rows of box on a coloured ground of crushed brick, is mean to be seen from a high vantage point, like the alleys that surround the ensemble or, even better, the windows of the first floor of the château. Exceptionally, the two basins feature no sculpted decoration. A simple spray of water animates them during the Grandes Eaux (fountain shows).

Like the North Parterre, the South Parterre features a marble base on three of its four sides. The bases are adorned with bronze vases. Only those of the north bass, on the château side, are original; they were designed by the goldsmith Ballin. The eighteen other vases of the eastern and western bases were added under Napoleon III, copied from the existing vases. Four pairs of large marble vases were installed in the corner of the parterre in 1701. Only two of them – placed in the north-east corner and made by Claude Bertin – are historiated, one of them showing Numa Pompilius, one of the legendary kings of Rome, entrusting the sacred fire to the vestal virgins and the other a sacrifice to Bacchus.

The main access to the parterre is via a staircase flanked by two marble female sphinxes straddled by cherubs. The model was by Jacques Sarrasin and the execution by the sculptors Jacques Houzeau and Jacques Lerambert, and the caster Ambroise Duval. Placed on top of the staircase of the Latona Parterre in 1670, they were moved to this spot in 1685. They now seem to incite the visitor to enter the parterre and go to the end where, once the balustrade is reached, the

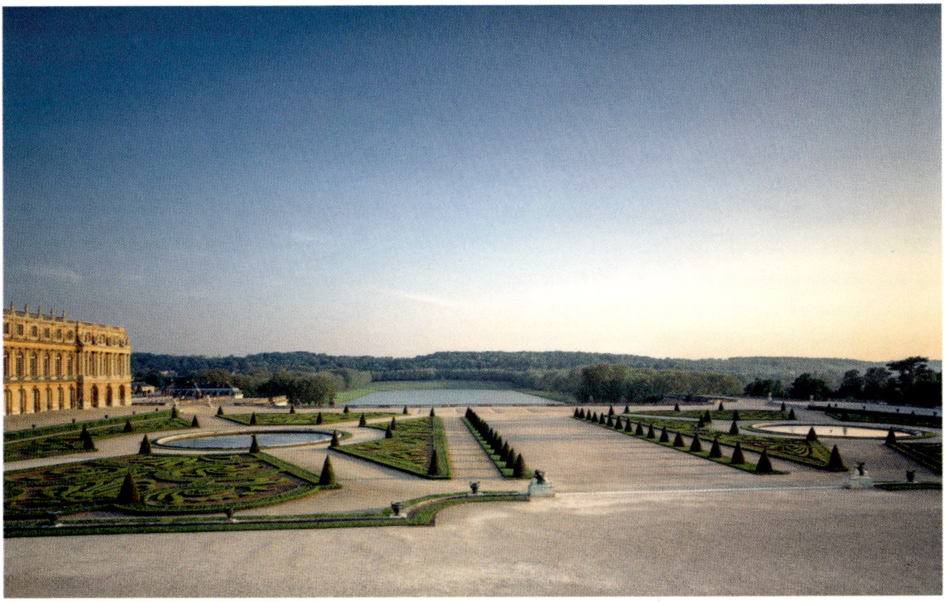

The South Parterre and the Lake of the Swiss Guards from the windows of the Queen's Apartments.

entire orangery parterre is unveiled.

To the west of the parterre, the balustrade is adorned with a marble *Sleeping Ariadne*, made after a classical original by Corneille Van Clève and completed in 1686.

The Cabinets des Animaux

To the west of the Water Parterre, the perspective is flanked by two fountains whose small dimensions and surrounding arbours earned them the name “cabinet”, an allusion to a *cabinet de verdure*. They are square basins whose elevated edge allows for the formation of an expanse of water flossing into a small canal. Completed in 1687, they are decorated with bronze groups whose jets contribute to the animation of the fountain. Each group depicts a combat between two animals. The victorious animal spits water into the upper basin, the vanquished in the lower basin.

North cabinet:

Lion Flooring a Boar by Jean Raon
Lion Flooring a Wolf by Corneille Van Clève

South cabinet:

Tigre Flooring a Bear by Jacques Houzeau
Bloodhound Flooring a Deer by Jacques Houzeau

All these animals were cast in bronze by the Keller brothers.

The presence of works from the Great Commission near each of these fountains explains why they are sometimes called the Evening Fountain or Diana Fountain (to the north) and the Daybreak Fountain (to the south), in reference to the statue *Evening, or Diana* by Martin Desjardins and the statue *Break of Day* by Gaspard Marsy. Near the Daybreak Fountain are two other works from the Great Commission: *Water* (Legros) and *Spring* (Magnier). Likewise, to the north, *Air* (Le Hongre) and *Noon* (Marsy) surround the Evening Fountain.

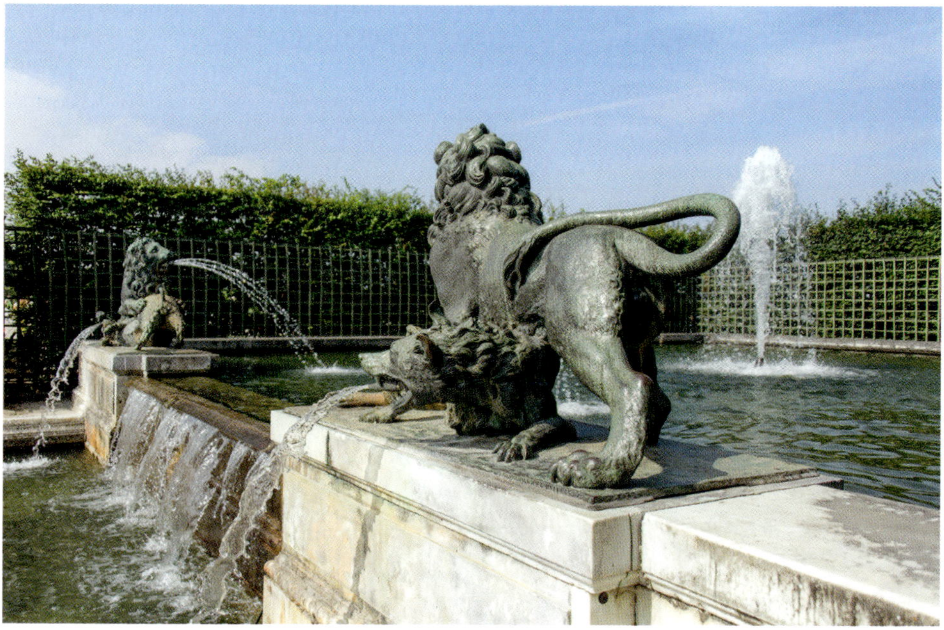

The North Cabinet des Animaux or Evening Fountain.

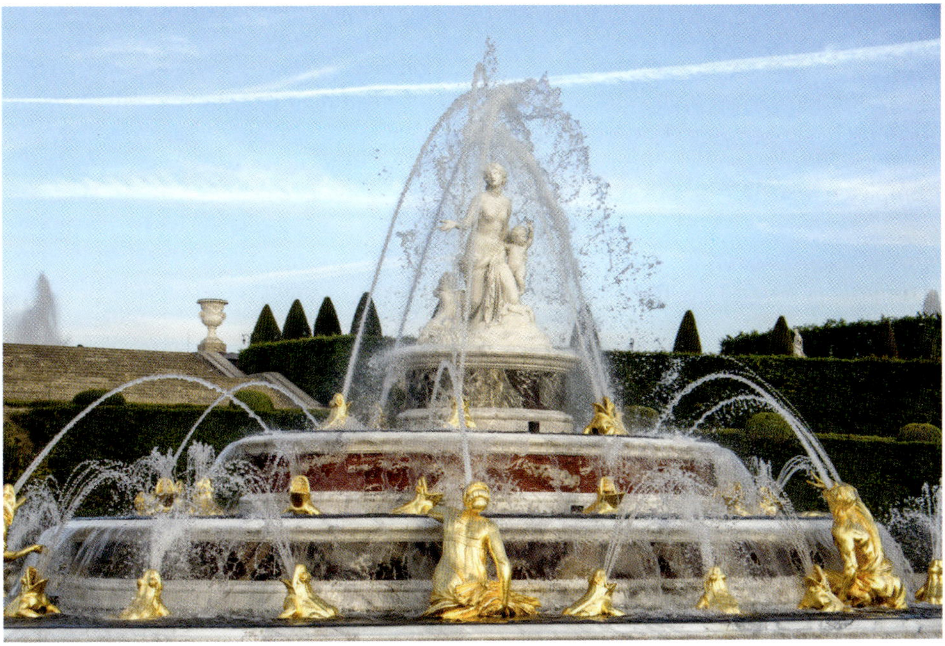

Latona Basin.

The Latona Parterre and the Latona Basin

At the end of the Water Parterre, the visitor reaches the top of a large staircase from which he can view the new landscape spreading out before him. There, he can see what was invisible from the château: the Latona Basin, the inclines surrounding it, highlighted by yews and statues, the lawn parterres, the two Lizards Basins as well as the top of the Royal Alley, not forgetting, on either side, the wooded areas of the groves. This viewpoint allows us to understand how Le Nôtre managed to organise the landscape by structuring it into the coherent large ensembles of wooded spaces, open ground and ornamental lakes.

The vast Latona Amphitheatre was built between 1665 and 1668. Dug out at the bottom of the stairs descending from the Water Parterre, the basin was given, in 1670, decoration sculpted by Gaspard and Balthasar Marsy, evoking an episode in the story of Latona. Seduced by Jupiter, Latona gave birth to Apollo and Diana. Pursued by the wrath of Juno, Jupiter's wife, Latona fled to Lycia where, stopping near a pond, she was pushed away by the peasants who refused to let her drink there and deliberately muddied the waters. To punish them for their insensitivity, Jupiter turned them into frogs. Latona exclaimed: "May you live forever in your pond!" The Marsy brothers depicted the moment when the goddess launched her curse at the heavens. The marble group was originally placed at the centre of the basin, on a small island encircled by tin reeds. It was surrounded by six statues of peasants being turned into frogs. Eighteen frogs were placed in a circle on the edge. This arrangement was completely changed by Jules Hardouin-Mansart between 1687 and 1689. The

Following pages:
The Latona Amphitheatre,
the Water Parterre and the château.

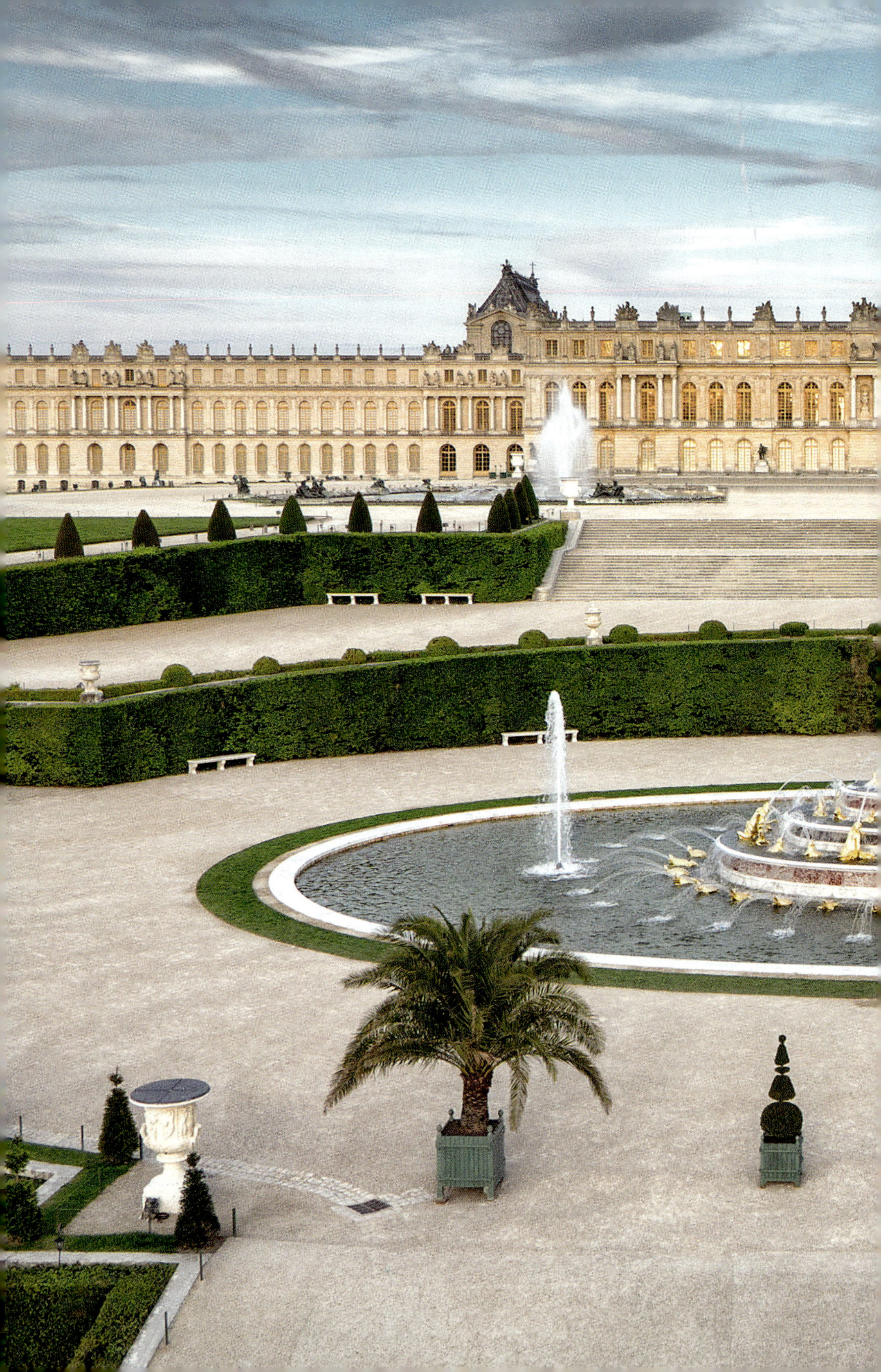

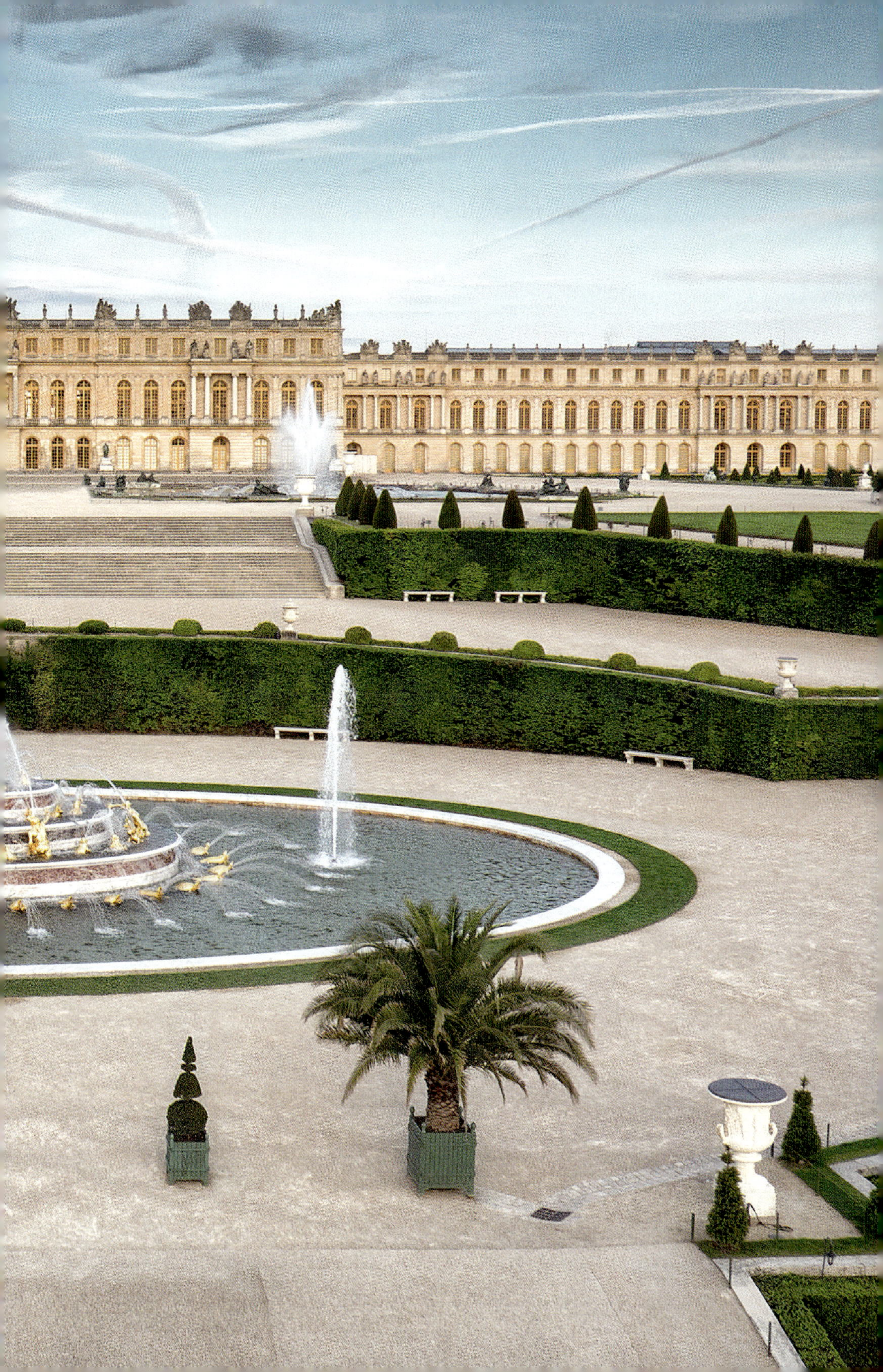

basin was then endowed with a large marble pyramid on whose terraces were placed the original sculptures as well as new frogs made by Claude Bertin. At the base, the fifteen turtles and fifteen lizards come in part from the two neighbouring circular basins where they accompanied two groups of peasants by the Marsy brothers; the others are the result of a complementary commission entrusted to Claude Bertin.

People have long wanted to see in the representation of this episode a direct allusion to the troubled time of the Fronde and see Anne of Austria in the figure of Latona, and Louis XIV and his brother in the two children. The transformation of the peasants of Lycia into frogs may thus have been a warning against any sort of opposition to royal authority by showing the humiliation of the Frondeurs. This widely spread hypothesis is not, however, supported by any texts from the reign of Louis XIV. All the descriptions of the garden, on the contrary, note its appropriateness to the Apollonian theme that reigns at Versailles.

Organised in sections of lawn, the Latona Parterre is surrounded by a gently sloping vast ramp along which clipped yews and statues alternate. The statues, apart from the three that belong to the Great Commission series, are all copies after famous classical models belonging to the most prestigious Roman collections and placed here by order of the king to show the degree of excellence of French sculptors. There are even two versions of some of these sculptures, such as *The Capitoline Urania* and *The Belvedere Antinous*. Going down the South Ramp, one will successively see: *The Heroic Poem* (Tuby), *Fire* (Dossier), a *Farnese Prisoner*, also known as *Tiridates* (André), *Farnese Callipygian Venus* (Clérion), *Silenus Carrying Bacchus*, or *Large Borghese Faun* (Mazière), *Belvedere Antinous* (Legros), *Farnese Mercury* (Mélo), *Capitoline Urania* (Carlier), *Belvedere Apollo* (Mazeline) and the *Dying Galatian Ludovisi* (Monier). On the north ramp, descending: *Melancholy* (La Perdrix), *Belvedere Antinous* (Lacroix), *Farnese Prisoner*, also known as *Tigranes* (Lespagnandelle), *Faun Playing the Flute*, also known as the *Small Borghese Faun* (Hurtrelle), *Medici Bacchus* (Granier), *Mattei Ceres* (Regnaudin), *Belvedere Hercules Commodus* (Coustou), *Capitoline Urania* (Frémery), *Medici Ganymede* (Laviron) and *Borghese Nymph with a Shell* (Coysevox). The later was replaced by a copy by Auguste Suchetet in 1891 and taken to the Louvre.

On the west side, the arbours circumscribing the Girandole Grove and the Dauphin's Grove are lined with a series of ten marble terms put up in around 1690.

In addition to the abundant statuary, visitors should not forget to pay particular attention to the marble vases that adorn the ensemble, beginning with the two imposing Sun vases executed by Drouilly and Dugoulon placed on top of the steps of the Grand Degré, replacing the female sphinxes of the South Parterre. They are decorated with suns with masks of Apollo surrounded by laurels and heliotropes. On the steps that dominate the Latona Basin, four other vases, made by the students of the French Academy in Rome after classical models. Finally, on the parterre, eight vases feature various scenes, including Mars' triumphs, a direct allusion to the king's military victories.

The Royal Alley

The plan of the Royal Alley dates to the original garden of the château of Louis XIII, but its aspect was regularly modified until the eighteenth century. It was originally no more than 15 metres wide and much more steeply inclined than it is today. In 1667 major levelling works reduced the declivity of the terrain and the dimensions of the alley were brought to approximately 45 metres. Initially decorated with stone terms, the alley received, from 1684, a vast commission of marble vases and statues, original creations or copies after classical originals. In 1680 a broad strip of grass gave it its present aspect as well as its other name, the Tapis-Vert. During the replanting of the gardens at the beginning of the reign of Louis XVI, the alley was lined with chestnut trees.

Among the most remarkable works of the Royal Alley are two sculpted groups by Pierre Puget, placed at the top of the alley on the orders of the king himself: *Milo of Croton* to the south and *Perseus Delivering Andromeda* to the north. The originals were transferred to the Louvre in 1819 and 1850 respectively; casts were made of them in 2013. The casts are now in Versailles in the locations occupied by the originals until the nineteenth century. Two copies of classical statues accompany them: *Castor and Pollux* by Coysevox and *Papirius and His Mother* by Massou, Carlier and Monier.

On either side, six pairs of marble vases alternate with statues and benches contrasting with topiary planted between the chestnut trees. On the south side, from top to bottom, are the following sculptures: *Fidelity* (Lefebvre), *The Richelieu Venus* (Legros), *Faun with Kid* (Flamen), *Dido* (Poultier), *The Mattei Amazon* (Buirette) and *Achilles at Skyros* (Vigier). To the north, from top to bottom: *Treachery* (Leconte), *Juno of Smyrna* (classical statute completed by Granier), *The Belvedere Hercules Commodus* (Jouvenet), *The Medici Venus* (Monier and Frémery), *Cyparissus* (Flamen) and *Artemisia* (Lefebvre and Desjardins).

Following pages:
The Apollo Basin and the Royal Alley

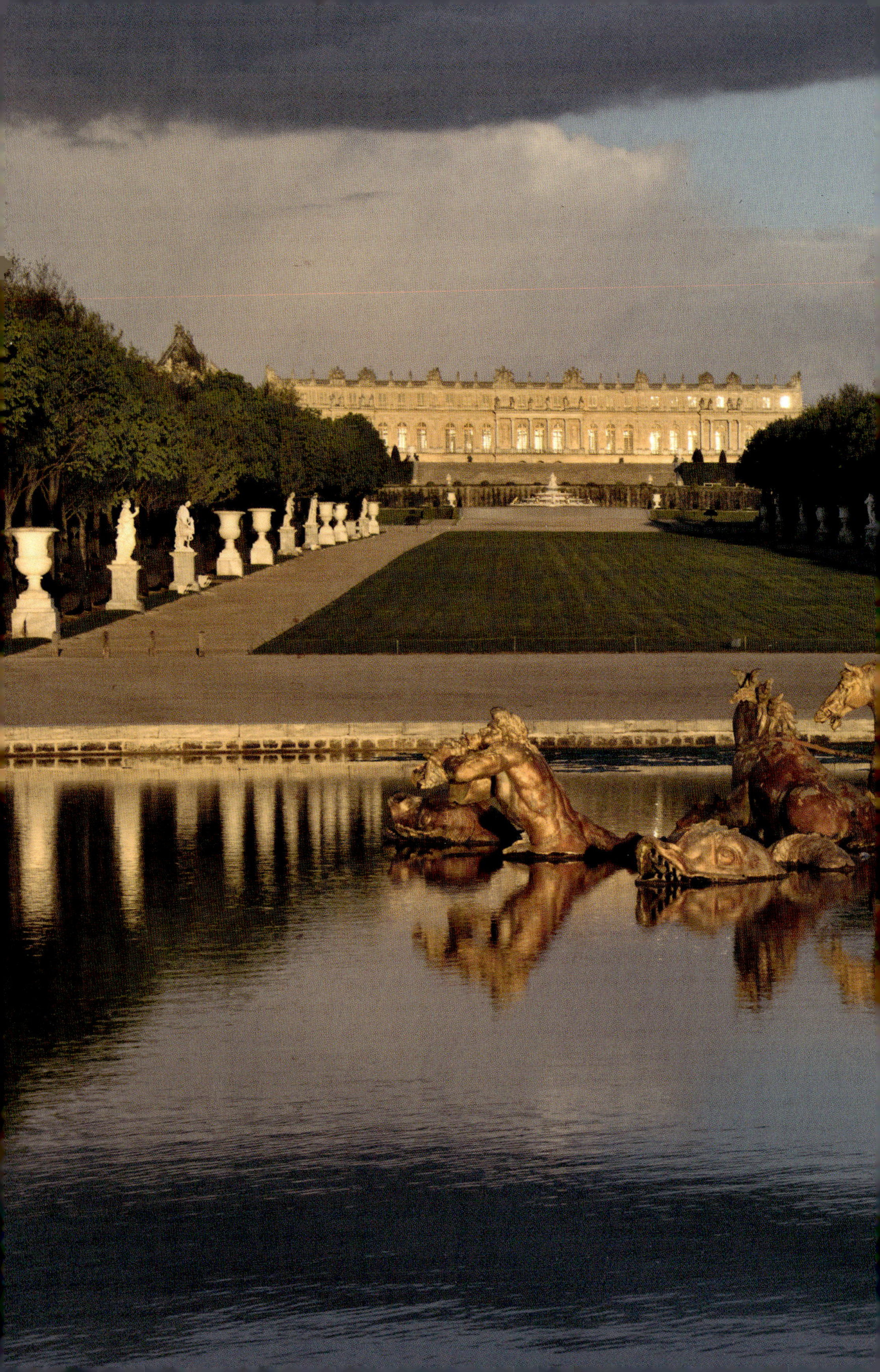

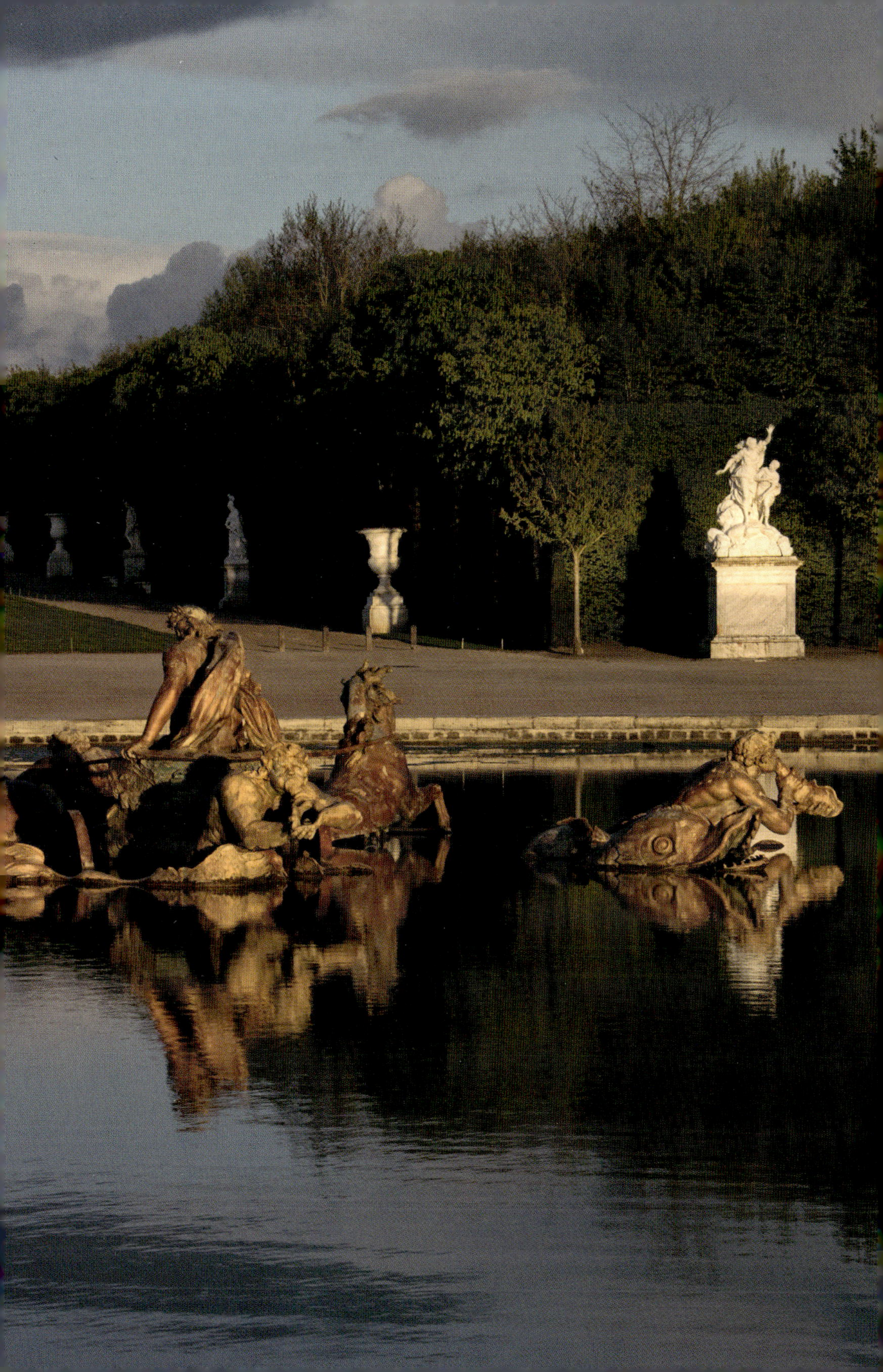

The Great Commission

This was the name given to a major commission of sculptures ordered by Colbert to decorate the Water Parterre from 1674. Charles Le Brun was charged with supplying the designs, while the execution of the twenty-four statues (six series of four) was entrusted to twenty or so sculptors who delivered their works until 1687. In the meantime, the radical modification of the plans for the Water Parterre led to the installation of the sculptures on the edges of the North Parterre and at the top of the Latona Amphitheatre. The allegorical and iconographical coherence of the series thus became secondary.

The six allegorical series are thus divided:

– the four seasons: *Spring* (Magnier), *Summer* (Hutinot), *Autumn* (Regnaudin) and *Winter* (Girardon);

– the four parts of the day: *Daybreak* (Marsy), *Noon* (Marsy), *Evening* (Desjardins) and *Night* (Raon);

– the four elements: *Earth* (Massou), *Air* (Le Hongre), *Water* (Legros) and *Fire* (Dossier);

– the four parts of the world: *Europe* (Mazeline), *Asia* (Roger), *Africa* (Sibrayque and Cornu) and *America* (Guérin);

– the four temperaments of man: *Choleric* (Houzeau), *Phlegmatic* (Lespagnandelle), *Sanguine* (Jouvenet) and *Melancholic* (La Perdrix);

– the four poetic genres: *The Lyric Poem* (Tuby), *The Heroic Poem* (Drouilly), *The Pastoral Poem* (Granier) and *The Satirical Poem* (Buyster).
Weakened by weather and pollution, all these works, which constitute a remarkable collection and an incomparable anthology of seventeenth-century French sculpture, were sheltered and replaced in situ by casts.

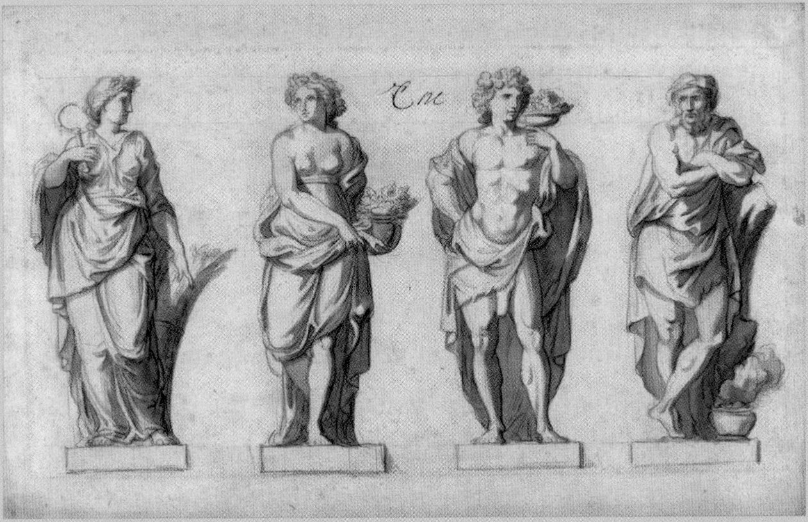

Studio of Charles Le Brun, *The Four Seasons*, plan for the Great Commission (1674).

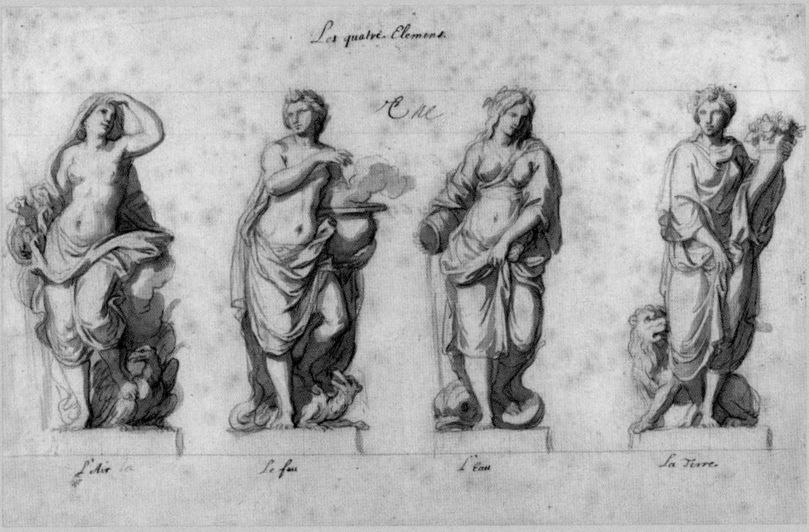

Studio of Charles Le Brun, *The Four Elements*, plan for the Great Commission (1674).

The Basins of the Seasons

The two alleys parallel to the Royal Alley, one to the north, the other to the south, are punctuated with intersections, four of which are occupied by basins evoking the four seasons. The first two basins, circular, were dug from 1662–63 in the bottom of the garden (the future Flora Basin, to the north, and Saturn Basin, to the south). In 1672 two other, octagonal basins were laid out closer to the château and the parterres (the Ceres Basin, to the north, and the Bacchus Basin, to the south). Between 1673 and 1677, the ensemble was given a rich decoration of lead, blending gold and naturalistic painting – each central group was accompanied by small groups of children arranged in the basin while the edges disappeared underneath exuberant lead motifs, themselves also gilt or painted naturalistically and taking up the themes of each of the seasons: flowers for spring; wheat sheaves combined with pigeons, rats and ants for the summer; vine branches for the autumn; and icicles for the winter. From 1681, Jules Hardouin-Mansart lightened up this primitive decoration by having the independent groups of children transferred to the Feasting Chamber Grove. In 1684 the decoration of the edges was entirely removed. During the transformation of the Feasting Chamber Grove in 1705, the secondary groups were once again removed and sent to Trianon where they still may be found. The children of the Summer Basin were transferred to the Château de Meudon in 1697.

Ceres, or *Summer* by Regnaudin (1673)
The harvest goddess, crowned with ears of wheat, lies on a bed of wheat sheaves decorated with wildflowers such as poppies and cornflowers. Three cherubs are placed near her.

Flora, or *Spring* by Tuby (1674)
Flora is surrounded by flowers and four cherubs who play with garlands of intertwined roses, cornflowers, heliotropes and anemones.

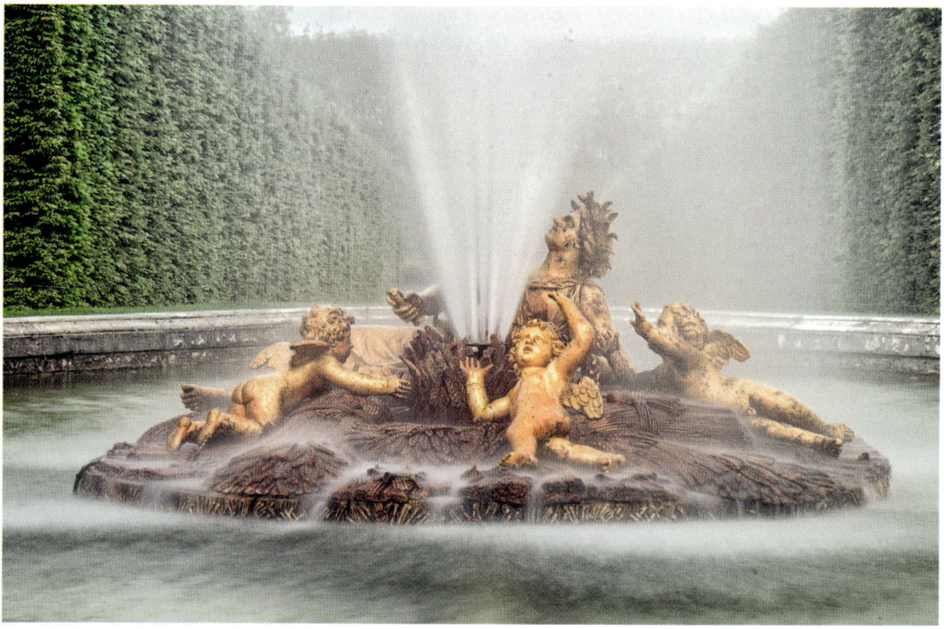

The Ceres or Summer Basin.

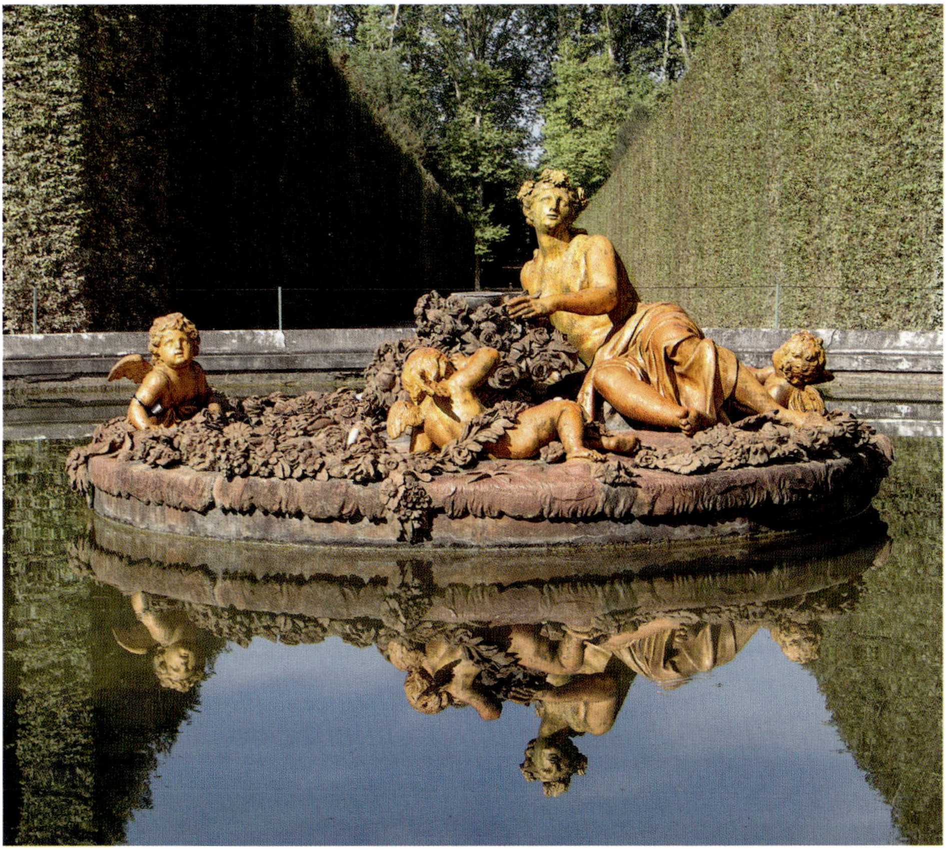

The Flora or Spring Basin.

Bacchus, or *Autumn* by the Marsy brothers (1674)
Crowned with vine branches, Bacchus leans on a crater that he seems to want to fill with grapes. Wallowing in the bunches of grapes, four small satyrs take to drink. Overcome by drunkenness, one of them has fallen asleep.

Saturn, or *Winter* by Girardon (1677)
On a small island edged with shells and icicles, Cronos (Saturn in Roman mythology) is represented by a winged old man. He holds the bag that was supposed to contain his son Zeus whom he prepared to devour and who his wife Rhea saved by replacing him with a stone. There are four cherubs around him, chilled to the bone, two of whom seem to be trying to warm themselves up at an imaginary fire that one of them may be trying to fan by blowing on it.

In the garden there is a single point of view from which the visitor can see the four basins from the same observation point. This remarkable viewpoint is located between the Latona Basin and the entrance of the Royal Alley and allows the visitor, by being turned towards it, to have the Bacchus Basin to his left and the Ceres Basin to his right; the diagonal open through the Girandole Grove leads the eye to the Saturn Basin, while that of the Dauphin's Grove overlooks the Flora Basin.

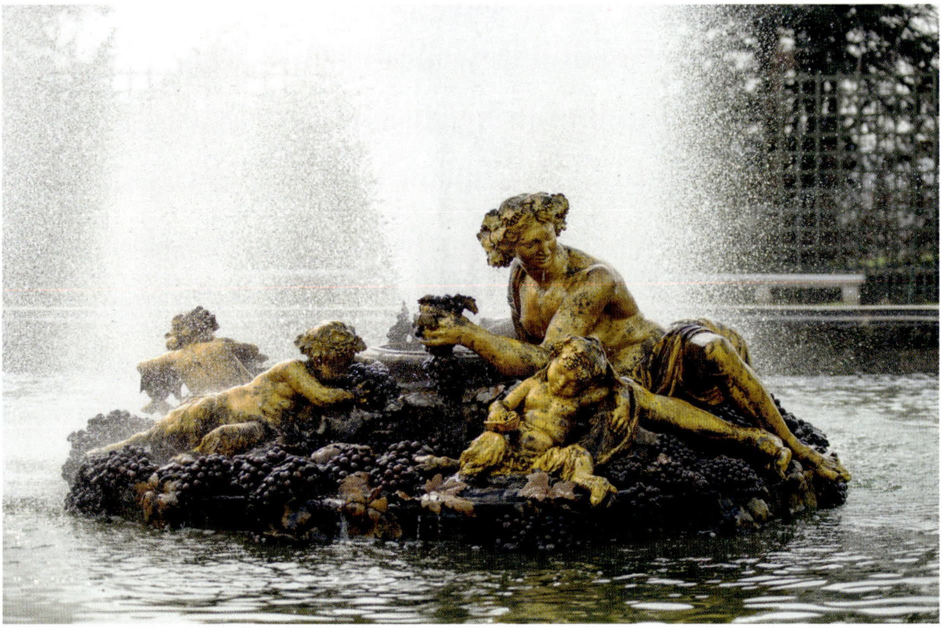

The Bacchus or Autumn Basin.

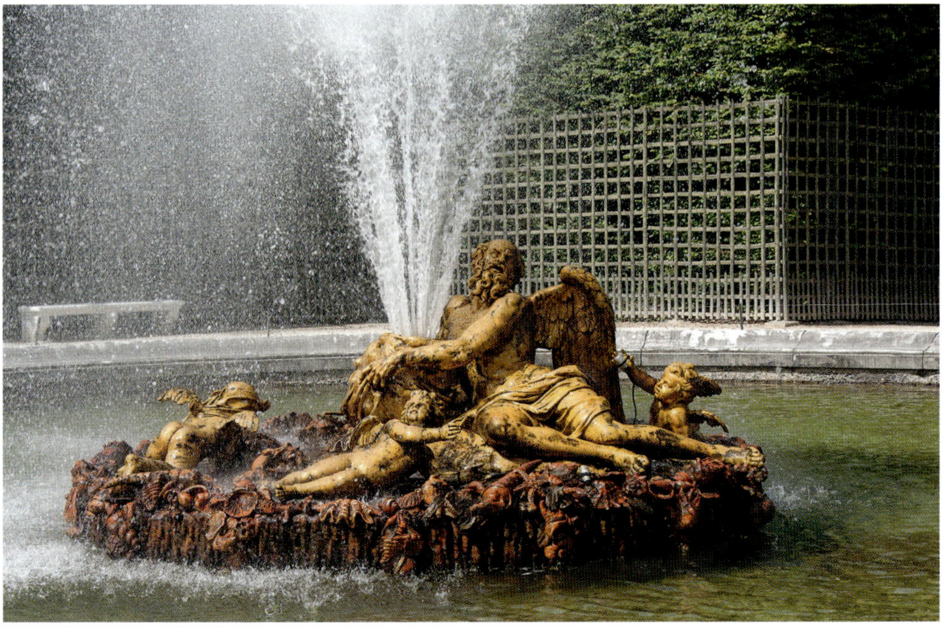

The Saturn or Winter Basin.

The Orangery

A first orangery was designed by Louis Le Vau from 1663. The site chosen was practical, south-facing and allow the building to be supported by the incline. Staircases bordered a parterre where, in warm weather, fragile plants were shown, particularly the orange trees of which Louis XIV proved to be an avid collector. From 1683, under the supervision of Jules Hardouin-Mansart, Le Vau's orangery was replaced, slightly more to the south, by a building twice the size with a surface area that was six times larger. Under the terrace of the South Parterre, Mansart designed a vast ensemble of three galleries forming a U, the largest measuring 155 metres long, the two others 114 metres. The parterre is protected by two gigantic staircases, known as the Hundred Steps, whose masonry buttresses the South Parterre. The building façade is treated like that of the ground floor of the château, decorated with banded rustication. Powerful double Tuscan columns highlight the avant-corps, which break the monotony of the walls. The ensemble gives an impression of extraordinary power. The visitor should be encouraged to walk down to the parterre and go to the feet of the columns to perceive fully the dimensions of the building. On the side of the Bacchus Alley and the Saturn Alley, a large façade with an avant-corps supported by two columns gives access to a vestibule that now houses the marble bath from the former Bathing Apartments of Louis XIV. From the top of this vestibule, the view of the central section – 13 metres high – is remarkable, especially when the trees brought in for the winter form a forest there. Dazzled, the ambassadors of the king of Siam who visited it in 1686 said: "The magnificence of the king is great for having made a superb building to serve as a house for the orange trees." The present collection features a few thousand plants, includes

Following pages:
The Orangery Parterre and the South Wing.

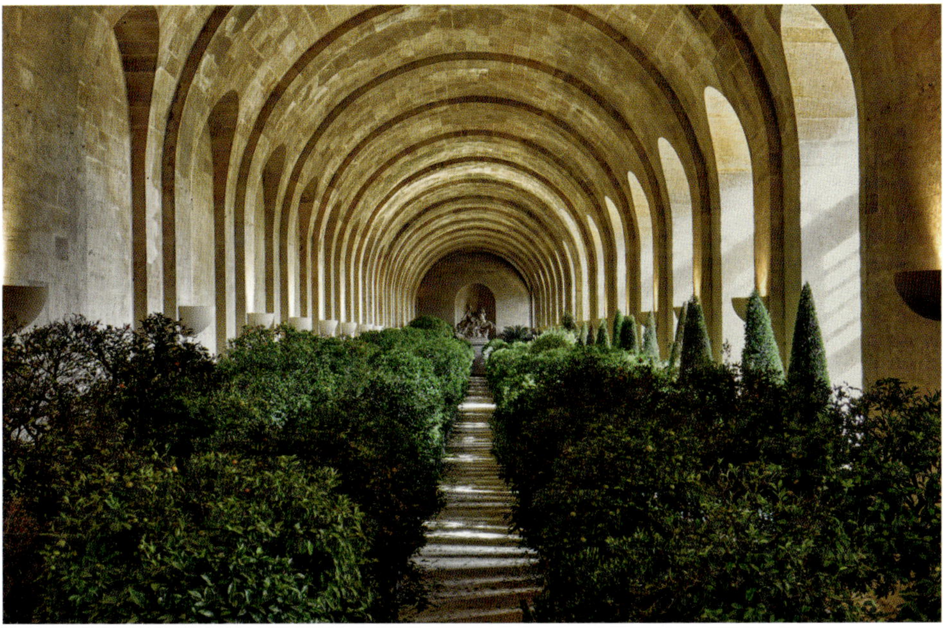

The Orangery gallery during the winter. In the distance is the equestrian statue of Louis XIV by Bernini.

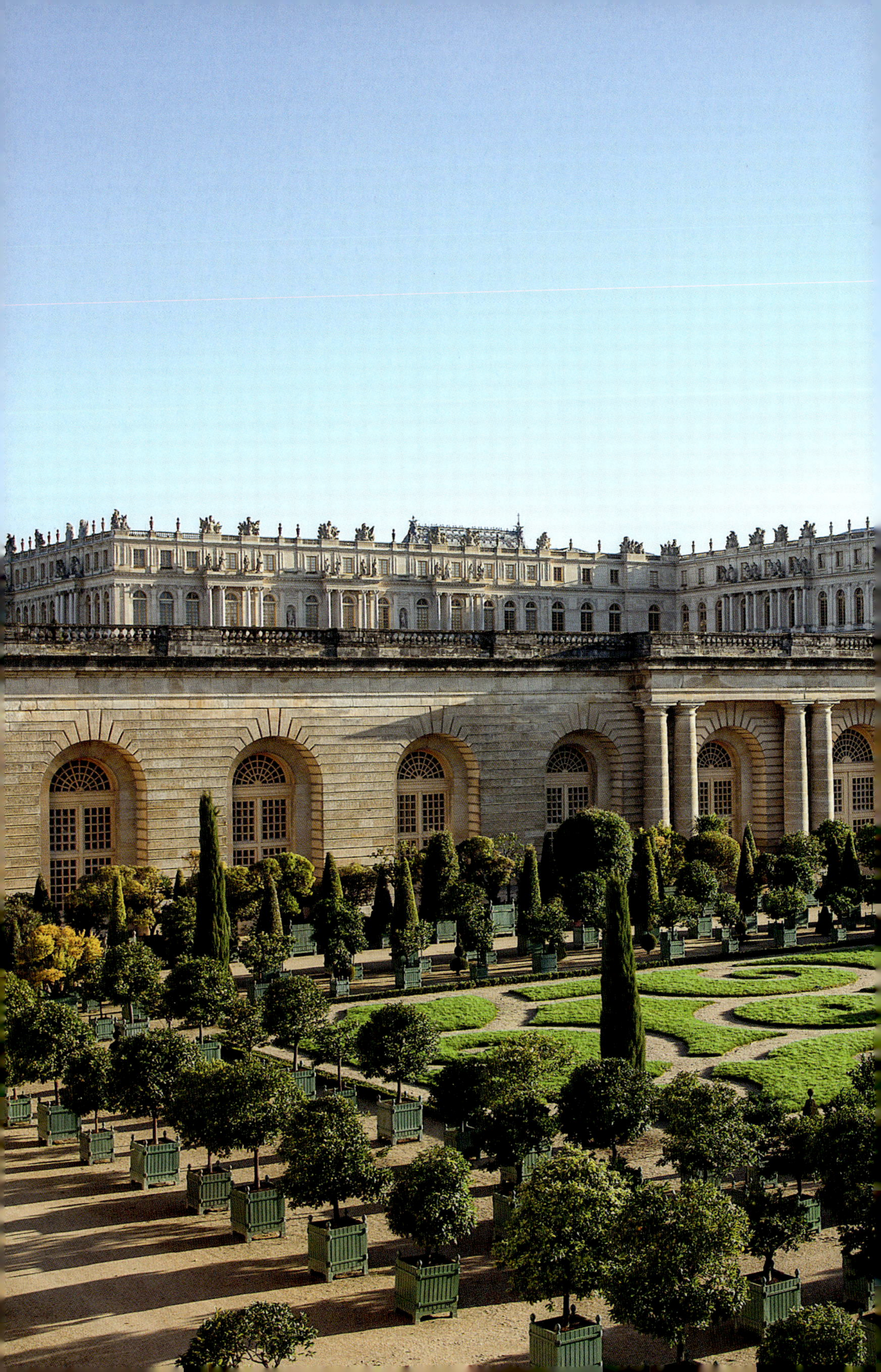

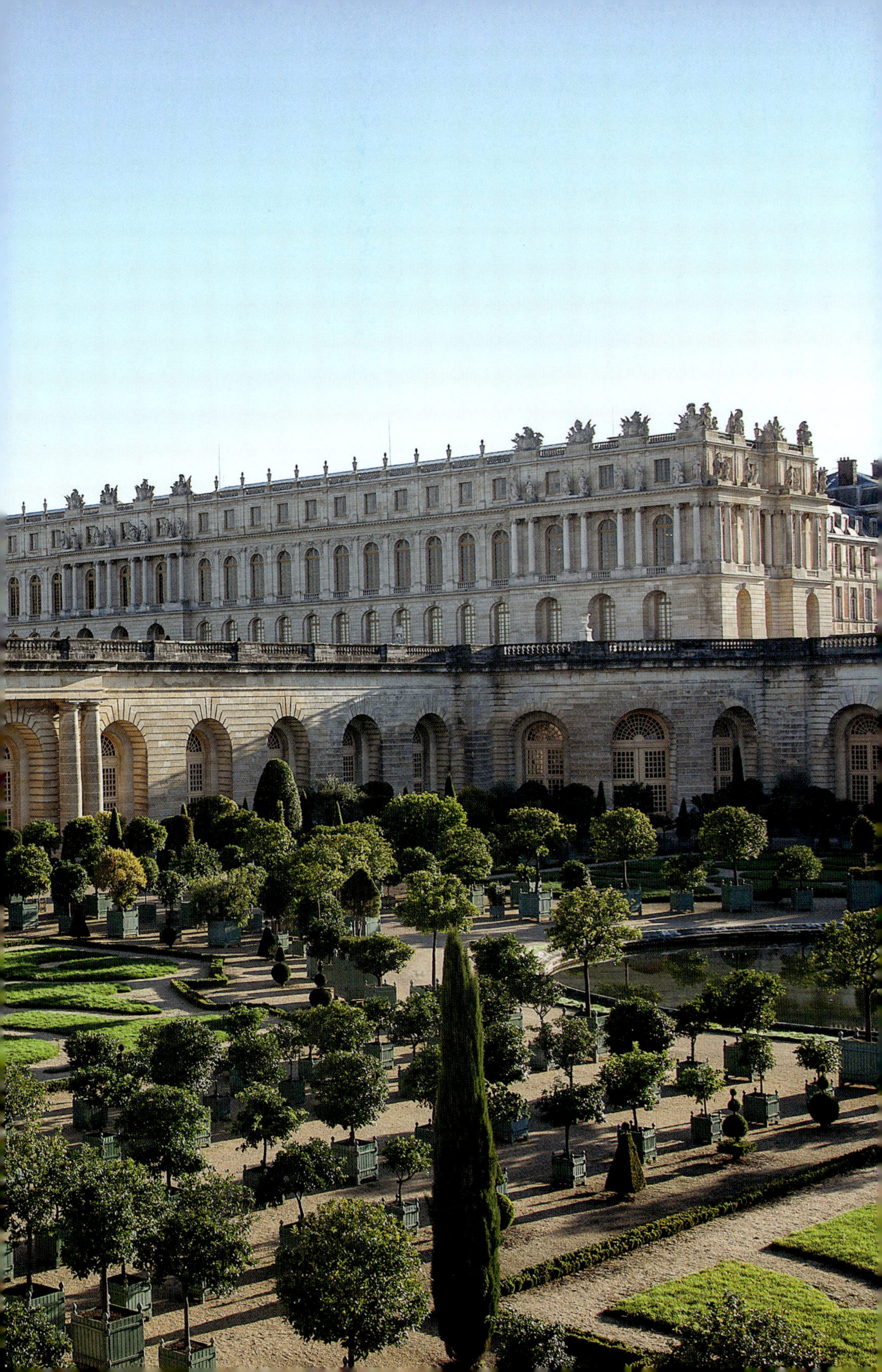

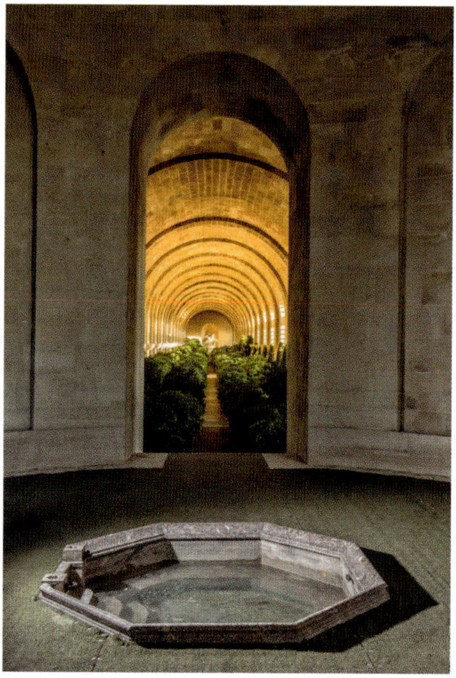

The vestibule of the Orangery and the marble tub from the former Bathing Apartments of Louis XIV.

orange trees, lemon trees, bitter orange trees, laurels, pomegranate trees and palm trees. It is heir to the collection of Louis XIV, who had concentrated in Versailles almost all the finest plants of the royal houses, continuing to acquire them in Spain and Italy, or be given them as gifts by attentive courtiers. The tall double-glazed windows and the thickness of the walls (4–5 metres) guarantee an interior temperature that never goes below 5°C and allows a climate conducive to the resting of the plants to be maintained.

In 2002 the parterre that spreads out in front of the Orangery once again features the original design of its cut grass divided in to six compartments bordered with alleys and containing a vast circular basin. A balustrade allows the visitor a view without obstacles towards the Lake of the Swiss Guards. At the end of the parterre, in line with the Hundred Steps, two sets of railings are punctuated with pillars topped with vases of flowers and lead to two monumental railings framed by massive pillars, each bearing a group in stone by Saint-Leu dedicated to the loves of the gods: on the east railing, *Venus and Adonis* (Leconte) and *Vertumnus and Pomona* (Legros); on the west railing, *Zephyrus and Flora* (Leconte) and *Aurore and Cephalus* (Legros). The groups were installed in 1687.

The Lake of the Swiss Guards

This vast stretch of water was first designed to clean up this part of the garden located below the château and the city, which the runoff made marshy and unhealthy. Under Louis XIII, a first pond was laid out on the site of the present King's Vegetable Garden. But it was not effective enough and a second pond, with the evocative name "stinking pond" – located more to the west on the Saint-Cyr road – was unable to resolve the problem. In 1675 Louis XIV decided to have the present basin dug by the Regiment of Swiss Guards, which left its name to the pond. The impressive surface area of the basin (12 hectares) contributed to structuring the landscape of the garden up to the Colline de Satory which marked its horizon. When pondering the uneven terrain that rapidly rises at the end of the stretch of water, Le Nôtre thought of building a vast cascade for a while. In the end, it was Bernini's equestrian *Louis XIV*, which was transformed by Girardon into *Marcus Curtius*, that was installed there as a boundary stone marking the south end of the garden. The Italian sculptor's work did not please the king, who refused to recognise it as his own portrait but did not dare send the statue back. A few discreet modifications sufficed to transform it into a hero of Roman history. Now replaced in situ by a cast, the masterpiece is in the

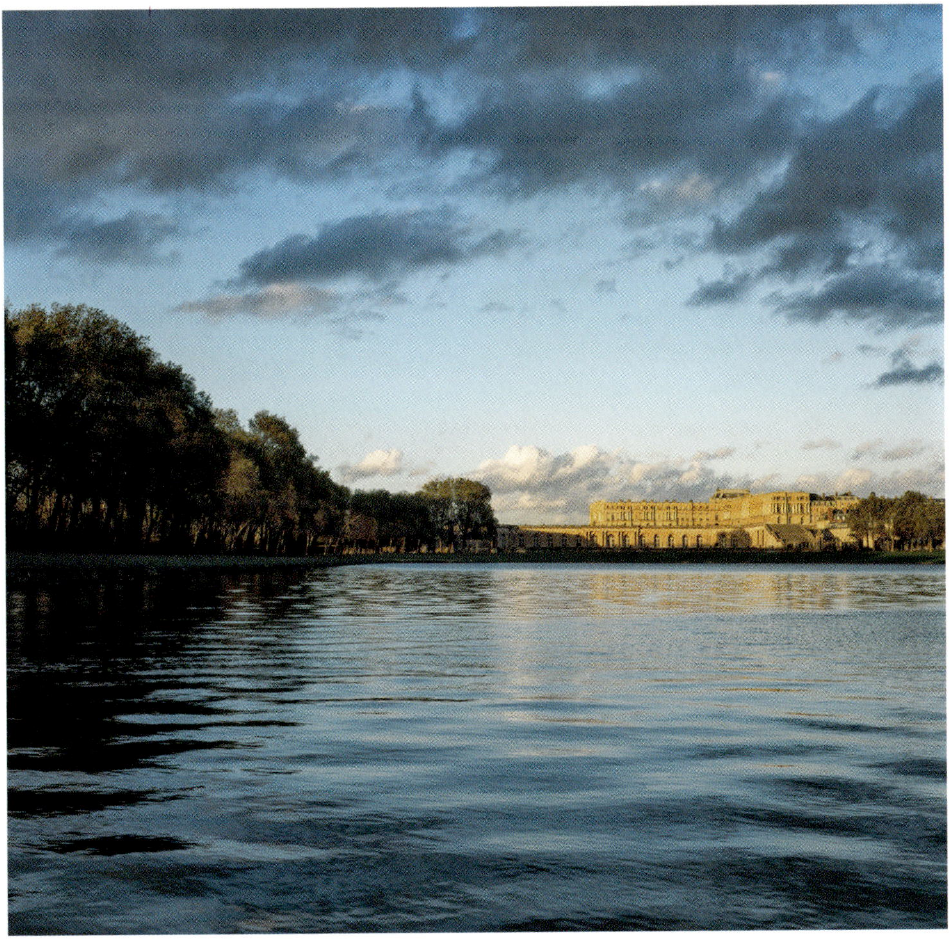

View of the Orangery and the château from the Lake of the Swiss Guards.

Orangery. The visitor who undertakes the walk to this statue is rewarded by a very beautiful and rather unusual view of the château, which seems literally placed on the orangery and is at one with it.

THE SOUTH GROVES

The Queen's Grove formerly the Labyrinth Grove

Located immediately to the west of the Hundred Steps, the present Queen's Grove occupies the exact site of the Labyrinth Grove created in 1665 by the express will of the king. Initially comprised only of plants, made up of winding alleys with complex plans, the Labyrinth Grove was gradually decorated with fountains and sculptures dedicated to the bestiary of Aesop's fables. In 1674 there were 330 naturalistically painted animals, divided over 39 fountains, each illustrating a fable explained by a quatrain by Isaac de Benserade painted on a lead plaque. The ensemble was completed in 1680. The main access to the labyrinth was at the north-east corner of the grove (near the door of the present Orangery). Visitors were welcomed by the statue of Aesop and by that of Cupid holding Ariadne's thread (now in the château), and found themselves facing the first basin representing the fable entitled *The Owl and the Birds*: at the centre of the fountain, an eagle owl received all the jets of water spread at him by a multitude of birds perched in a trellis. Benserade's quatrain, placed on the edge, summed up the moral of the scene: "The horn owl, tho' Minerva's bird / And for his wisdom priz'd; / Was for his hideous grab and hoot, / By the whole tribe despis'd." The correct circuit allowed the visitor to traverse the grove and to see each fountain without ever passing the same place twice.

Fragile, the labyrinth was repaired several times during the eighteenth century. Whether it would be preserved or removed was discussed during the overall replantation of the garden undertaken by Louis XVI in 1775. Like other groves deemed to have had fallen out of fashion and to be too expensive to maintain, it was sacrificed in the end. The lead statues,

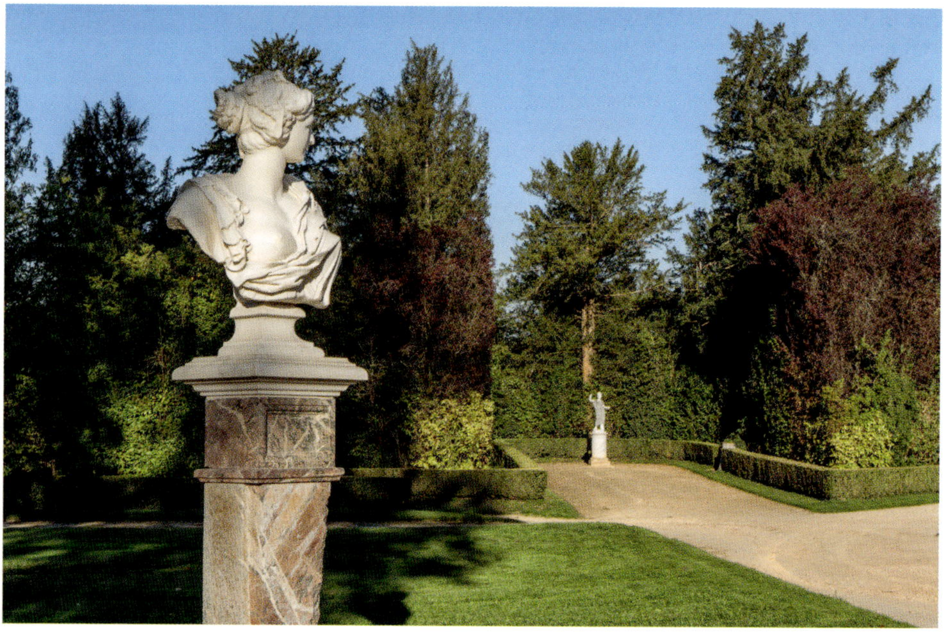

The Queen's Grove.

first carefully taken down and preserved, were scattered after the Revolution. Only thirty-five animals now survive in the château collections.

A new grove with a much simpler layout, replaced the Labyrinth Grove. Made up of a vast central area planted with tulip trees and a covered perimeter crisscrossed with alleys and punctuated with small *salles de verdure*, the grove was first called the Venus Grove because its centre was supposed to contain a bronze version of the renowned *Medici Venus*. Its current name dates from the nineteenth century. In August 1784, it served as a setting for one of the episodes of the notorious Affair of the Diamond Necklace. It was in one of its alleys that Cardinal de Rohan thought he was going to meet Marie-Antoinette but it was a lookalike skilfully exhibited by the swindlers who then managed to filch the most expensive piece of jewellery in Europe and thus bring about a terrible scandal from which the queen, although innocent, never really recovered.

Restored several times in the early nineteenth century, replanted during the reign of Napoleon III, the Queen's Grove was seriously damaged by the successive storms that ravaged the park in the late twentieth century. Its sculpted decoration underwent several changes. In 2008 a bronze *Faun with Kid*, executed in 1843 by Charles Ingé after a classical model, was placed in the centre. The busts surrounding it (*Faun, Woman with Diadem, Woman with a Chignon, Young Man*) are anonymous seventeenth-century French works. To the east, a bronze version of the *Borghese Gladiator* by Nicolas Coustou (1683) was installed in around 1855, responding to a polychrome marble *Minerva* (white and grey-blue marble), allegory of invincible Virtue, erected to the west.

The Ballroom Grove

The Ballroom Grove is the last of the groves laid out by Le Nôtre in the gardens of Versailles. Works began in 1680. In 1685 the Grand Dauphin, the son of Louis XIV, inaugurated the grove with a dinner. The location of the grove, below the Water Parterre and the Latona Amphitheatre, inspired Le Nôtre to make use of the significant different in level to create a large cascade using for a support the embankment to the east. It is the only cascade in the gardens of Versailles because the lack of relief and water mean that it was difficult to lay one out, unlike at Marly, for example, whose site is wonderfully suitable.

Two winding alleys, one to the south, the other to the west, lead to the centre of the grove. Their ingenious layout means that the vast amphitheatre in the arena, led to by whose two pebble slopes, is only discovered at the last moment. Grass-covered terraces, highlighted by clipped box and served by staircases, surround the whole like an ancient circus and are interrupted to make way for any imposing cascade. The central area was originally dug with a small circular canal with two cascading levels, forming a small island to which led four swing bridges. In 1707, during the works to simplify the groves that had been entrusted upon him by the king, Jules Hardouin-Mansart removed this area.

The cascade itself rises eight levels and is supplied at the top by two simple small fountains and three urns covered with burrstone and shells. At both ends, four narrower cascades, with sheets of water, framed by banisters covered in red Languedoc marble break up the uniformity of this aquatic wall and magnify its effects.

Trees in the Queen's Grove

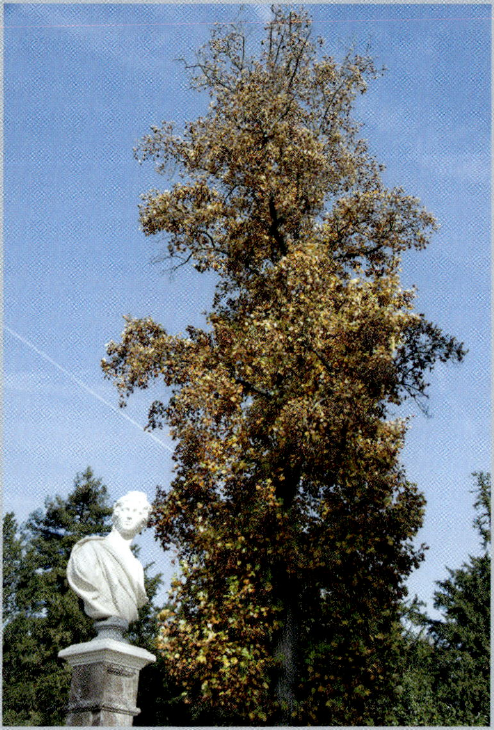

Tulip Tree
Liriodendron tulipifera

Native to the eastern United States, this tree is appreciated for its fragrant tulip-shaped flowers and curious trefoil leaves, which take on a golden tone in the fall.

It was introduced from Virginia to England in 1638.

In 1775 the Queen's Grove at Versailles was planted with a first *salle* of tulip trees, enlarged three years later. In October 1788, Abbé Nolin, director of the royal nurseries, had the seeds of these tulip trees specially gathered by Madame Lemoine, gardener to the king at Versailles, so that they could be grown later.

In April 1789 a new plan for the layout of the grove requiring the removal of some of the tulip trees was presented by the painter Hubert Robert, illustrator of the king's gardens since July 1784.

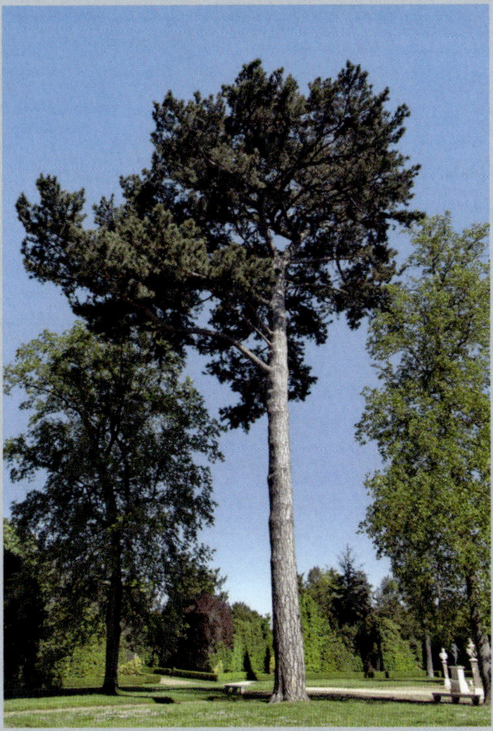

Corsican Pine
Pinus nigra subsp. *laricio*

André Thouin, who headed the Jardin du Roi in Paris, noted in 1786 that the Corsican pine, one of the largest trees of the northern hemisphere, merited to be multiplied in gardens, as it was more robust that other pines. It was above all valuable for masting: in Toulon, it was exclusively used for this purpose.

According to Jean Vincent, the pine in the Queen's Grove, which rose over 30 metres high in 1960, was probably one of the first specimens introduced from Corsica to Versailles.

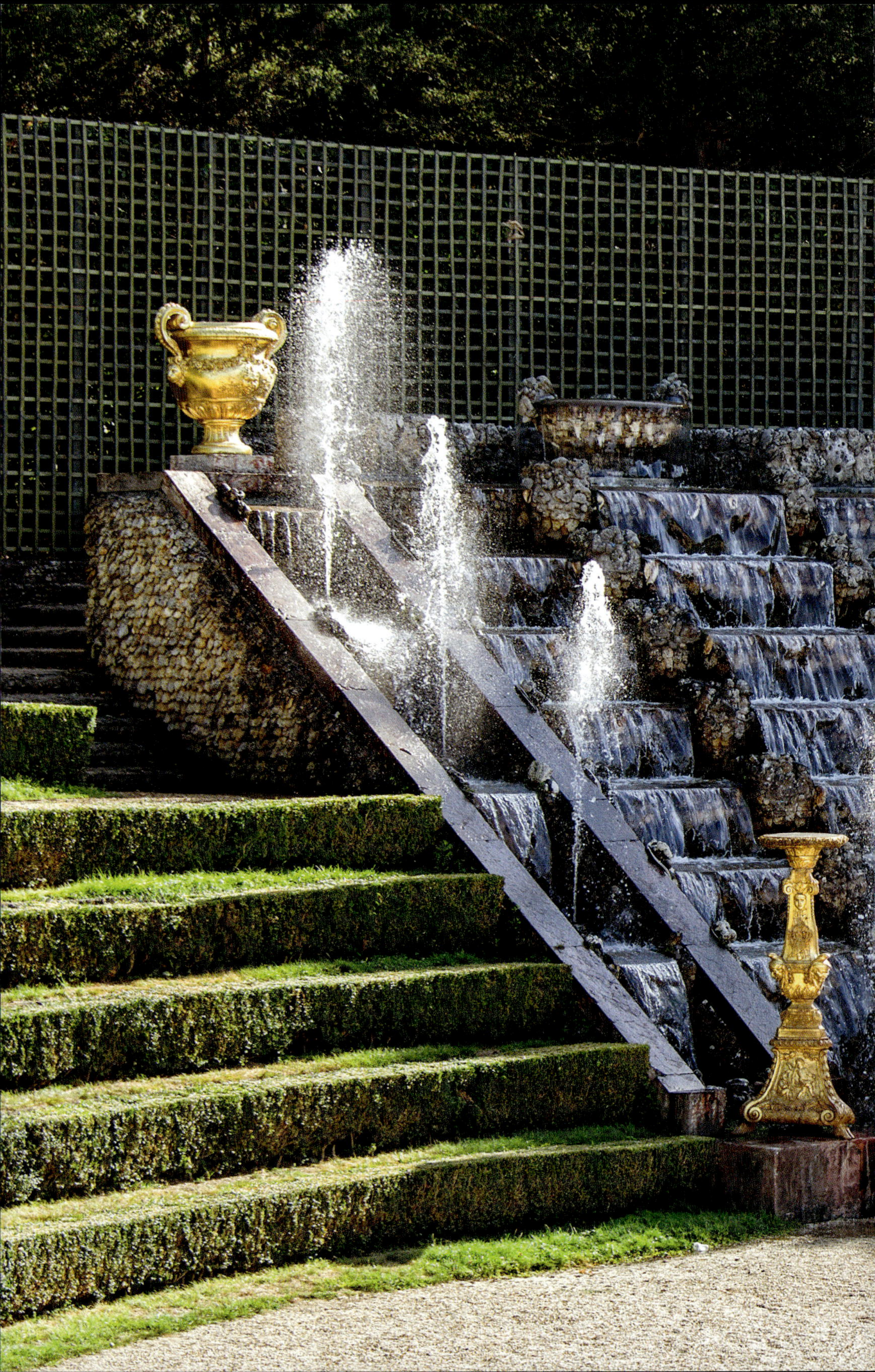

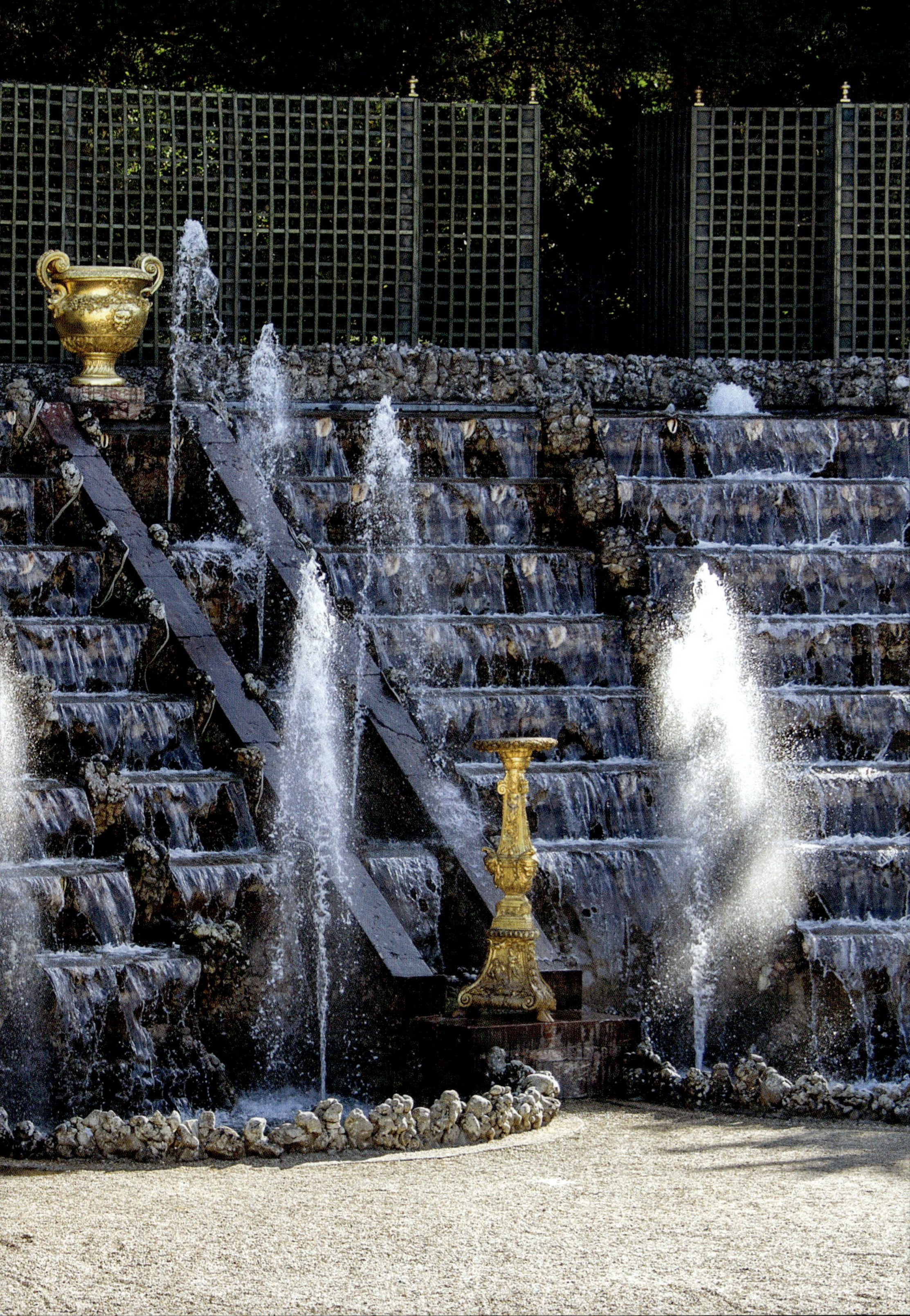

Preceding pages:
The Ballroom Grove.

The decoration of the walls is a fine example of rocaille art, very popular until the late seventeenth century for decorating ornamental grottoes and fountains, making use of various materials such as burrstone, shells and oddly shaped sandstone concretions nicknamed *gogottes*, which are found notably in the forest of Fontainebleau.

The grove was decorated with imposing gilt lead furniture comprising vases and *torchères guéridons* designed by Jacques Houzeau whose production was entrusted to various sculptors. The four vases at the top of the cascade are the work of Louis Le Conte. Endowed with handles with lion or dolphin heads, the vases feature a decoration of floral garlands topped by comedy masks. On either side of the two entries, four other, simpler vases by Étienne Le Hongre each develop a particular scene: to the west, *Triumph of Neptune and Amphitrite* and *Marine Triumph of Children*; to the south, *Children's Bacchanal* and *Dancing Figures*. The tripod torchères come in two different models. Those placed at the foot of the cascade, by Legros and Massou, rest on ox hooves. Their bases feature child musicians and dancers. On the upper level, faun heads wearing Phrygian caps and framed by small bells are topped with musical instrument trophies and comedy masks. The top of the torchère is encircled by a crown of flowers. Framing the two access ramps, four other torchères, by Jouvenet and Mazeline, are supported by lion paws and decorated with icicles, shells and small cartouches representing aquatic birds. On their bases, bas-reliefs represent musical instruments. The upper sections of the shafts are decorated with figures of dancers and musicians, flanked by faun heads. Overhanging the tier opposite the cascade, the group of *Marsyas and Olympus*, made after a classical model between 1680 and 1684 by Jean-Baptiste Goy, comes from the former Water Theatre Grove and was placed here in 1912.

The Girandole Grove and the Dauphin's Grove

The Girandole Grove is one of the oldest groves in the garden. Its plan was attested from 1663 and it was laid out at the same time as the Dauphin's Grove, located on the other side of the Royal Alley, to make up the ensemble known as the "Deux-Bosquets". Their layouts, strictly identical, are inscribed in a square in which the alleys lined with trellises formed a rigorous geometric path that leads to a central intersection. From 1669, a circular basin was laid out in the middle of each of them. In 1682 the edge of the south grove basin was given a rocaille decorated while its centre was adorned with a basket of naturalistically painted

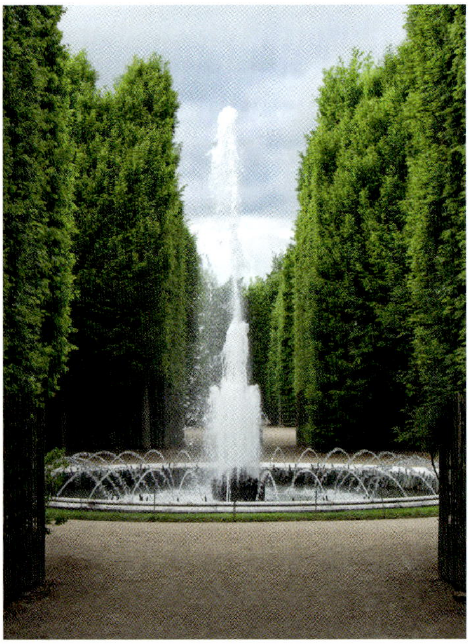

The Girandole Grove.

metal flowers. The water effects designed for this fountain formed a liquid girandole as soon gave its name to the grove. The basin was removed at the end of the reign of Louis XV. During the overall replanting of the grounds under Louis XVI, the grove was radically transformed, planted with lime trees arranged in a quincunx. In 2000, after the damage caused by the storm of December 1999, it was replanted according to the original plan and a new basin was installed. The sculpted terms are, for the most part, works made in around 1660 for the Château de Vaux-le-Vicomte after models by Poussin. Purchased by Louis XIV from Fouquet's widow in 1683, they were transported to Versailles and placed in the Deux-Bosquets.

The Mirror Basin and the King's Garden

At the western end of the southern groves – because of a recurrent drainage problem in this part of the garden – Le Nôtre had built a large rectangular basin, oriented east-west, and ending in a half-moon in its western section in 1671. Endowed with a small central island adorned with jets of water, this basin was called the Royal Island or Love Island. The following year (1672), the Mirror Basin was added to the east. The semicircular basin is bordered to the east by a steep *vertugadin* crowned with classical statues. The two *Draped Woman*, the *Apollo-Pothos* and the *Venus* placed in the niches of greenery adorned with marble benches were installed in 1821, replacing other classical statues removed over the years. The space was framed by two vases with ivy decoration, both made in around 1687, one by Jean Drouilly (to the north), the other by Barthélemy de Mélo (to the south).

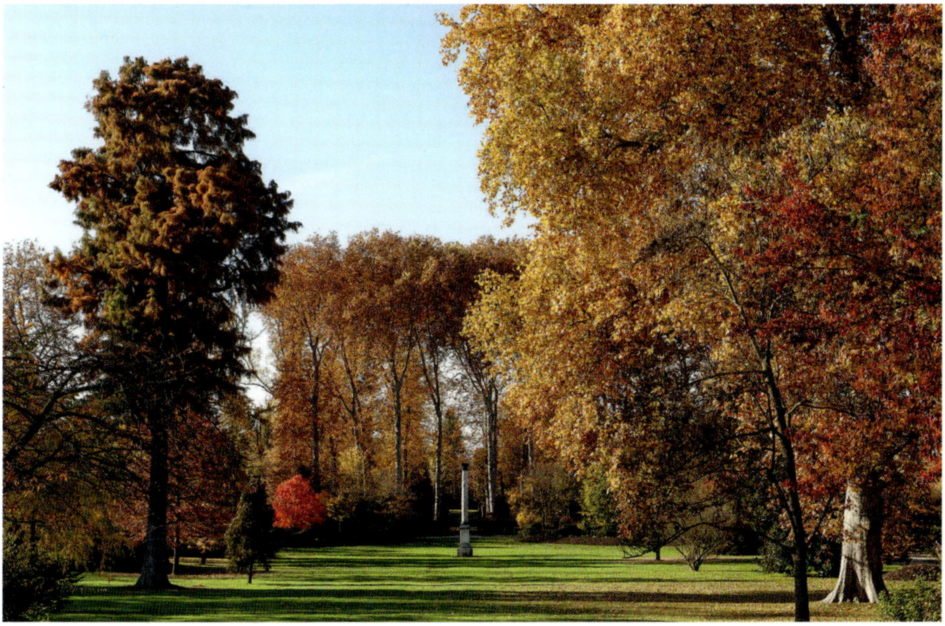

The King's Garden.

Trees in the King's Garden

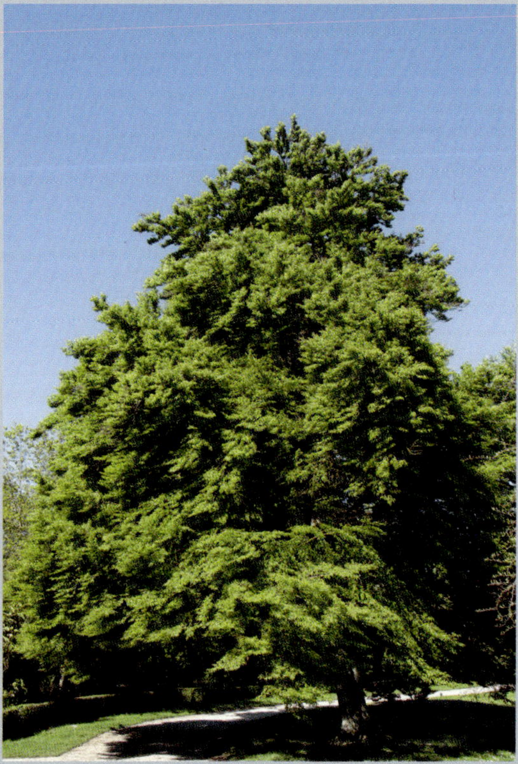

Fern-Leaved Beech
Fagus sylvatica 'Asplenifolia'

The fern-leaved beech, a variety of the common beech, is an ornamental species first cited in 1804. Its narrow, long and serrate leaves sport magnificent red and orange hues in the fall.

In 1847 the Versailles/Trianon nurseries grew 220 plants from three stools.

In 1960 one of these beeches, 3.2 meters in circumference, seemed to be in danger in the King's Garden. A young tree was then planted beside it, and they were known as "father and son" at the time. The old tree was cut down after 1989.

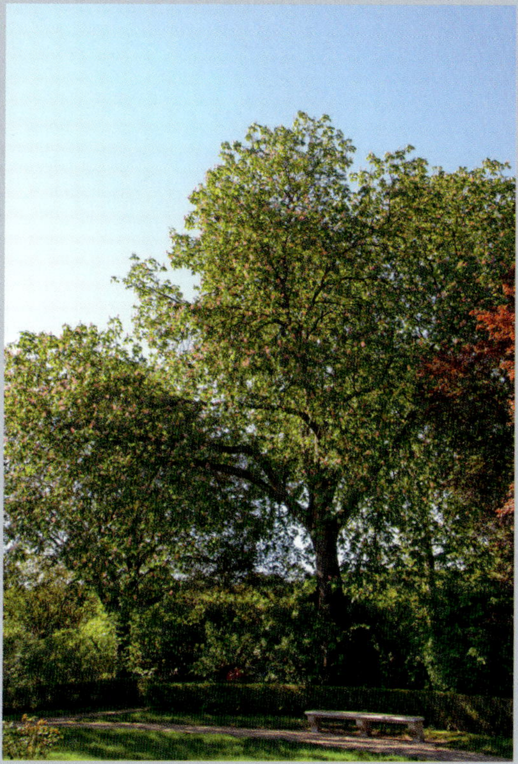

Briotii Red Horse Chestnut
Aesculus x carnea 'Briotii'

In 1858 a new variety of horse chestnut with red flowers, *Aesculus rubicunda* 'Briotii', was obtained by Pierre-Louis Briot (1804–1888), head gardener of the Trianon nurseries since 1834. This variety was then commercialised by Jean-Jacques Moser, a horticulturist in the Rue Saint-Symphorien, Versailles.

This magnificent variety of red horse chestnut was planted in the King's Garden in 1948.

In May-June, its lovely ornamental effect is due to its inflorescences in spiculate bunches, dark red with orangey spots in the upper parts of the flower. This variety produces little or no fruit.

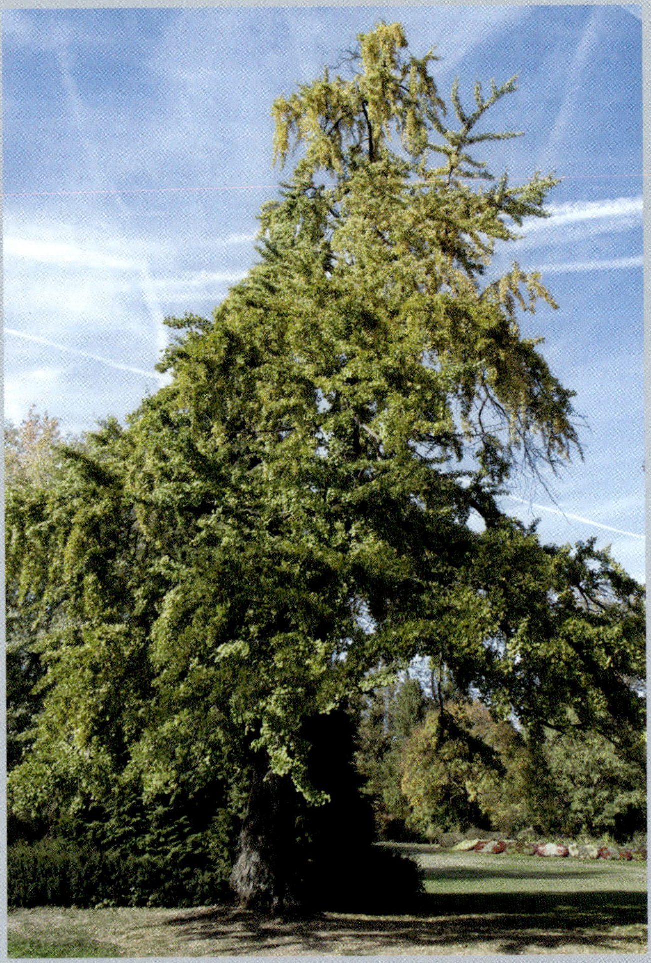

Ginkgo
Ginkgo biloba

Native to China, the ginkgo was grown in 1788 in John Williams's English nursery in Sèvres, where it was classified as a "precious tree". All the stocks grown in Europe until then had been male, as the species was dioecious. A female graft from the Jardin Botanique de Montpellier was grafted on to one of the two male ginkgoes in the Trianon nursery after 1830, thus enabling sexual reproduction – and no longer vegetative reproduction – of the tree.

In 1847 two "couples" of ginkgoes from the Versailles/Trianon nursery had supplied sixty-six plants. This stock may have come from the Versailles royal nurseries.

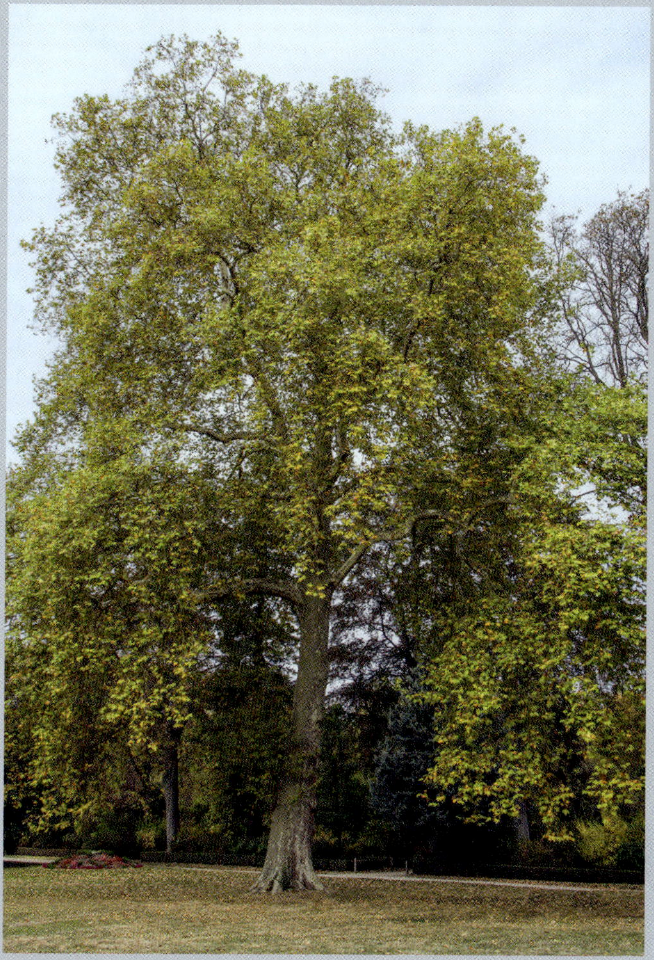

London Plane
Platanus x hispanica

According to Jean Vincent, it was the finest and largest of the trees in the King's Garden in 1960, 40 metres high and 5.5 metres in circumference. A cross between a *Platanus orientalis* L. and a *Platanus occidentalis* L., the London plane is often grown to decorate parks and roadsides.

Obtained in England from the Oxford Botanic Garden in around 1670, it was admired for its vigour and rapid growth.

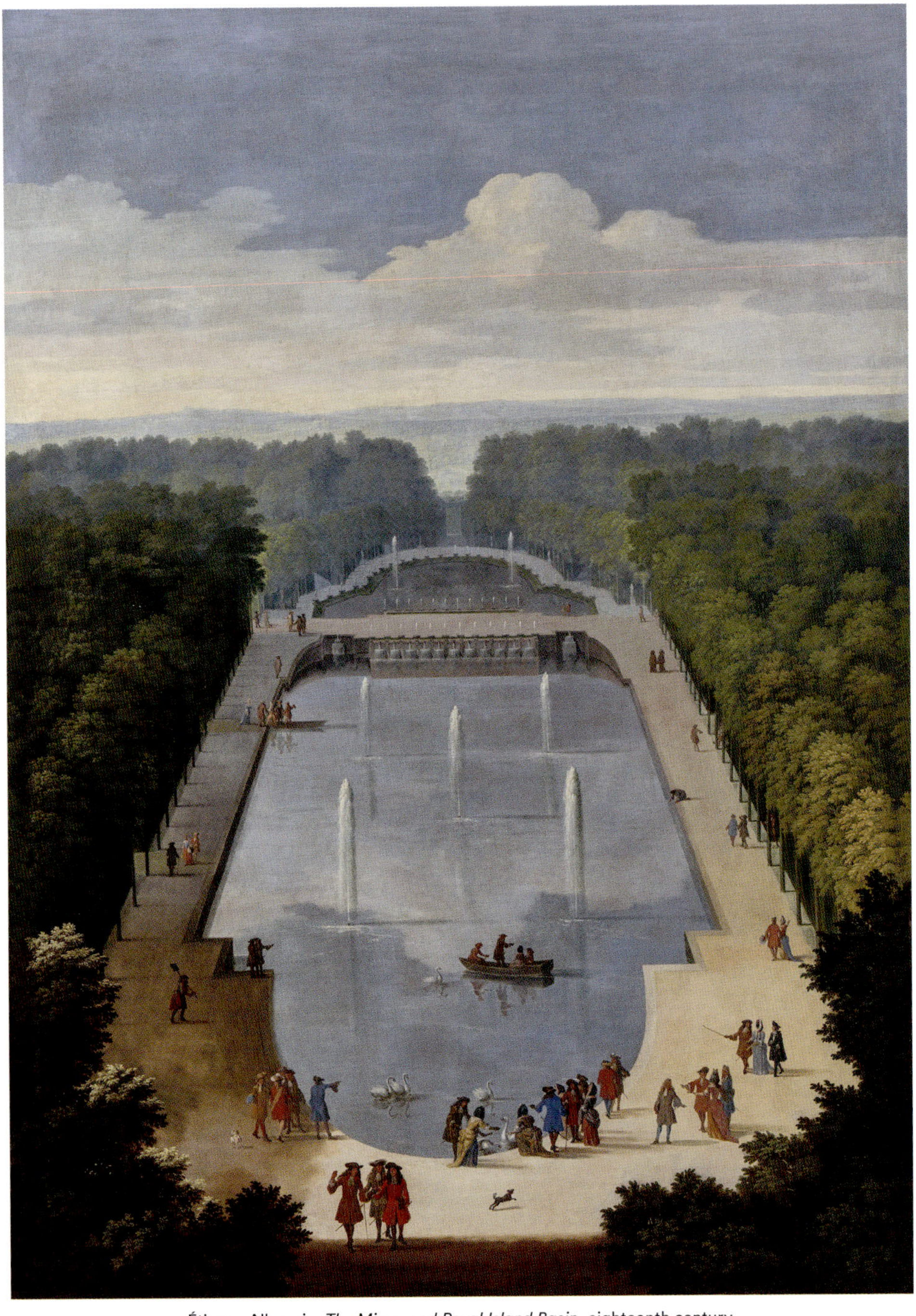

Étienne Allegrain, *The Mirror and Royal Island Basin*, eighteenth century.
Only the Mirror Basin survives. The Royal Island Basin, in the foreground, was replaced by the King's Garden.

Le Nôtre had played on the difference of level between the two pools to lay out, from 1680, a series of fountains with basins placed along the retaining wall of the alley of separation. Beginning in 1704, like many of the groves in the garden, the Royal Island was the object of simplifications and these basins were removed. The water features were then simplified and reduced to five lances, which responded to the two jets of the Mirror Basin. In 1688 copies of famous classical statues, the *Farnese Flora* copied by Jean Raon and the *Farnese Hercules* copied by Jean Cornu, were placed on the western end of the Royal Island. In the eastern section of the garden, two vases, completed in 1683 and copied from classical models by Jean Rousselet, represent a *Dionysian Sacrifice* (to the north) and the *Drunkenness of Silenus* (to the south).

During the Revolution and the Empire, the Royal Island Basin suffered from a lack of maintenance, which gradually transformed it into a swamp. In 1816 Louis XVIII commissioned the architect Alexandre Dufour to fill the pool and replace it with a garden. The garden was laid out during the winter of 1816–17. It was originally isolated by a trellis painted white which followed the exact plan of the former basin. Landscaped, the new garden was organised a vast stretch of lawn adorned with flowerbeds and shrubs. Particular attention was paid to the choice of species. In the centre, a Languedoc marble column, placed on a pedestal, originally supported a statue. Two Rousselet vases complete the remarkable ensemble.

The Colonnade Grove

Designed by Jules Hardouin-Mansart, the Colonnade Grove, completed in 1688, celebrated the triumph of architecture in the gardens of Versailles. Rocailles, trellises and topiary here give way to the majestic nobility of antiquity, the polychrome marbles, and an abundant sculpted decoration to which contributed the greatest sculptors of the reign of Louis XIV. The water itself, rising out of the basins in perfectly mastered jets, highlight the harmonious lines of the ensemble by forming a second liquid colonnade.

In 1678 André Le Nôtre had designed in this spot a grove of a particular genre,

Following pages:
The Colonnade Grove.

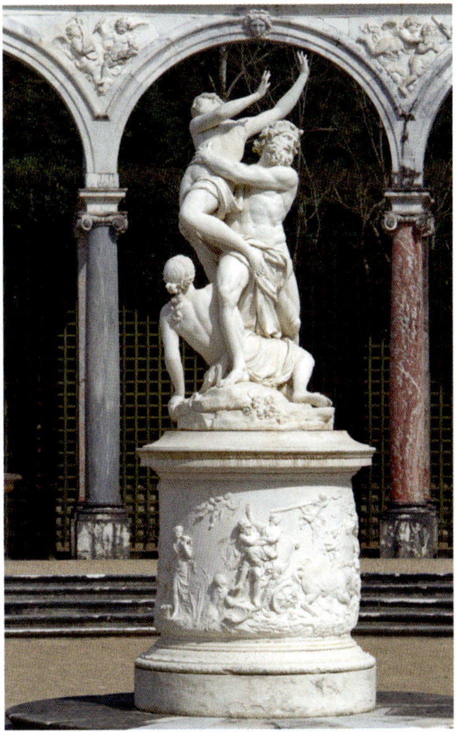

François Girardon, *The Abduction of Proserpina by Pluto*, in the Colonnade Grove.

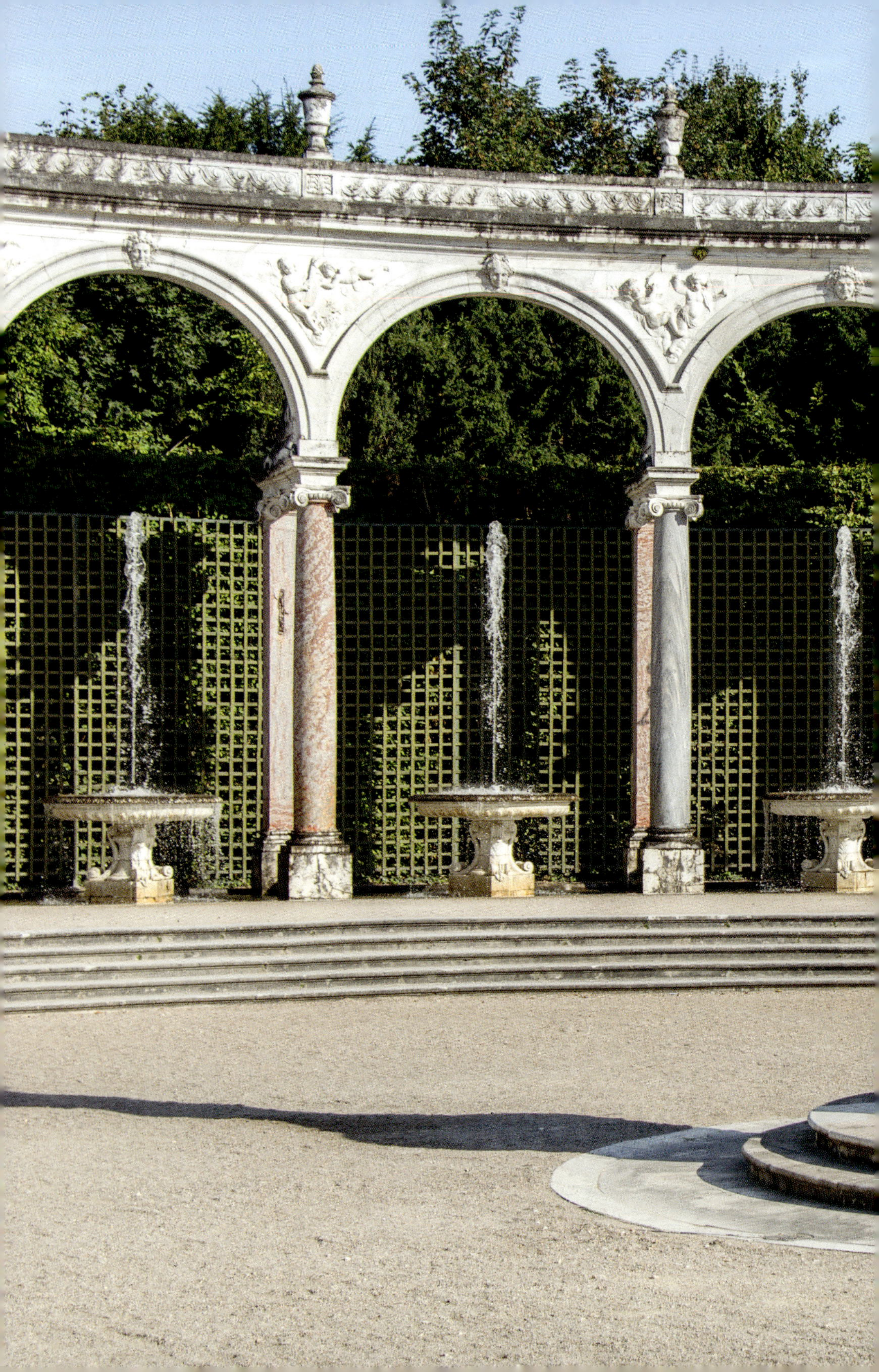

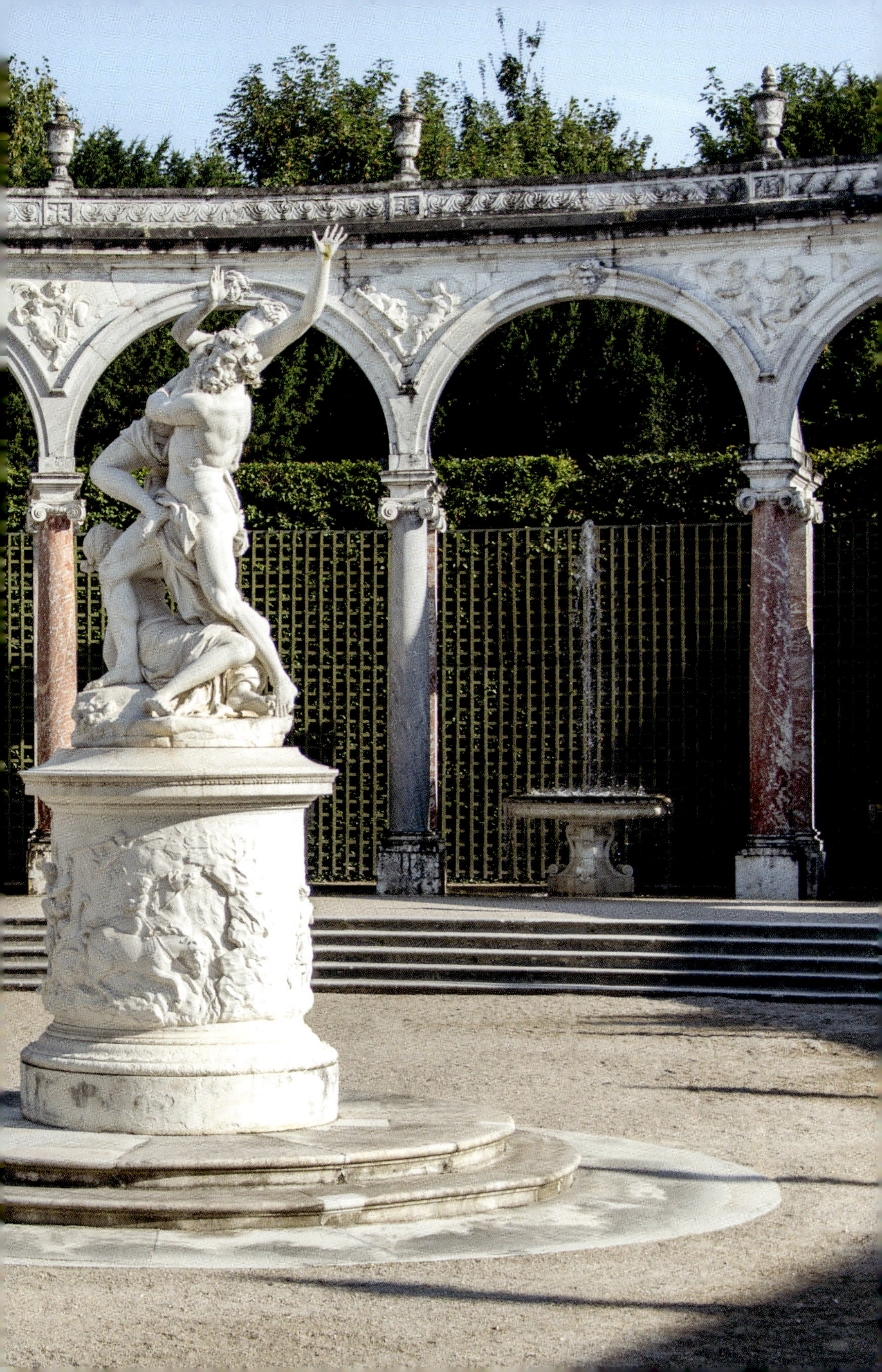

the Springs Grove. It was made up of a multitude of streams meandering under the foliage and which the visitor would step over to go from small island to small island. Here and there, small jets of water enlivened the current. This charming grove was destroyed in 1684 to give way to Hardouin-Mansart's majestic construction. However, Le Nôtre was so fond of his Springs Grove that he recreated it at Trianon a few years later. Inspired by the construction of trellises, which were then very popular in European gardens, Hardouin-Mansart designed a vast peristyle with a diameter of over 40 metres formed by thirty-two red Languedoc marble pilasters serving as counterforts and echoed by thirty-two Ionic columns. The columns are in three different types of marble: Languedoc red, blue-grey and violet Breccia for the columns framing the entrances. The arcades, the circular cornice and the vases topping it are in Carrara marble. The ensemble features a circular canal into which flow the basins placed in the centre of each arcade. Originally, Hardouin-Mansart had only planned a single entrance to the Colonnade, the western one, so that the edifice could be considered a closed space. In 1704 three other entrances, to the north, east and south, were created, resulting in the removal of the basins and the interruption of the circular channel at three supplementary points. Two of the three basins removed were reused in the new pools that the king had made at each end of the neighbouring Chestnut Grove. The third is now found at the centre of the round Great Basin of the Jardin des Tuileries.

The virtuoso sculpted decoration focuses on the arcades whose keystones feature alternating male and female mascarons alternant figures and spandrels feature bas-reliefs representing cherub musicians that, in a way, accompany the symphony of the waters. No less than fifteen sculptors were required, from 1685 to 1688, to complete this project: Coysevox, Regnaudin, Magnière *fils*, Van Clèves, Leconte, Lespingola, Dugoullon, Granier, Cornu, Le Hongre, Mazière, Flamand, Drouilly, Vigier and Tuby. In 1696 in the centre of the grove, reached by a circular staircase of five steps, one of the masterpieces of French sculpture was placed at the location of a fountain: *The Abduction of Proserpina*, by François Girardon.

The group depicts the abduction of Ceres' daughter by the god Pluto, in front of the nymph Cyane who is powerless to prevent it. The circular pedestal, completed in 1699, features the successive episodes of this mythological narrative (which inspired Lully to write an opera in 1680): to the right of a palm tree, the companions of Proserpina, daughter of the goddess Ceres, are surprised while they are gathering flowers; the following scene shows Pluto, god of the underworld, dragging the young woman to an infernal sojourn and the flaming rock open to let him through; Pluto, on his chariot, looks threateningly at the nymph Cyane, whom he warns to be quiet or be turned into a stream (which will happen, as suggested by the reeds that from which the nymph seems to emerge); finally, the third sequence is dedicated to the wrath of Ceres, who, desperately seeking her daughter, sets fire to the harvest that she flies over in her chariot drawn by dragons. Only the intervention of Jupiter appeased the goddess's ire and saved the Earth from going up in flames: Ceres kept her daughter six months of the year and Proserpina stayed with Pluto the six other months. Originally, this sculpture was supposed to be part of a series of four groups dedicated to mythological abductions and each symbolising an element. Only three groups were completed, the last never being executed.

In 1955, because of the fragility of the marble, the group and its plinth were replaced by a copy; the original is now in the château orangery.

The Chestnut Grove

The elongated shape of this grove evokes a gallery. In 1678 Le Nôtre, in all likelihood with the help of Jules Hardouin-Mansart, laid out in this spot a new grove that took on the name Water Gallery. In 1681 the king decided to exhibit there, as in an open-air museum, twenty or so of the finest classical statues he had just purchased in Italy. To highlight them, an extravagant ensemble of marble and water features was designed. The grove then took the name Ancients Grove and was considered one of the marvels of Versailles. The visitor could stroll through an elongated island, paved with black and white marble and decorated with statues, topiary and fountains. In 1704 Louis XIV decided to considerably simplify the grove, whose maintenance proved to be costly. Canals, marble and fountains

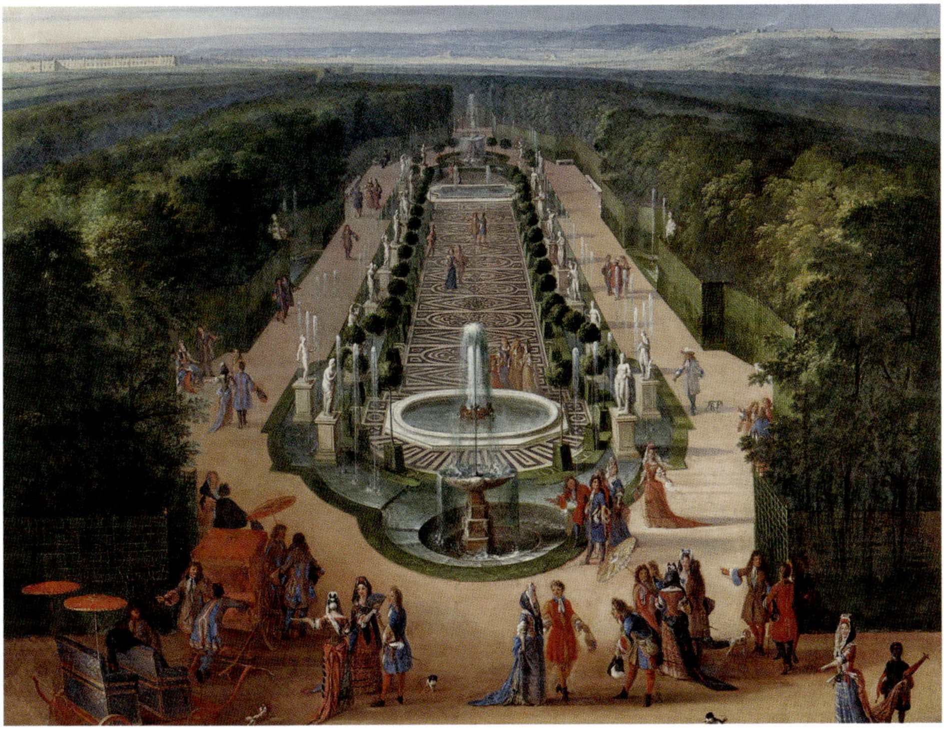

The Ancients Grove painted in 1688 by Jean-Baptiste Martin the Elder (detail). The Chestnut Grove now occupies the site of this former grove.

The *fêtes* of Louis XIV

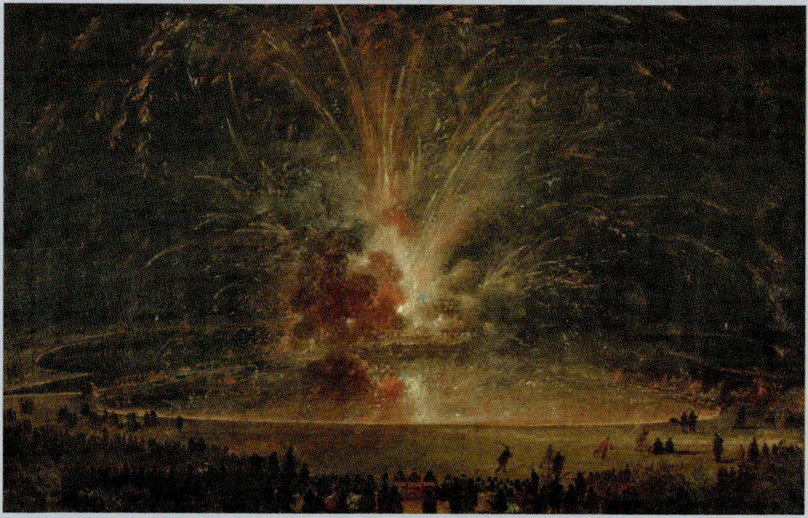

Fireworks, 9 May 1664. Launched above the future Apollo Basin, it closed the *fête* Les Plaisirs de l'Île Enchantée.

The gardens of Versailles served as the setting for several *fêtes*, memories of which still exist thanks to abundant descriptions, numerous archival documents, and a rich engraved and drawn iconography. Three of the most remarkable of them were held between 1664 and 1674, at a time when Versailles was not yet the official residence of the king and his court, but more of a place of leisure where the monarch liked to come to entertain himself. The *fête* Les Plaisirs de l'Île Enchantée (May 1664), held in a new garden, could be considered one of the founding acts of Versailles. For several days, the young king, twenty-five years old, hosting like a private individual, invited a very limited circle of guests to magnificent entertainments featuring comedies, ballets, theatre, *carrousel*, various jousts, lottery, strolls and refreshments. For the occasion, Molière wrote *La Princesse d'Élide* and, above all, *Tartuffe* there. Four years later, on July 18, 1668, a new *fête*, which was called the Grand Divertissement Royal, eclipsed the pomp of the first one. This time, the king chose to concentrate the various elements of the festivities on a single evening, but he revived the concept of itinerancy that had presided four years earlier, since each of the entertainments on offer that evening follow a carefully organised itinerary allowing the latest embellishments of the gardens to be discovered and admired: the Latona

Amphitheatre, the new Royal Alley, the Star Grove, the Grotto of Tethys and the Labyrinth. At the intersection where the Saturn Basin would later be dug, Molière produced *George Dandin* for the first time. An overall illumination and grandiose fireworks ended the evening.

For the *fête* of 1674, the last great *fête* of the reign, intended to celebrate the second conquest of the Franche-Comté, Louis XIV chose a new format. Entitled Les Divertissements de Versailles, the *fête* comprised six days spread out over July and August. The first day, 4 July, was marked by a performance of Lully's *Alceste* in the Marble Courtyard. On 11 July, the court attended a concert in the Trianon gardens, followed by a supper in the Feasting Chamber Grove. On 19 July, in front of the Grotto of Tethys, the troupe of Molière, who died the previous year, performed *Le Malade imaginaire*. On 28 July, there were fireworks over the canal, followed by a midnight supper served in the Marble Courtyard. On 18 August, at the Orangery the king and his court attended the first performance of Jean Racine's *Iphigénie*, then gigantic fireworks over the canal. Les Divertissements de Versailles ended on a high note on 31 August with the illumination of the Grand Canal: 5 kilometres of banks were lit by means of canvas flats and oiled paper, lit from behind. The court embarked on the canal, and this ride to the sound of violins brought an end to the most spectacular *fête* that Versailles had ever known.

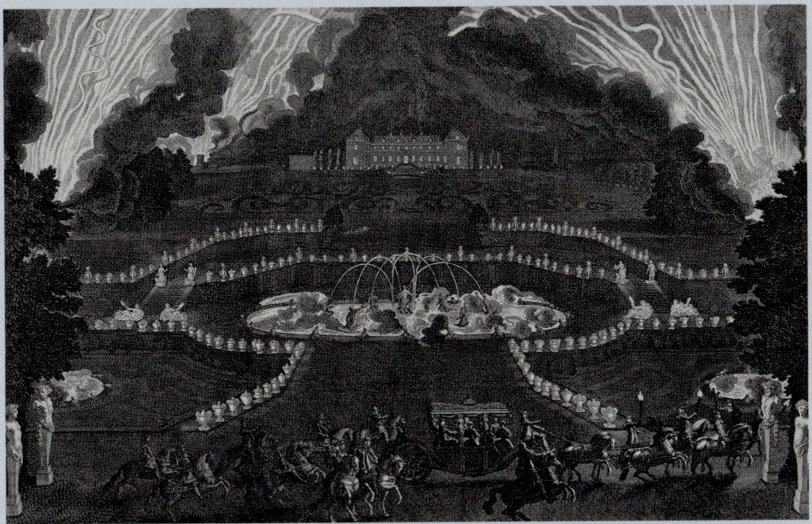

Fireworks, 18 July 1668. The château, in the distance, had not yet been modified by Le Vau. In the foreground, the royal coach passes in front of the Latona Basin represented it its original configuration.

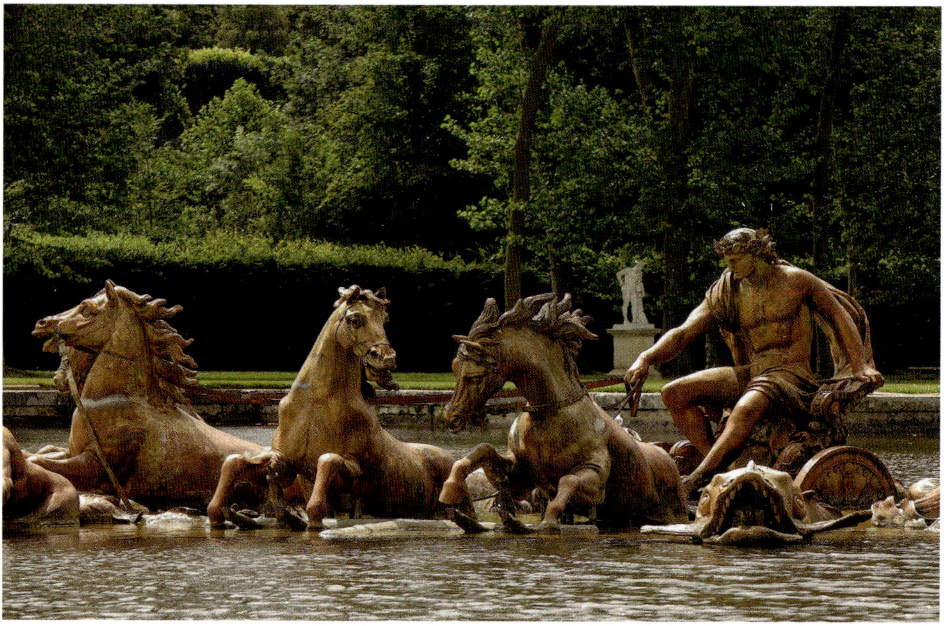

Jean-Baptiste Tuby, *Apollo on His Chariot*.

disappeared; the statues found other allocations in Versailles and Marly. Planted with a double row of horse chestnut trees, very popular as ornamental trees and which left their name to the new grove, the site of the former gallery was henceforth decorated with eight busts. Only two statues remained in place: *Belvedere Antinous* to the south and Meleager to the north. The eight present busts, placed on Languedoc marble plinths installed in the nineteenth century, represent Roman emperors (*Marcus Aurelius, Hadrian, Otho* and two busts of *Septimius Severus*), as well as *Alexander the Great, Hannibal* sculpted by Girardon after a classical model and a bust of Apollo.

At each end of the grove, two circular ornamental pools each received a basin from the neighbouring Colonnade Grove.

The Apollo Basin

At the bottom of the Royal Alley, the Apollo Basin marks the western edge of the garden. Beyond the railings is what is now known as the Great Park. From the reign of Louis XIII, when Versailles was still just a simple hunting lodge, a first circular basin, known as a *rondeau*, was dug into the base of the natural slope to drain the water. Enlarged in around 1660 to attain its present shape and dimensions (nearly 120 metres long by 80 metres wide), it was named the Lake of the Swiss Guards. In 1664 it served as the setting for Les Plaisirs de l'Île Enchantée – a *fête* held by the king for his court – hosting in its centre a floating stage with architectural decoration upon which a magnificent ballet was danced. In 1670, after the widening of the Royal Alley, the basin was decorated with an imposing gilt lead group representing *Apollo on His Chariot*, drawn by four horses and surrounded by tritons and sea monsters. The sculptor

Jean-Baptiste Tuby depicted the moment the sun god sprang out of the sea to begin his race around the Earth. The full dimension becomes apparent when the water of the fountain is running; the group then seems to be endowed with movement and gives the impression that it is really surging out of the frothing basin.

The perimeter of the vast parterre in the middle of which stands the Apollo Basin has always been a prime location for sculptures. Louis XIV had classical pieces installed there, which rubbed shoulders with masterpieces of French sculpture. The entrance of the Royal Alley is thus marked by two important groups: to the north, *Aristaeus and Proteus* by Sébastien Slodtz (completed in 1723) and, to the south, *Ino and Melicertes* by Pierre Granier (completed in 1691). The terms accompanying them represent gods and goddesses. To the north: *Syrinx* by Mazière, *Jupiter* and *Juno* by Clérion and *Vertumnus* by Le Hongre, followed by a classical piece, *Silenus Carrying the Infant Bacchus*. To the south, *Pan* by Mazière, *Flora*, or *Spring* by Arcis and Mazière, *Bacchus*, or *Autumn* by Dégoullons and Raon and *Pomona* by Le Hongre in front of a large classical *Bacchus*. Along the alley leading to the canal, the classical statues placed there by Louis XIV were, for the most part, replaced in the nineteenth century by other classical pieces of lesser importance or by seventeenth-century French and Italian works.

The Grand Canal and Little Venice

In the seventeenth century, the taste for large, rectilinear stretches of water extending to infinity manifested itself in several gardens. These canals were filled by quick currents or resulted from the harnessing of a stream or river (Tanlay, Vaux-le-Vicomte and Chantilly) or were simply vast basins supplied by drainage or the wastewater of fountains, as at Fontainebleau, Sceaux and Versailles, the canal thus playing a utilitarian as well as decorative role. Located at the lowest point in the gardens, the Versailles canal began in 1668, in line with the Royal Alley. Successive modifications (widening, digging of the transversal arms) gave it its definitive aspect in 1673. The following year, Louis XIV held in Versailles a

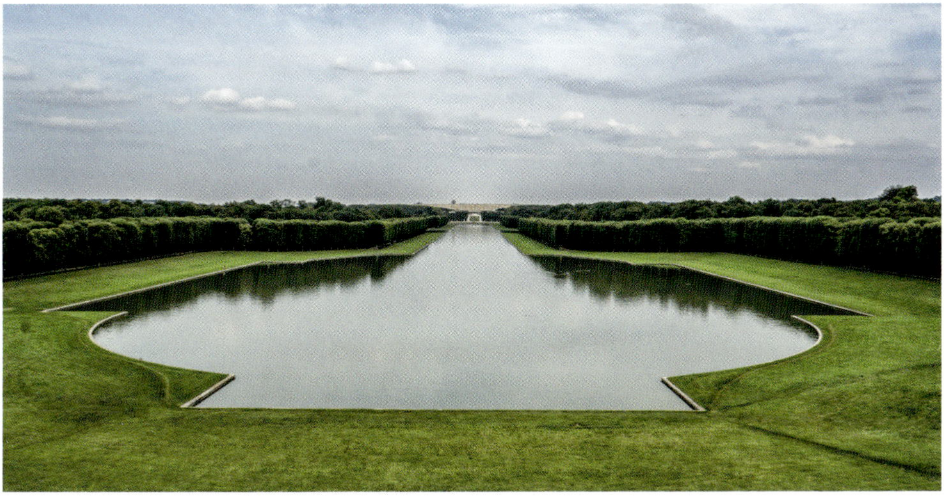

The west end of the Grand Canal widens into a vast basin. The château is nearly 3 kilometres away.

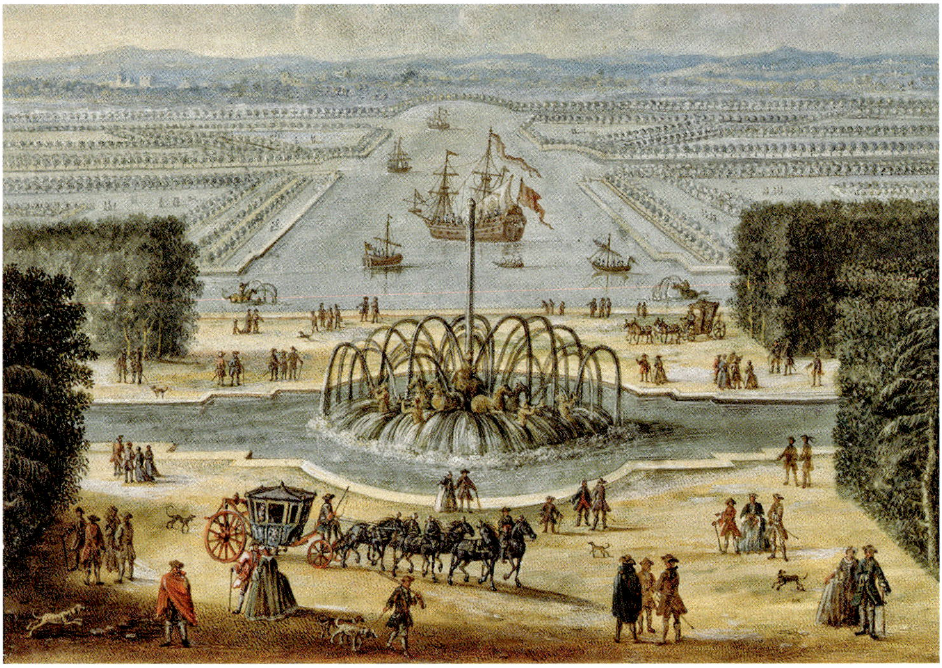

This eighteenth-century gouache shows the Apollo Basin and the Grand Canal on which floats part of the royal flotilla.

memorable *fête* one of whose highlights was the overall illumination of the canal on whose waters the entire court had embarked. In 1676 he had two lead groups representing children and marine horses placed in the rounded basin that marks the beginning of the canal, on either side of the staircase used for embarkation. The two groups were later removed.

The dimensions of the canal are impressive: the large arm measures 1,700 metres long and the small arm, 1,000 metres (600 metres for the Menagerie arm, to the south, and 400 metres for the Trianon arm to the north). At its narrowest section, it is 60 metres wide. Its total surface area is 23 hectares (nearly three times that of the Place de la Concorde in Paris). The entire basin is fringed with stone tablets and surrounded by a wide strip of grass delimited by sandy alleys that follow its plan.

The shallowness of the canal (approximately 2 metres deep) did not stop a large flotilla from developing from 1669. These small boats, quite varied in nature, constituted both a leisure fleet and an experimental fleet. First there was a small boat built in Toulon as well as a few gilt and painted rowboats in different sizes. During the winter of 1674, gondolas, a gift to the king from the Republic of Venice, arrived, accompanied by gondoliers who settled permanently in Versailles. Other gondolas were then built in Versailles by Venetian carpenters who had come to France especially. In addition to these light pleasure crafts, a fleet of scaled-down ships of the line gradually developed. In 1671 the canal was given a captain to command its fleet, the Marquis de Langeron, officer of the French royal navy. A first galley, built in Marseille and richly decorated, was launched in 1681, followed by a second in 1685, the *Grande Galère*, a reduced-scale model of the *Réale*. In 1670 the *Grand Vaisseau*, built in Le Havre, was launched, followed by the *Vaisseau de Versailles* (1685) and the *Triomphant* (1688). There was also a collection of foreign craft, including Neapolitan feluccas, English yachts and Dutch hoys. The flotilla was maintained by staff working and living in the building constructed for this purpose near the head of the canal. These low buildings whose overall plan resembled that of a miniature arsenal, were named Little Venice after the Venetian gondoliers and carpenters settled in Versailles; some families still lived there in the nineteenth century.

The Grand Canal was emptied several times over its history. Not maintained during the Revolution, it was restored at Napoleon's behest. During the First World War, it was camouflaged by a system of pontoons and nets so as not to serve as a landmark for German aviation. In 1939, at the beginning of the Second World War, it was purely and simply emptied for the same reasons as it was feared that the château and its estate would be bombed.

The Menagerie

At the end of the south arm of the Grand Canal, a vast circular basin and a wide staircase led to the Château de la Menagerie. The château, no longer extant, was built by Le Vau between 1663 and 1668, on a site meant to house the menagerie with which Louis XIV had wanted to endow Versailles. The appeal of the building especially resided in an octagonal pavilion covered with a dome, whose ground floor contained a grotto, and the first floor a vast salon of windows from which the animals, split up in a series of courtyards spread out like a fan, could be admired. After having been the setting for the walks of the court and having hosted a few *fêtes*, the estate was given by the king to his grandson's wife, the Duchesse de Bourgogne, for whom Jules Hardouin-Mansart built the two small square pavilions topped with slate roofs incorporated into the enceinte wall, the only vestiges still intact of the ensemble, destroyed in the nineteenth century as it had not been maintained.

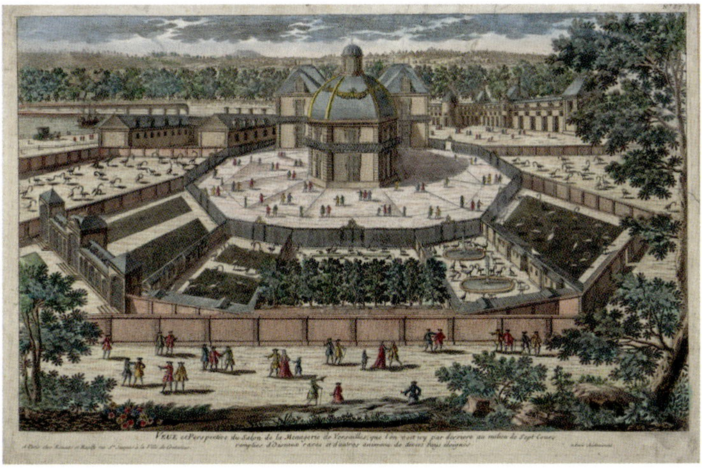

This eighteenth-century engraving shows the Château de la Menagerie and its rotunda dominating the courtyards reserved for animals.

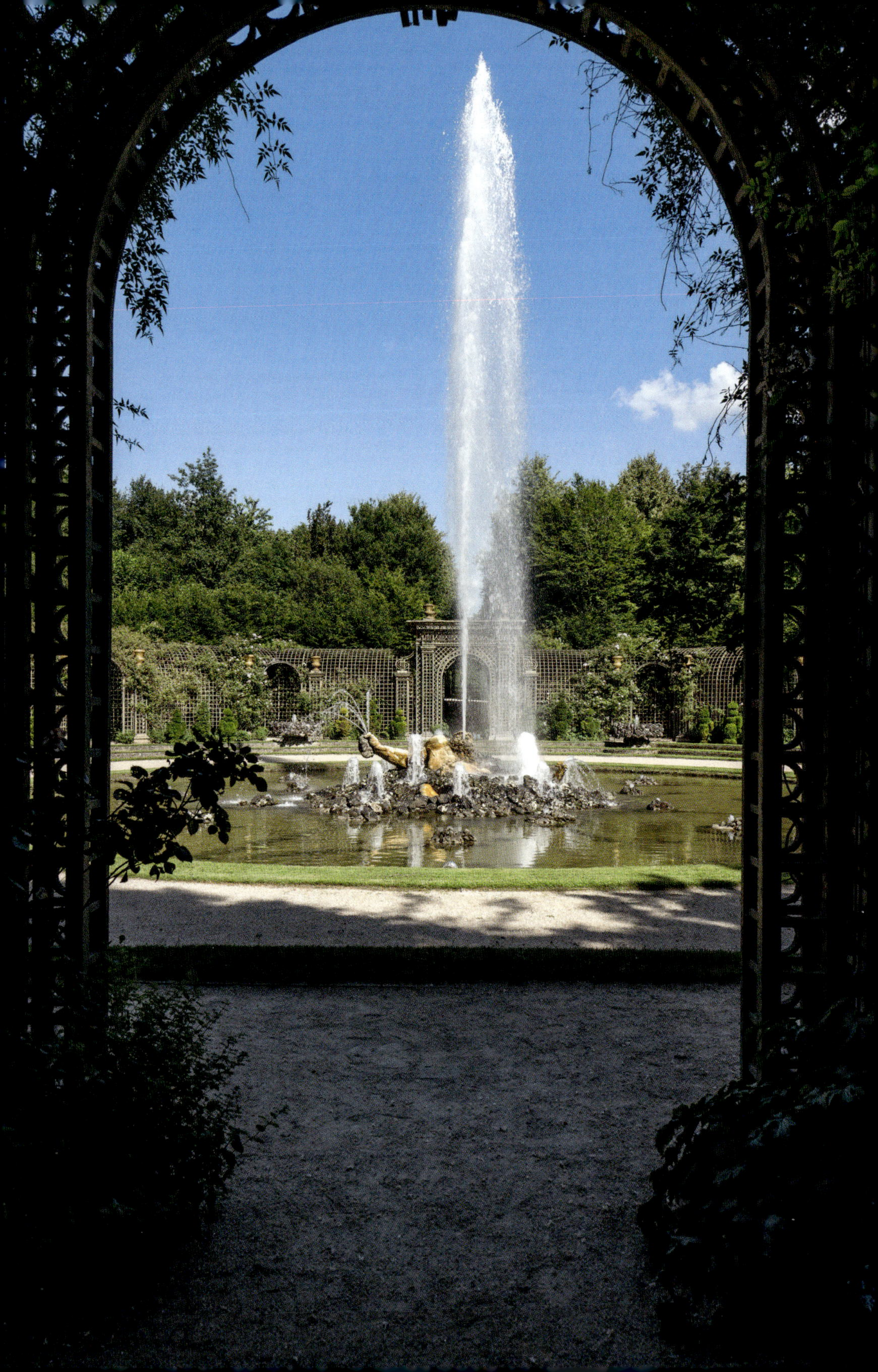

THE NORTH GROVES

The Enceladus Grove

A major refurbishment of the grove, undertaken in the late twentieth century, restored its original aspect, highlighting the know-how of seventeenth-century gardeners who had to master the art of trellis work to the point of using it in real architectural elements. The Enceladus Grove, surrounded by a wide octagonal gallery punctuated by pavilions topped with domes, is a fine example of this. Setting out and organising different spaces, the trellises also had the role of supporting and highlighting climbing plants, such as rosebushes and jasmine. They were decorated with gilt vases. Laid out between 1675 and 1677, the grove originally only comprised its trellis gallery and, in its centre, a vast circular basin for which Gaspard Marsy made a striking representation of Enceladus. This colossal gilt lead figure seeming to emerge from the rocks evokes the attempted revolt against Zeus led by the giant and his companions. Thrown at the heavens to dethrone the gods, they were broken by the immortals after violent combats known as gigantomachies in Greek mythology. Athena brought down Enceladus by hurling at him the island of Sicily under which he was buried. The half-buried giant seems to be letting out a final cry, which is conveyed by a powerful jet of water coming out of his mouth. Many wanted to see in this subject a warning against any attempt of revolt against royal authority. Without being as explicit, the scene depicted in the grove may nevertheless be interpreted as an allegory of the triumph of order over chaos.

In 1678 the grove was decorated with eight small fountains whose basins were made of concretions of sandstone. Yews clipped into the shapes of vases were also added. In 1706 the ensemble was

The Enceladus Grove.

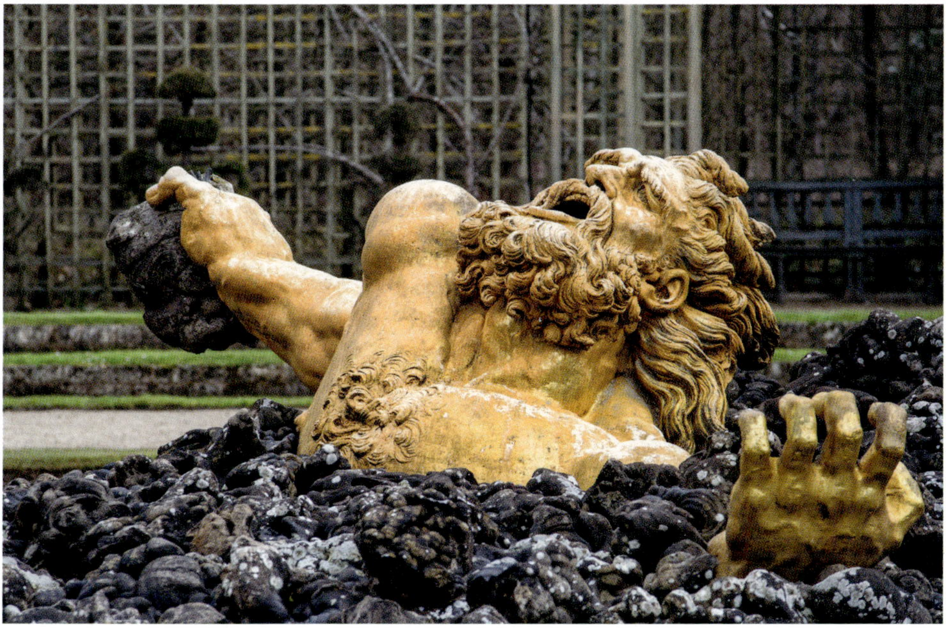

Gaspard Marsy, *Enceladus*.

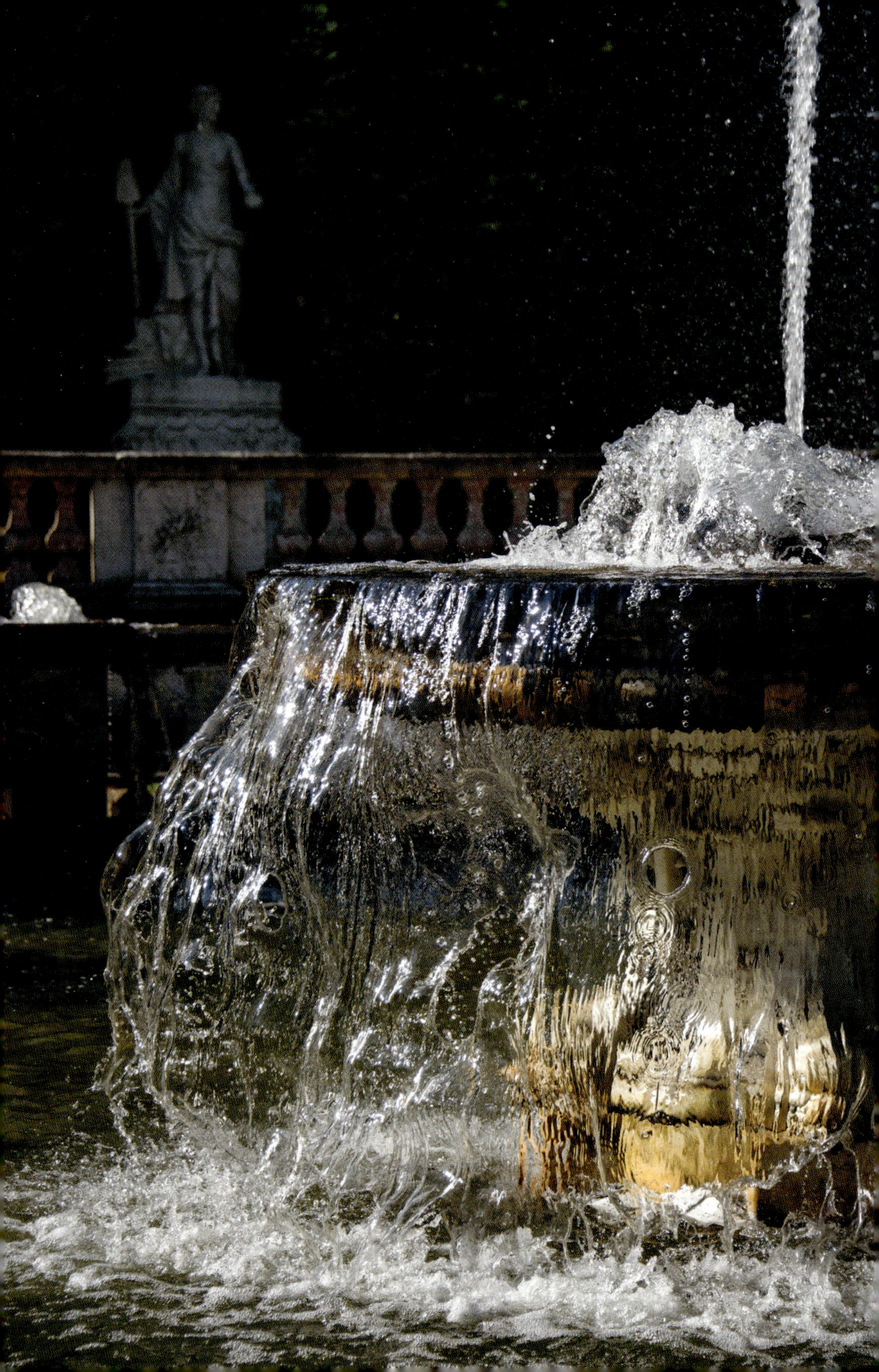

considerably modified by the removal of the trellis gallery, the fountains and the yews, which transformed the grove into a simple intersection of alleys with the basin at the centre.

The Domes Grove

Laid out between 1675 and 1680, this grove comprises a hexagonal basin surrounded by a marble balustrade and located below a second, circular balustrade. It bore many different names following the modifications of its decoration.

It was first called the Grove of Fame because of the presence of an allegorical gilt lead statue by Gaspard Marsy after a design by Le Brun, which adorned the centre of the basin. Fame was personified there by a large female figure blowing in to a trumpet that spit out water.

The Domes Grove Basin.

The first balustrade placed around the basin was in gilt metal, punctuated by eighteen pillars, which all spit out water. A channel serving as a handrail pours out in a sheet into the basin. The original balustrade was, in 1705, replaced by the present one, whose white marble balusters, pillars and red marble handrail echo the red marble balusters, pillars and white marble handrail of the upper enclosure. In 1677 it was adorned with forty-four bas-reliefs by François Girardon, Pierre Mazeline and Gilles Guérin that represented trophies from all nations. Between 1676 and 1681, with the construction of two pavilions on either side of the basin, Jules Hardouin-Mansart made his first intervention at Versailles. These two white marble edifices, open on their four sides and richly decorated with gilt lead, are topped with domes, which gave their name to the grove. Inside the pavilions, the visitor could admire a rich pavement of polychrome marbles and other bronze gilt trophies. Suffering from a lack of maintenance and threatened with

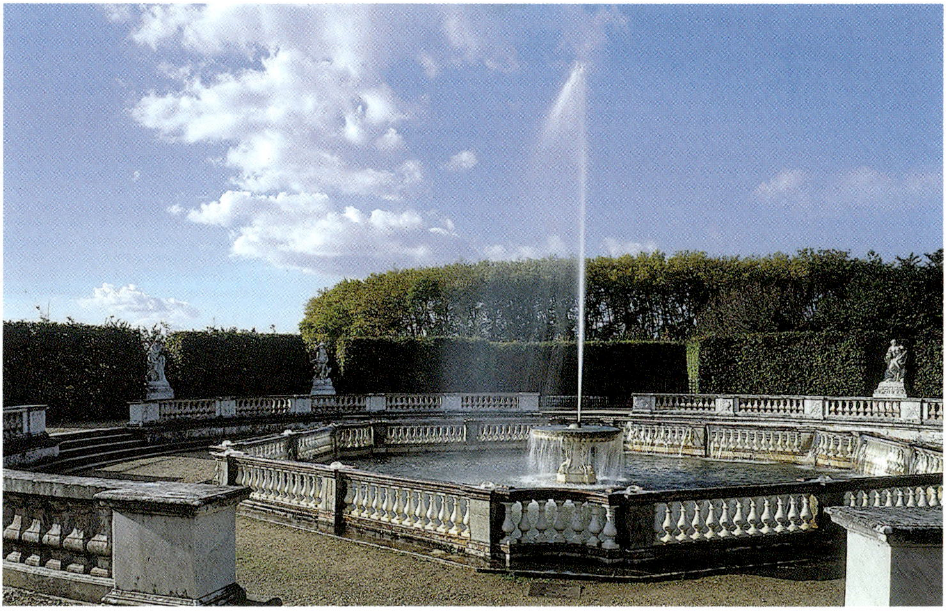

The Domes Grove.

ruin, the edifices were destroyed in 1820. There are still, however, material traces of their location on the ground. Between 1684 and 1705, the grove was home to the statues of the Grotto of Tethys whose demolition was rendered inevitable by the construction of the North Wing of the château. In reference to Girardon's central group, *Apollo Served by the Nymphs*, it took the name of Grove of Apollo's Baths. When this work was once again moved, the grove took on its present name. In 1708 the sculptors Poirier, Lespingola and Hardy completed a new basin supported by dolphins for the centre of the pool, giving the ensemble its definitive aspect.

The statuary adorning the grove has been modified several times. On the other hand, the plinths are those made in 1677 for the grove. The works now in situ are for the large part modern copies, the originals having gradually moved to more sheltered locations because of their growing fragility: *Amphitrite* by Nicolas Massé after Michel Anguier, *Galatea* by Jean-Baptiste Tuby (copy), *Dawn* by Philippe Magnier (copy), *Acis* by Jean-Baptiste Tuby (copy), *Daybreak* by Pierre Legros (copy), *Callisto* by Anselme Flamen (copy) and *Arion* by Jean Raon.

The Obelisk Grove

This open grove comprises a rectangular basin flowing through four water staircases with five steps into a canal located below. In the centre of the basin, a clump of lead reeds generates, when the water is flowing, a powerful spray rising 23 metres high and made up of 231 jets, which resembles a liquid obelisk. Laid out between 1704 and 1705 by Jules Hardouin-Mansart, the grove replaces an earlier, more complex ensemble by Le Nôtre, laid out between 1671 and 1674: a quatrefoil rectangular island, decorated by four small round basins, surrounded by a canal equipped with jets and itself surrounded by four circular basins. The centre of the island, which was reached via two small swing bridges, was raised by two steps in order to form a vast central reservation lined with topiary. In 1674 Louis XIV hosted a brilliant dinner there and sometimes enjoyed holding his council there, activities which earned the grove the name Feasting Chamber Grove or Council Chamber Grove. In 1681 the exterior basins and the canal were endowed with sculpted elements from the four basins of the seasons that the king had resolved to simplify, retaining only the central groups. After the transformation of the grove, these elements were sent to decorate the Trianon basins.

The Star Grove

This grove is now one of the most isolated ones in the garden. It is, however, one of the first groves of the lower section of the garden to have been laid out according to a particularly complex plan: after entering the grove, the visitor first gained access to a vast circular alley surrounded by trellises. To move further ahead, he has to find one of the three narrow, winding alleys that allow him to reach a new pentagonal alley. The five corners of the alley, each marked

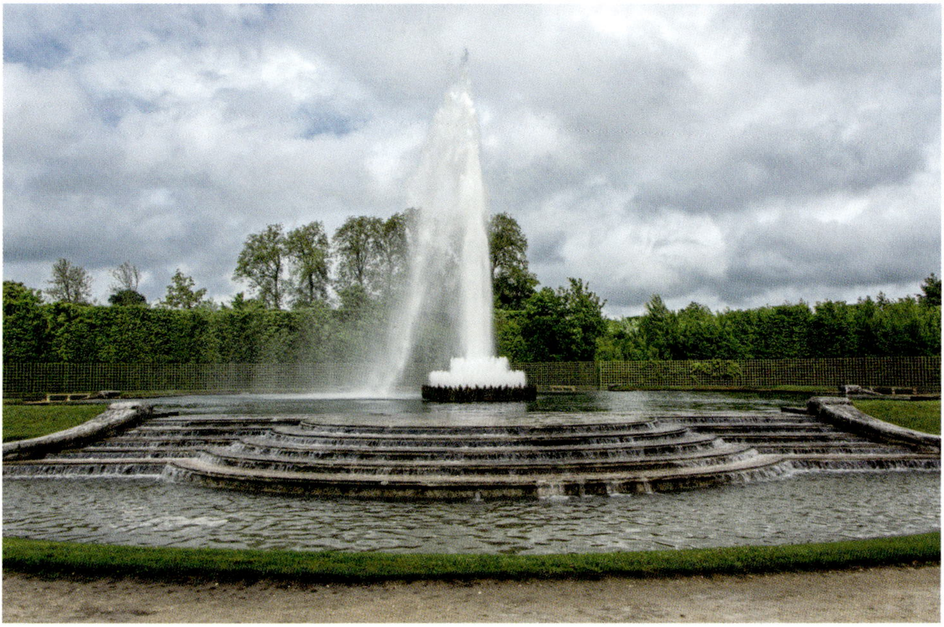

The Obelisk Grove.

by a small circular basin, are starting points for five rectilinear alleys that lead to the centre of the grove to which this novel plan, reminiscent of that of a star, naturally gave its name. In 1670–71, the central basin was decorated with a rocaille border and a central rock from which flowed a spray of water. The ensemble then took the name Water Mountain Grove. In the early eighteenth century, the layout of the alleys was profoundly modified and its labyrinthine aspect replaced by axes that allowed the wood to be crossed without a detour. The overall replanting of the garden attempted to partially reuse the original layout of the grove without, however, completely restituting it.

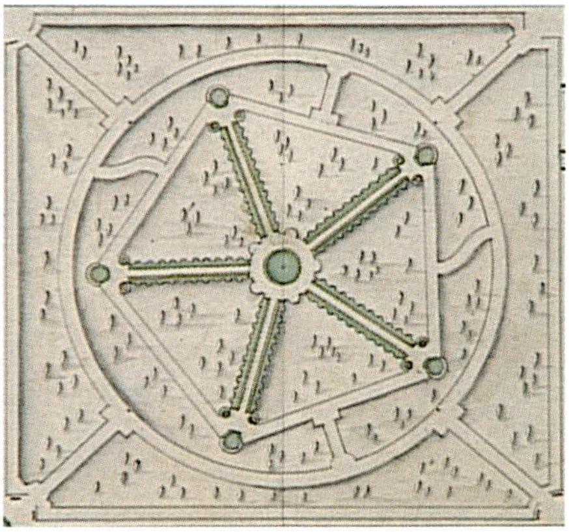

Seventeenth-century plan showing the former state of the Star Grove. Two small straight alleys were already added to the two original winding alleys to go from the circular alley to the pentagonal alley.

The Grove of Apollo's Baths

The present grove occupies the site of two former groves which were joined together in the late eighteenth century when Louis XVI, while the entire garden was being replanted, decided to create a new ensemble in the new landscaped garden style. Between 1670 and 1674, in the upper section of the wood, Louis XIV had laid out the stunning Marsh Grove, said to have been inspired by Madame de Montespan herself. It was a vast rectangular basin whose edge was decorated with tin reeds and four lead swans placed in each of the corners of the basin, all of it concealing jets of water that converged towards the centre of the ornamental lake. The lake was occupied by a small island also edged with reeds from which rose a bronze oak with tin foliage whose branches shoot off jets of water. All these ornaments were painted naturalistically. Two *buffets d'eau* and two marble tables placed on the sides of the grove rounded out this refined but fragile ensemble. The basin, tables and *buffets* disappeared in 1704–05, replaced by a new fountain meant to host the three large groups of the former Grotto of Tethys, moved to the Domes Grove in 1684: *Apollo Served by the Nymphs* by Girardon, as well as the two groups of the *Horses of the Sun* by Guérin and the Marsy brothers. Each was topped by a tall gilt lead canopy and placed on a plinth from which the water flowed to fall in a cascade into a basin. The grove then naturally took on the name Grove of Apollo's Baths.

The lower section of the wood, located to the west, was never landscaped under Louis XIV despite several projects.
In 1736 Louis XV had a small octagonal pavilion built there by Gabriel for the amusement of his son; it was decorated

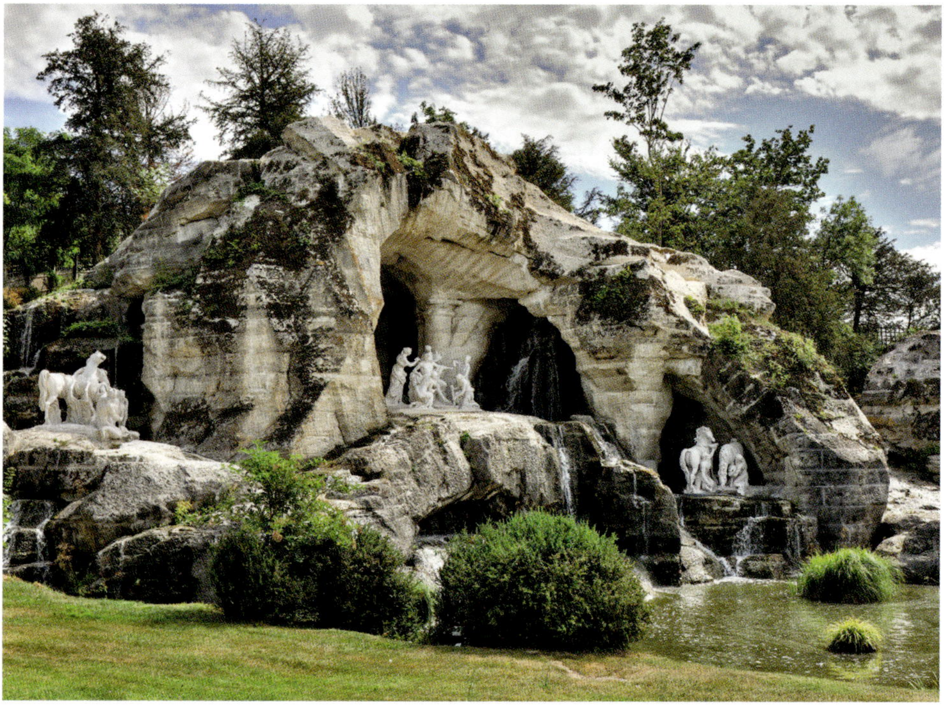

François Girardon, *Apollo Served by the Nymphs.*

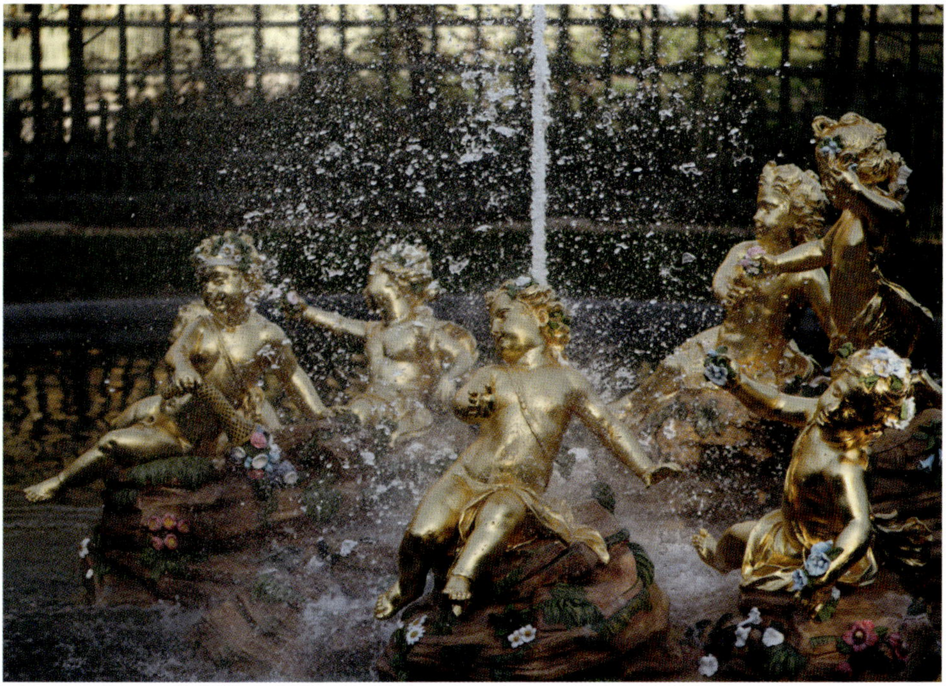

The Isle of Children or Golden Children Basin.

with a small fountain. The "Petit Bosquet du Dauphin" was short-lived, disappearing a few years later.

During the overall replanting of the garden ordered by Louis XVI at the beginning of his reign, the Grove of Apollo's Baths was in a poor state and it was decided to transform it radically. In 1778 the painter Hubert Robert's project was chosen and laid out. By uniting the two parts of the wood, the artist created a vast ensemble covered with winding alleys that gradually let to a vast clearing where a small lake was topped by an enormous artificial rock. In the centre, a grotto contains the Apollo group. Powerful columns that seemed to have been carved out of the rock evoke the Palace of the Sun while surrounded with cascades, the two groups of horses are arranged below. While affirming a new aesthetic, Hubert Robert respected the memory of the first Grotto of Tethys, conserving its theatrical spirit.

In 2008, because of their fragility and the inevitable damage caused by bad weather and pollution, the three groups – considered absolute masterpieces of seventeenth-century French sculpture – were, like the most valuable statues of the garden, taken indoors and replaced by copies.

The Water Theatre Grove and the Golden Children Basin

The recent creation of a contemporary grove on this long-neglected site revived the memory of one of the older marvels of the gardens of Versailles: the Water Theatre. Designed by André Le Nôtre with the collaboration of the fountain designers Denis and Francini to highlight the variety

Following pages:
The Grove of Apollo's Baths.

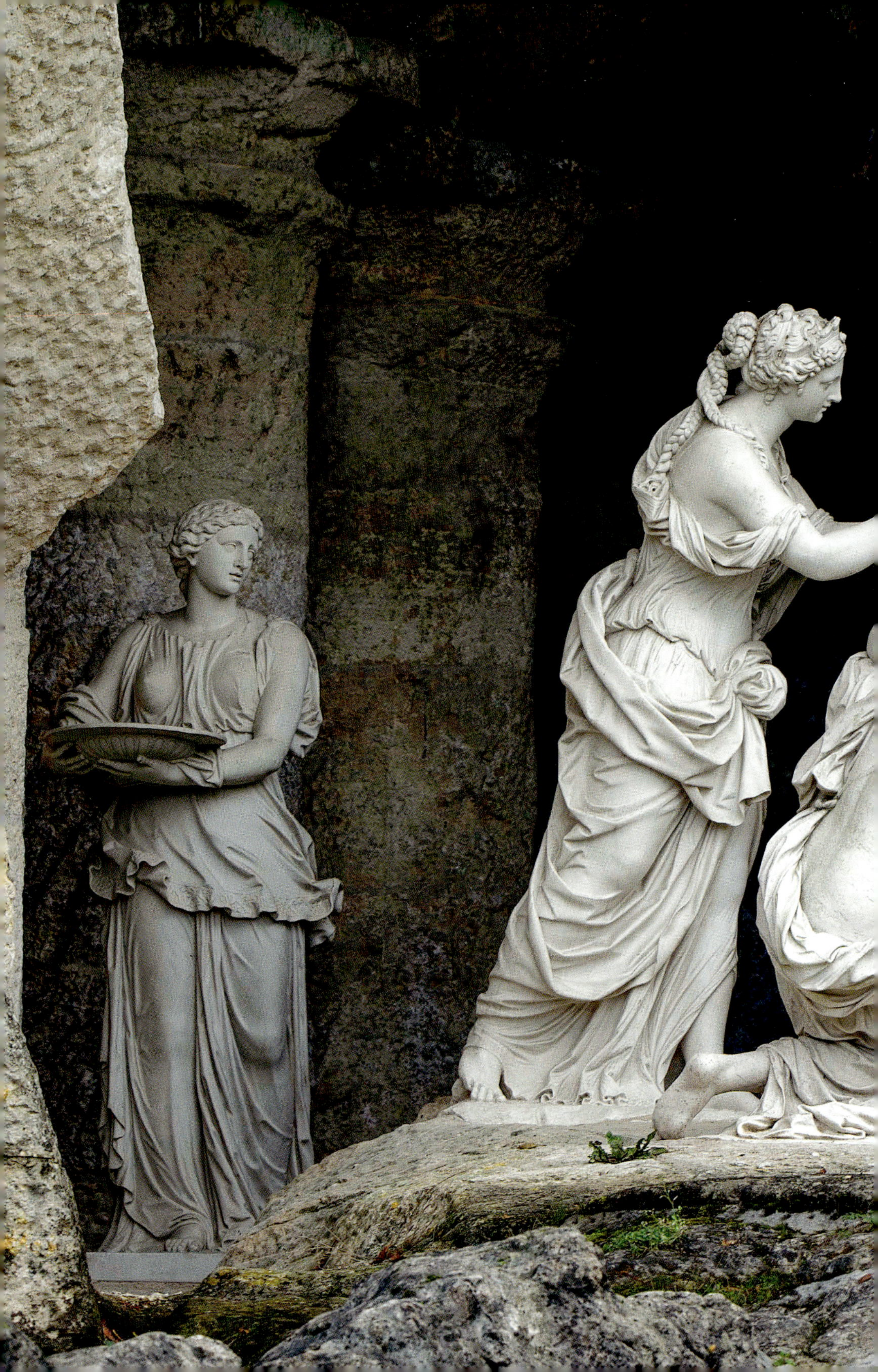

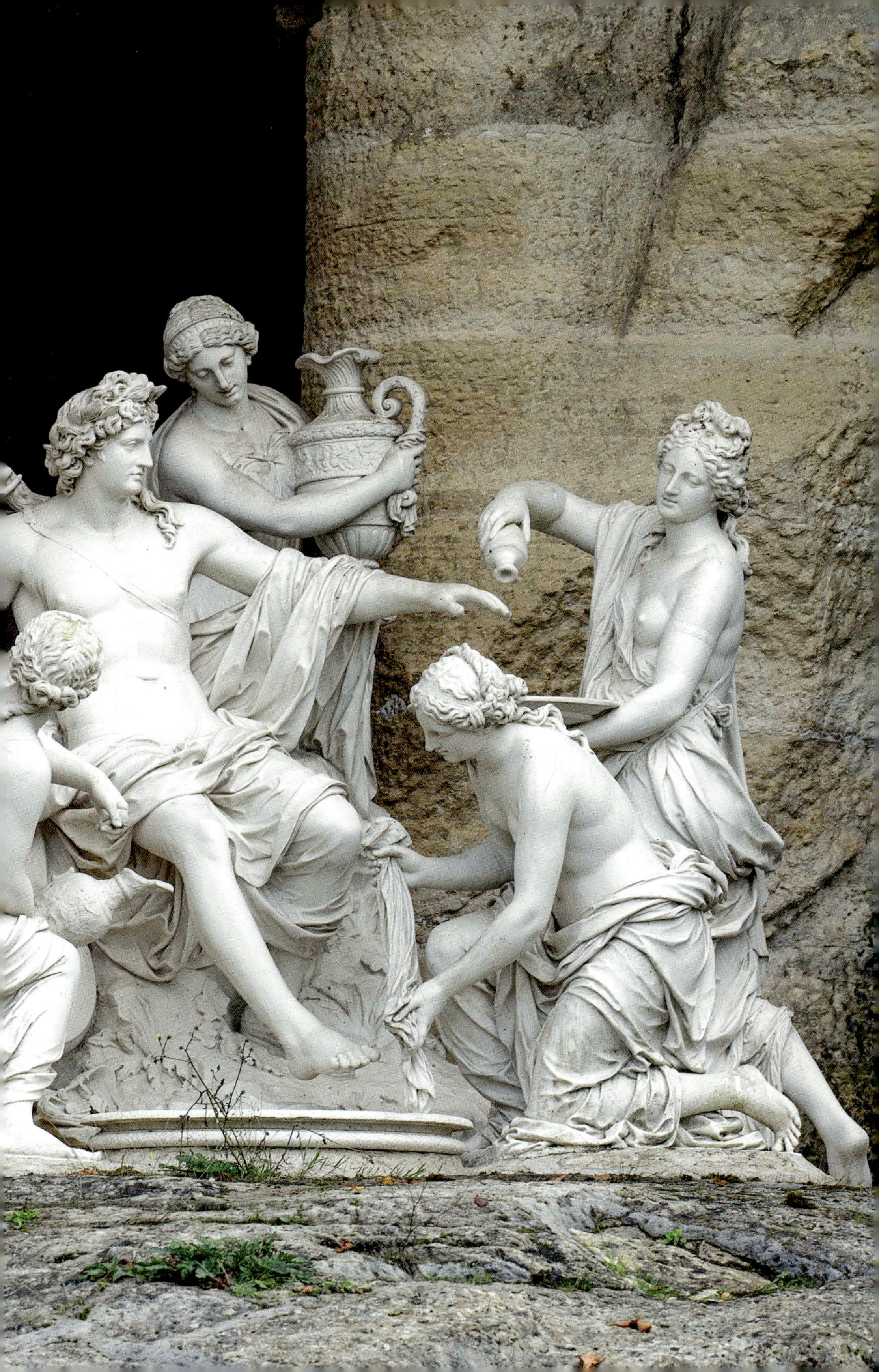

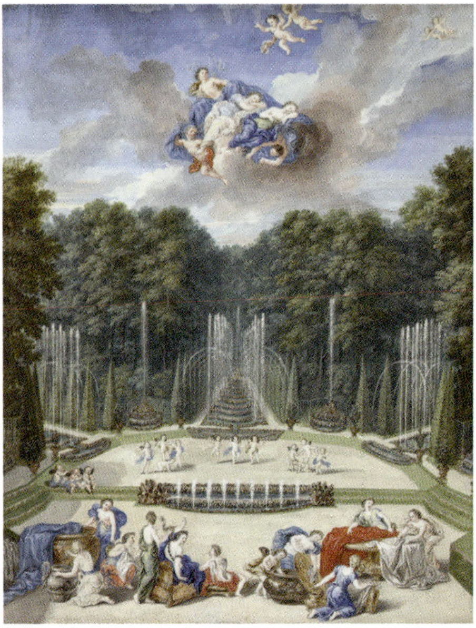

The former Water Theatre Grove by Jean Cotelle (eighteenth century).

of water features, the grove was completed in 1674. Its layout, which in large part inspired the present plan, featured two distinct spaces, like in a real theatre: the auditorium, located to the north, and the stage, to the south. The stage, raised by a few grass-covered steps with a small water staircase in the middle, marked the starting point of three perspectives treated as cascades and ending, in the distance, in allegorical fountains evoking *Valour, Strength* and *Wealth*. The space dedicated to the auditorium was surrounded by arbours, each sheltering a small round basin in which a jet of water rises. Fragile and fallen out of fashion, the grove disappeared during the replanting of the garden ordered by Louis XVI and its centre was then occupied by a simple circle of lawn that gave it its name, "Rond-Vert".

In 2015 the renovation of the grove was entrusted to the landscape architect Louis Benech and the artist Jean-Michel Othoniel. Both were inspired by the original design but did not create a pastiche of it. The water displays that made the name of the grove under Louis XIV served as a starting point for the new design. The moving 1,750 glass

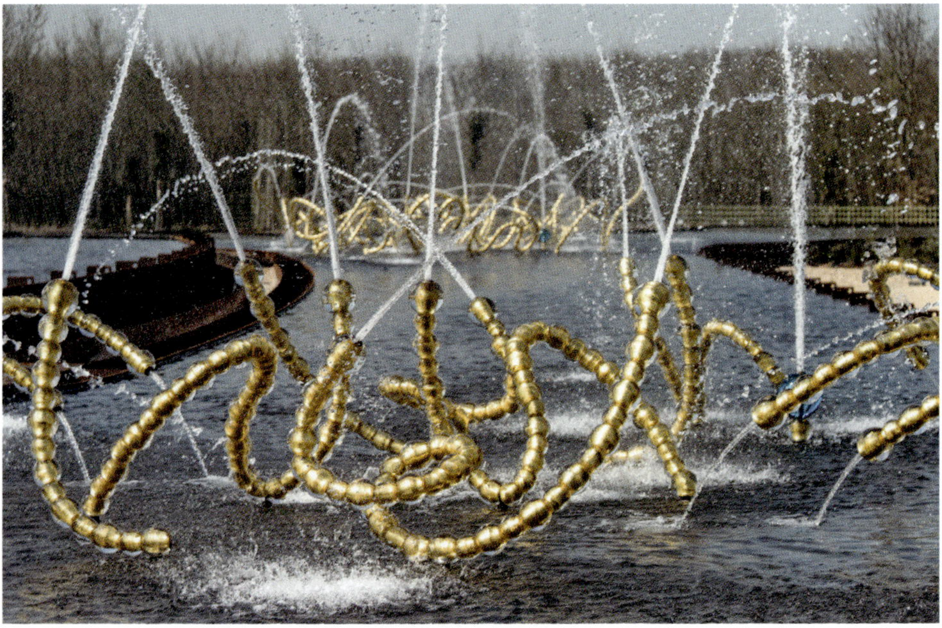

The Water Theatre Grove today.

beads decorated with gold leaf that are deployed in the basin are directly inspired by choreographic writing and represent, in three dimensions, three seventeenth-century dance steps inspired by Raoul Auger Feuillet's book, published in 1700, *La Chorégraphie ou l'art de décrire la danse*.

To the west of the Water Theatre, a circular trellis surrounded by arbours conceals a basin dug in 1704 and decorated with a group of eight gilt lead cherubs frolicking around a small island in the shape of a rock, strewn with naturalistically painted flowers. These charming figures, the work of the sculptor Jean Hardy, were originally intended for the garden of Marly but were installed in Versailles in the end in 1709, a period when childhood was a decorative them of which the king was particularly fond.

The Three Fountains Grove

The two woods bordering the Water Alley were rapidly landscaped by Louis XIV. To the west, from 1665–66, Le Nôtre laid out a simple alley that the hydraulic engineer Francini decorated with a multitude of water jets forming a vault above the strollers. The "Bosquet du Berceau d'Eau" was radically transformed between 1677 and 1679, and then became the Three Fountains Grove. Like many other groves, it suffered from a lack of maintenance in the early nineteenth century and disappeared, returning to its natural state. It was recreated exactly as it was between 1998 and 2005, after a long preliminary study comparing archaeological vestiges and old plans kept in the archives and whose results enabled its renaissance.

As it was originally, the space is organised according to the downward slope of the terrain and divided into three distinct levels connected by cascades. At the lowest level is an octagonal basin with rocaille decoration whose jets form a fleur-de-lis; a grassy slope edged with cascades leads to an intermediary level occupied by a square basin enlivened by a water arbour with arching jets; finally, two grassy slopes frame a vast cascade formed by lead double shell lead to a final level where a column of water spouts from a circular basin. The ensemble is surrounded by a bench highlighted with yews. Because of its terracing and the variety of its water features, the grove presents multiple viewpoints to the visitor, who should explore from top to bottom and from bottom to top to appreciate all its diversity.

The Triumphal Arch Grove

A pendant to the Three Fountains Grove, the Triumphal Arch Grove is located to the east of the Water Alley. It replaced an initial feature known as the *Pavillon d'Eau*, created in 1671. Significant modifications, begun in 1677 and completed in 1684, radically transformed it, making it one of the most magnificent groves in the garden at the time. Playing on the difference in level that leads from the North Parterre to the Neptune Basin, Le Nôtre organised the space into two *salles vertes* joined by an alley flanked by small waterfalls. Stunning gilt lead structures and marble fountains amplified the water features. In the upper section, no longer extant, a vast metal gilt triumphal arch, the work of Pierre Mazeline, featured multiple jets of water, which then flowed in cascades into a vast basin. Two tall marble *buffets d'eau*, flanked by metal gilt obelisks rounded out the ensemble. The lower section, which also featured *buffets d'eau*,

Following pages:
The Three Fountains Grove.

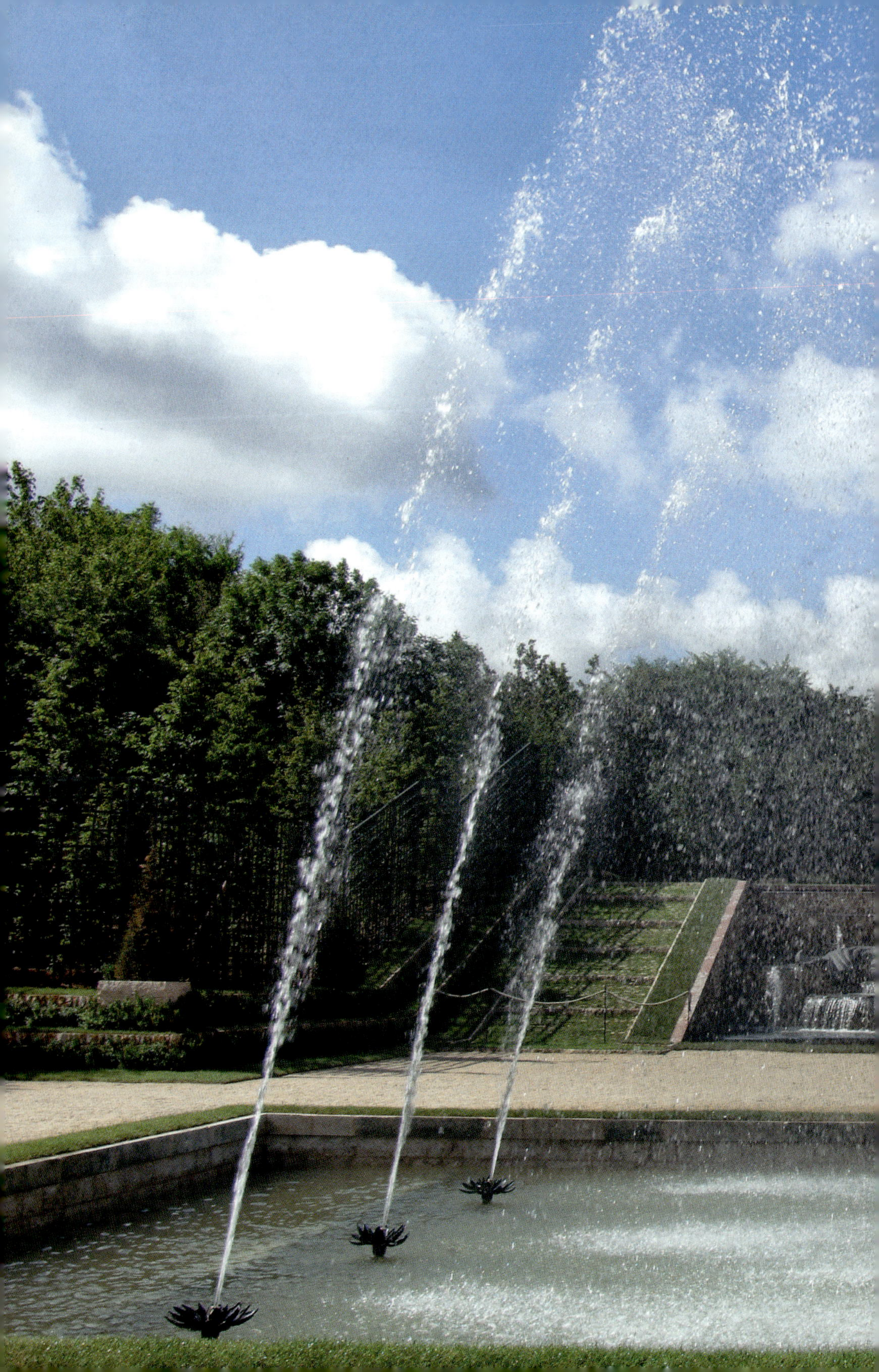

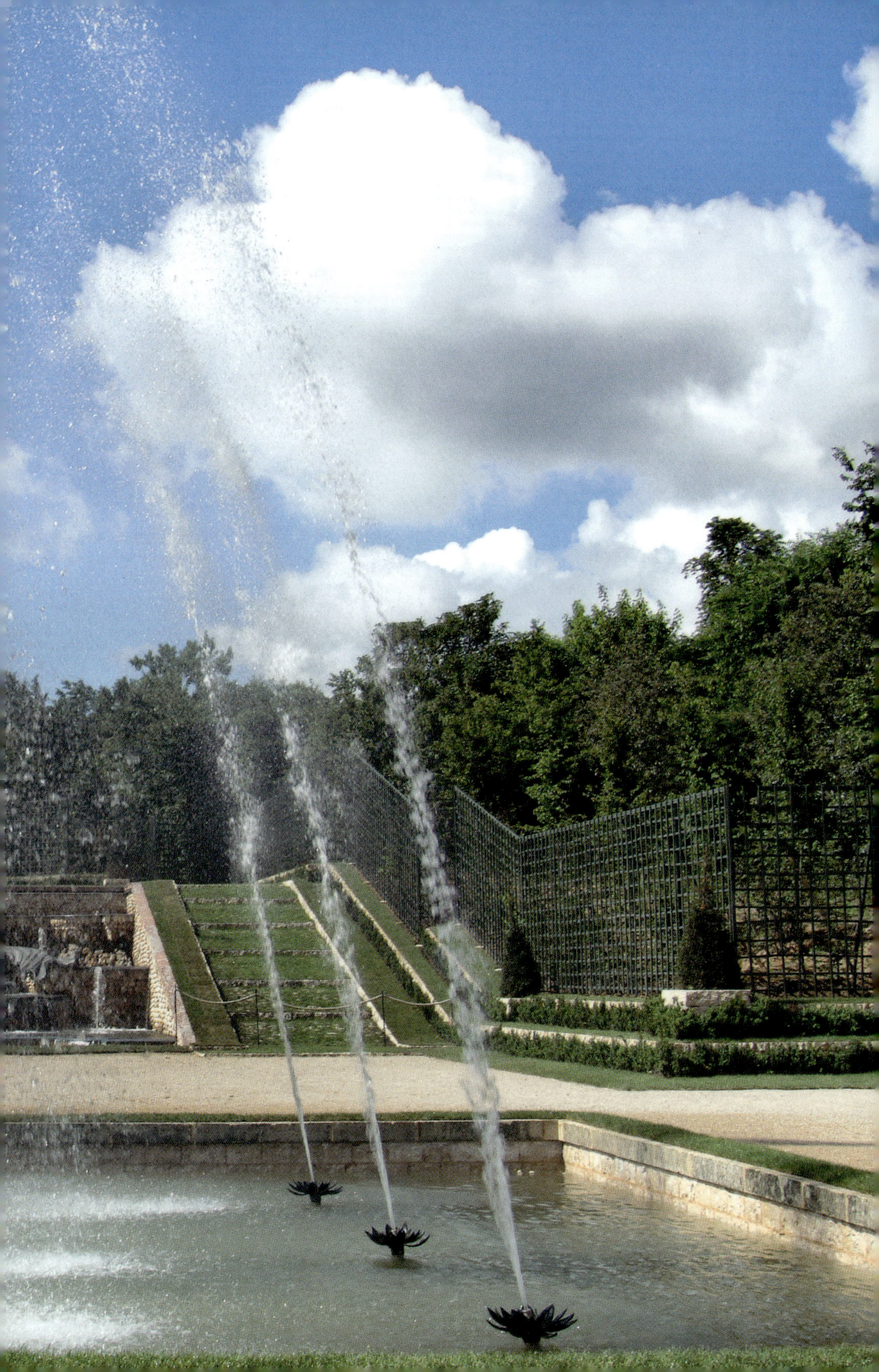

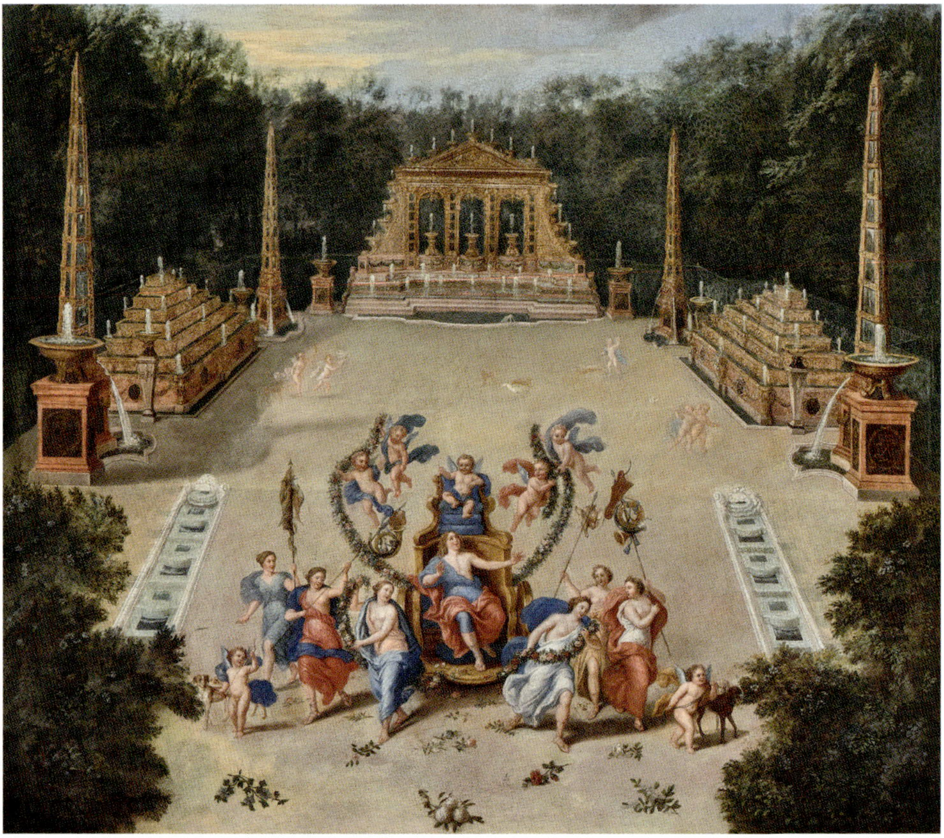

Jean Cotelle, *The Triumphal Arch Grove* (detail), this view shows the upper section of the grove, no longer extant.

has only retained the diamond-shaped basin containing the majestic allegory of France triumphant. The composition, the work of the sculptors Girardon, Tuby and Prou, celebrates the king's military triumphs and is a reminder of the victories of the Dutch War (1672–78) and the more recent ones of the War of the Reunions (1683–84). On a white marble base with three steps decorated with icicles, France, the crest of whose helmet conceals a rooster, holding a lance, sits on a triumphal chariot. In her left hand, she holds a shield decorated with fleurs-de-lis surrounding a Rhodian sun. Along the chariot wheels, two military trophies accompany two captive warriors, each of whom seems to be crushing one of the emblematic animals of the conquered powers: to the left, Spain symbolised by a lion; to the right, the Holy Roman Empire, symbolised by an eagle. On the step below, two overturned shields serve as small intermediary basins from which water flows while, on the front of the fountain, the hydra of discord and war breathes its last in splashes of water.

The fountain of France triumphant in the Triumphal Arch Grove.

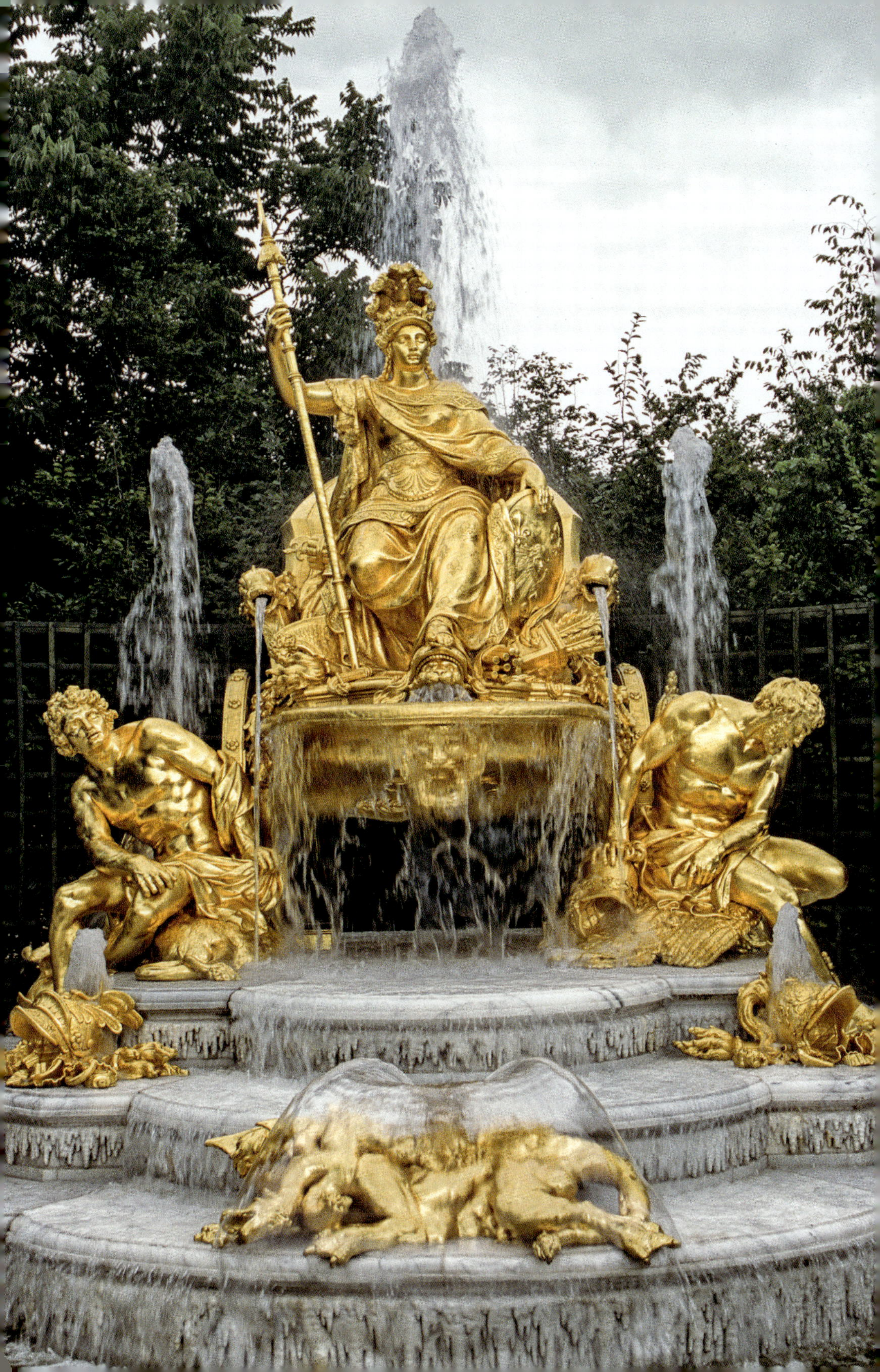

THE WATER ALLEY AND ITS BASINS

The Pyramid Fountain

At the end of the North Parterre, the Pyramid Fountain marks the entrance of the Water Alley, which gently slopes down towards the Neptune Basin. This striking composition was designed by Girardon, who completed it in 1672. Made out of lead and entirely gilt originally, it is in the middle of a basin whose form, originally quatrefoil, was modified in 1683 to become circular. The structure of the ensemble bears witness to great originality. The four basins – decreasing in size – that make it up are supported, from bottom to top, the first by lion paws and tritons, the second by young tritons, the third by dolphins and the fourth by crayfish. The ensemble is topped by a vase from which flows the water that supplies the whole.

The Fountain of the Bathing Nymphs

The incline of the Water Alley allowed for a basin – invisible from the North Parterre and which one only discovers after advancing along the alley – to be laid out. This basin receives the overflow of the Pyramid Fountain above and then to supply the fountains of the Water Alley. In 1670 a large lead relief, which used to be gilt, by Girardon showing nymphs bathing and playing among the reeds was placed on the retaining wall. The other reliefs surrounding it were made by Legros, Le Hongre, Magnier and Legendre. They represent river deities – identifiable by their urns pouring water – and cherubs bearing a basket of fruit or shells, or playing with a dolphin. The two smallest reliefs are adorned to the east by a dolphin and a crayfish and to the west by two dolphins. The south wall is adorned with four terms on rusticated pilasters representing fauns, whose heads and hooves were made from bronze. When the fountains flow, this remarkable sculpted

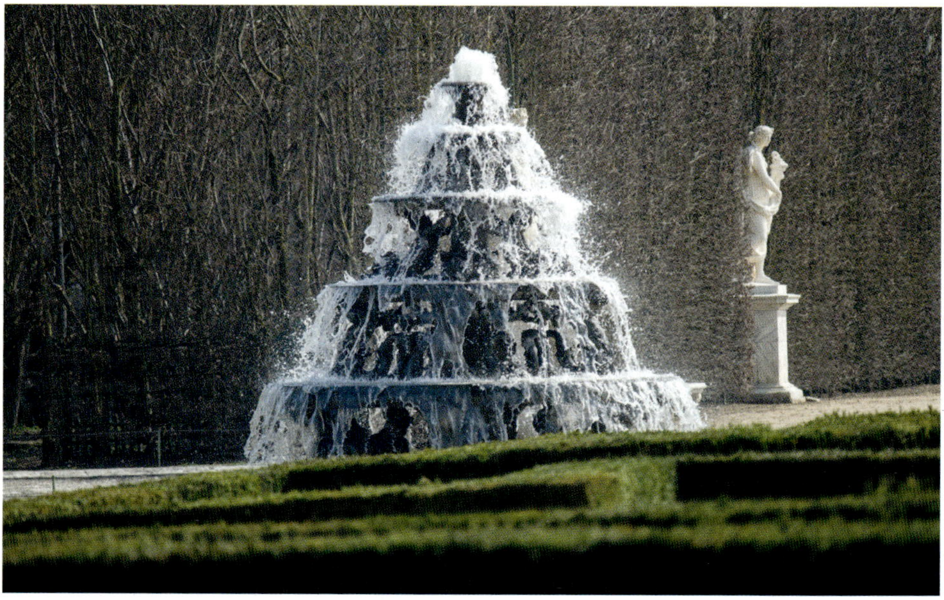

The Pyramid Fountain.

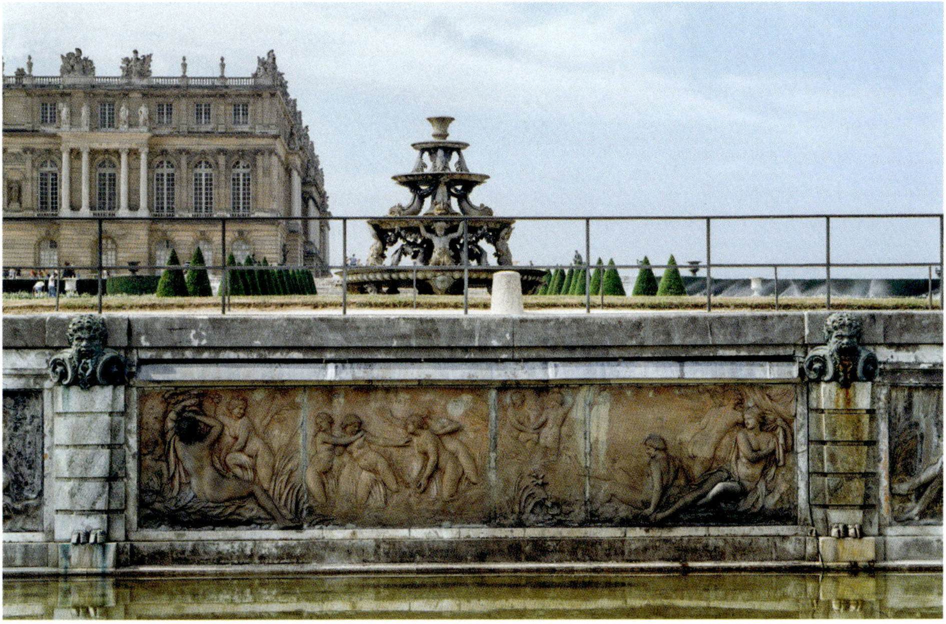

The Fountain of Bathing Nymphs.

ensemble is decorated by an expanse of water that falls in front of Girardon's relief, enlivening the scene while lightly veiling it.

The Water Alley

The Water Alley, also known as the Alley of the Marmosets links the North Parterre to the Dragon Basin. Beginning in 1668, a major decorative project – inspired by the architect Claude Perrault and revised by the painter Le Brun – led to the creation of fourteen fountains, divided into two rows of seven, place on either side of the alley. Initially in gilt lead, the fountains represented, by identical pair, groups of children, cherubs, young tritons or young satyrs each carrying a basket of naturalistically panted fruit or flowers. They were made by the sculptors Legros, Le Hongre and Lerambert. Finished in 1670, the series was completed in 1678 by either supplementary groups made by Massou and placed at the bottom of the alley, around the Dragon Basin. Between 1684 and 1688, the ensemble was modified: the lead groups were replaced by identical bronze versions and the baskets by Languedoc pink marble. Topiary was then added between each of the basins, the ensemble surrounded by a strip of lawn.

Moving down the alley, we come successively across, in pairs:

- *Three tritons*
- *Three children dancing and holding bunches of grapes*
- *Two cherubs and a girl*
- *Three children dancing*
- *Three child musicians*
- *Three satyrs*
- *Three children as terms*
- *Three children hunting, accompanied by a dog*
- *Three children fishing*
- *Three boys*
- *Three girls*

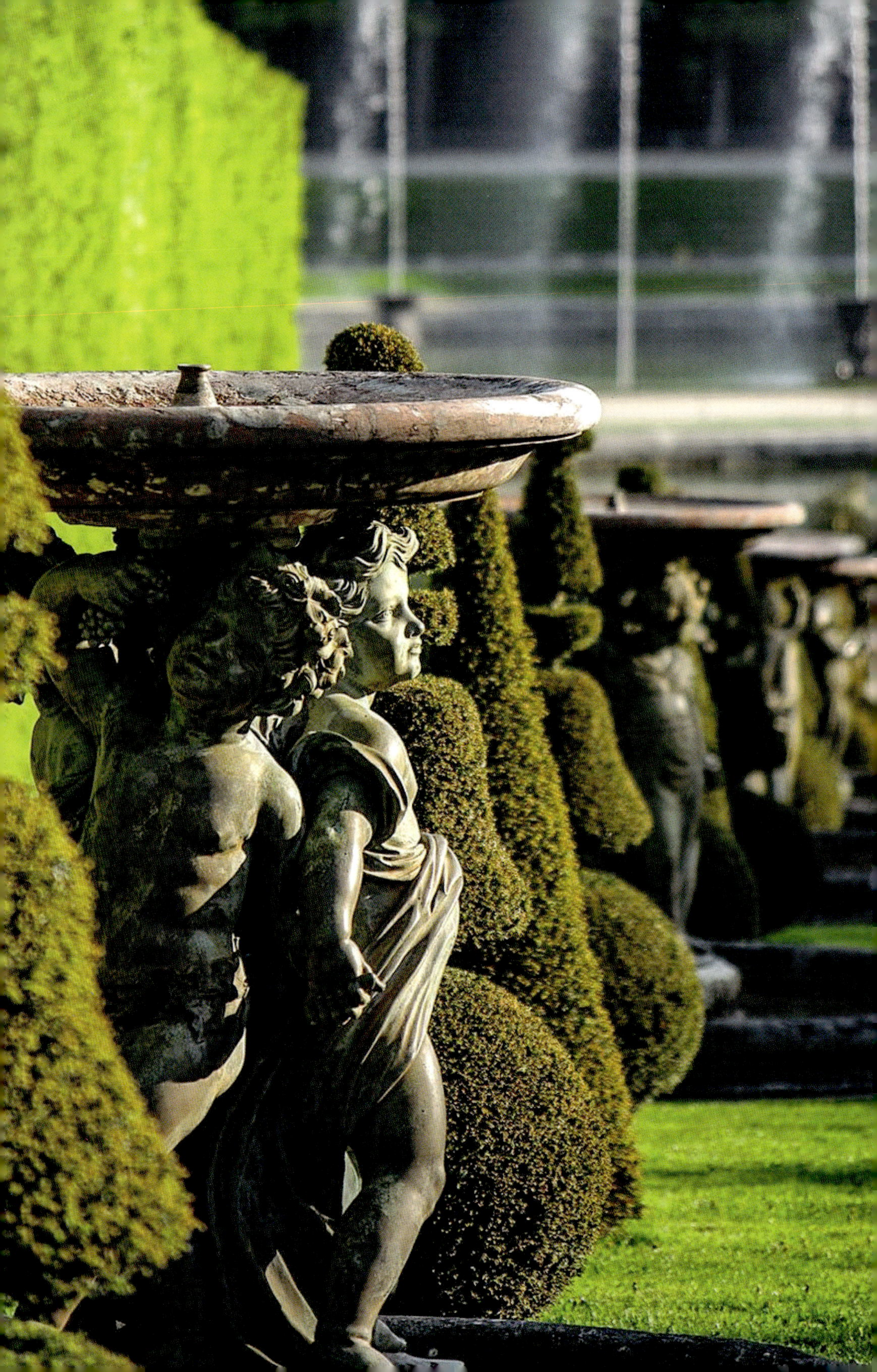

The Dragon Basin

The first circular basin, dug from 1663, was initially known as the *Grand Rondeau*. In 1667 it was given significant sculpted decoration by the brothers Balthazar and Gaspard Marsy, evoking the combat of Apollo and the serpent Python. In mythology, the sun god fought the dragon that guarded a sanctuary dedicated to Gaia at Delphi. As he was the victor, he could establish his oracle there. In another version, recounted by Ovid, the young Apollo killed the serpent that Juno had pursue Latona, the god's mother, and his sister Diana.

Enlarged in the early eighteenth century to attain its present dimensions, the basin saw its sculpture entirely replaced in the late nineteenth century. The present elements, produced on a larger scale than the original ones, are the work of the sculptor Tony Noël and were completed in 1889. In accordance with the original composition, cherubs straddling swans and accompanied by dolphins shoot their arrows at the dragon whose powerful torso, oriented southwards, rises above the waters. Out of the monster's mouth escapes, like a cry of agony, a powerful jet that the art of the fountain designers allows to be regulated two different ways: the *grande manière*, when the water rises nearly 30 metres, was reserved for the king, while the jet ordinarily only rose 11 metres.

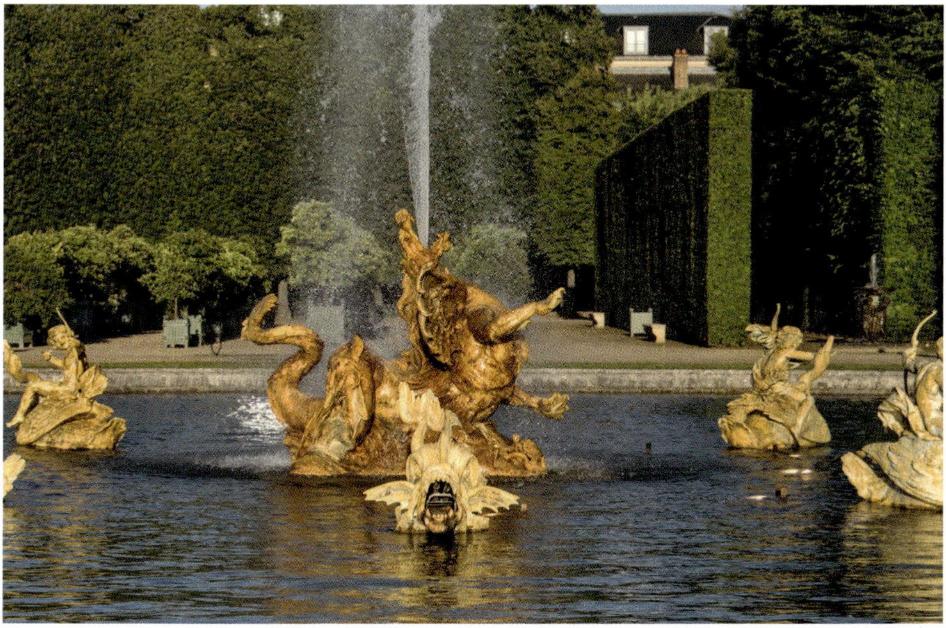

The Dragon Basin.

The Water Alley or Alley of the Marmosets. In the distance, the jet of the Neptune Basin.

The Neptune Basin

Dug between 1678 and 1682, this vast ornamental lake was first known as the *Pièce des Sapins* because of the trees that lined it. Its location below allowed it to play a drainage role for this part of the garden. It seems that sculpted decoration having the god Neptune as its theme had been planned from the beginning, but the project was never executed under Louis XIV. It was his successor who completed the ensemble with the installation of large sculpted groups. The new Neptune Basin was inaugurated in August 1741.

On the south side of the basin, the retaining wall is bordered by a small canal or gutter decorate with lead vases whose varied decoration may be admired: lizards, shells, lobsters, serpents and aquatic foliage clearly announce the maritime theme of the basin. The wall itself is decorated with icicles and punctuated with twenty-four lead mascarons, all different, spouting water into the shells (it is the overflow of the gutter that thus streams into the basin). In 1738 the architect Jacques Gabriel slightly modified the shape of the basin to be able to place new groups commissioned by Louis XV in it. These lead groups, which, like the vases of the gutter, were originally gilded, feature various marine deities. In the centre, *Neptune and Amphitrite* by the brothers Lambert-Sigisbert and Nicolas-Sébastien Adam (1741): the couple is depicted sitting on a gigantic shell that serves as a chariot. Neptune brandishes his trident in an authoritarian gesture; Amphitrite lying by his side holds the sceptre of the seas. On either side rises a sea horse tamed by a vigorous triton and a walrus. Behind this creature, a nereid accompanied by a young triton offers a branch of coral to the goddess. Under the shell emerges a triton blowing into a conch, flanked by two sea monsters. To the west is *Ocean* by Jean-Baptiste Lemoyne (1740): the god is supported by a sea monster whose rostrum evokes that of a narwhal. Near him are a seal, a large crab and a sea serpent. To the east, *Proteus* by Edme Bouchardon (1739): charged with guarding Neptune's troops, the god, represented as a young man,

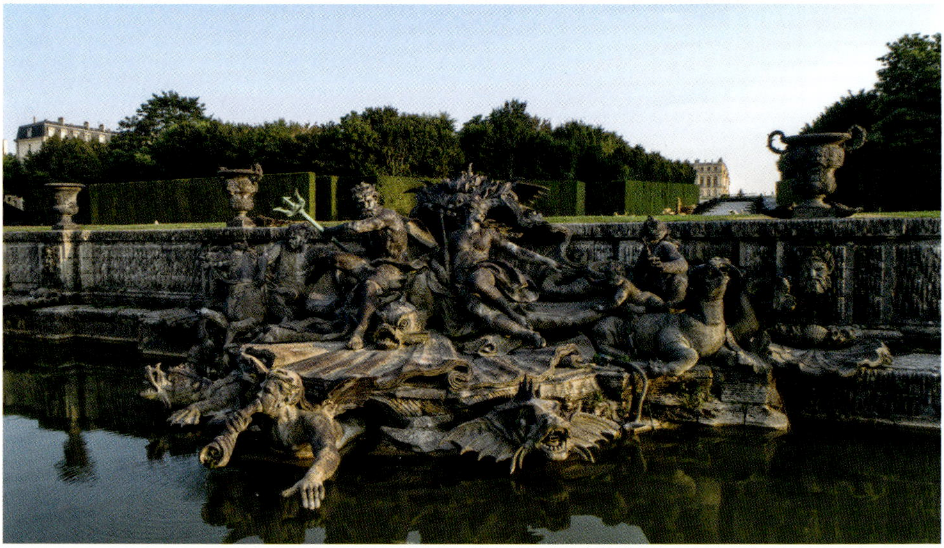

The Neptune Basin: *Neptune and Amphitrite* by the Adam brothers.

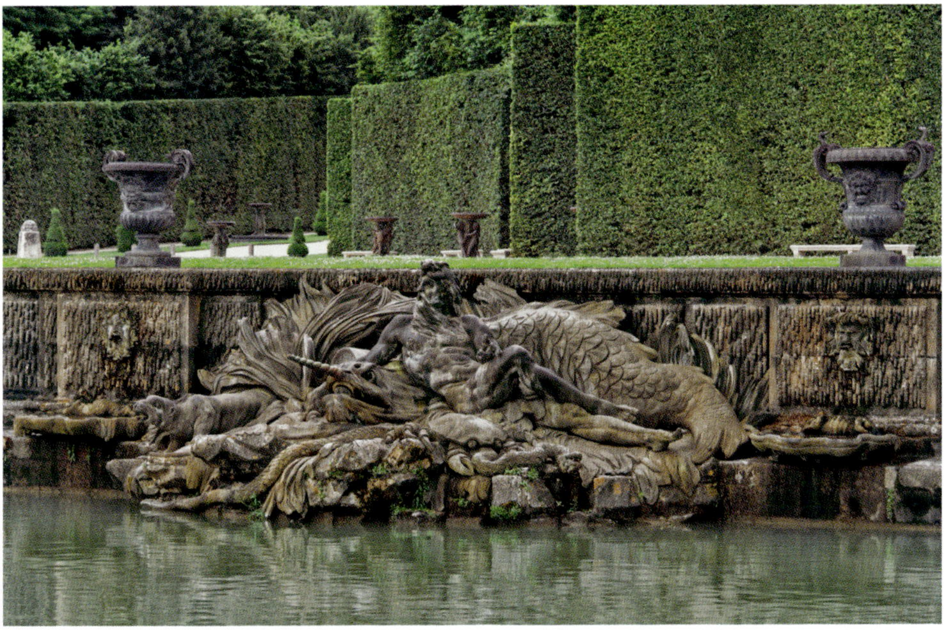

The Neptune Basin: *Ocean* by Jean-Baptiste Lemoyne.

clasps a dolphin. They are both placed in the centre of a vast shell from underneath which emerge the heads of two fish and two seals. Bouchardon also made the two dragons straddled by cherubs that flank the ensemble.

The fountains of the basin provide an exceptionally powerful and beautiful spectacle, thanks to the variety and number of jets required. No fewer than ninety-nine jets are thus distributed: eight in the basin, twenty for the *Neptune and Amphitrite* group, fourteen for the *Ocean* group, ten for the Proteus group, two coming out of the vases, twenty-three spurting directly from the gutter, and two corresponding to the two lateral dragons. Modern water features were recently installed, meant to “animate” very anachronistically the basin when its historic waters are switched off. The result was not impressive.

Opposite the basin, on the north side, two female figures (*Cesi Juno*, also known as *Berenice*, and *Mattei Ceres*, also known as *Faustina*), copied in the seventeenth century after classical models, frame Domenico Guidi’s famous group *The King’s Renown*, commissioned in 1677, completed in 1686, and placed here in 1702 to replace Bernini’s equestrian statue of Louis XIV. Fame, personified by a winged woman, holds a portrait of the king in a large medallion and writes his history on a book held by Time, represented by an old man; trod on by Fame, Envy, in the guise of an old woman, eats her heart. The medallions made out behind represent the great men of antiquity whose glory has been eclipsed by that of the king. Hacked off during the Revolution, the royal profile was remade by the sculptor Jean-François Lorta in 1816.

Following pages:
The Neptune Basin.

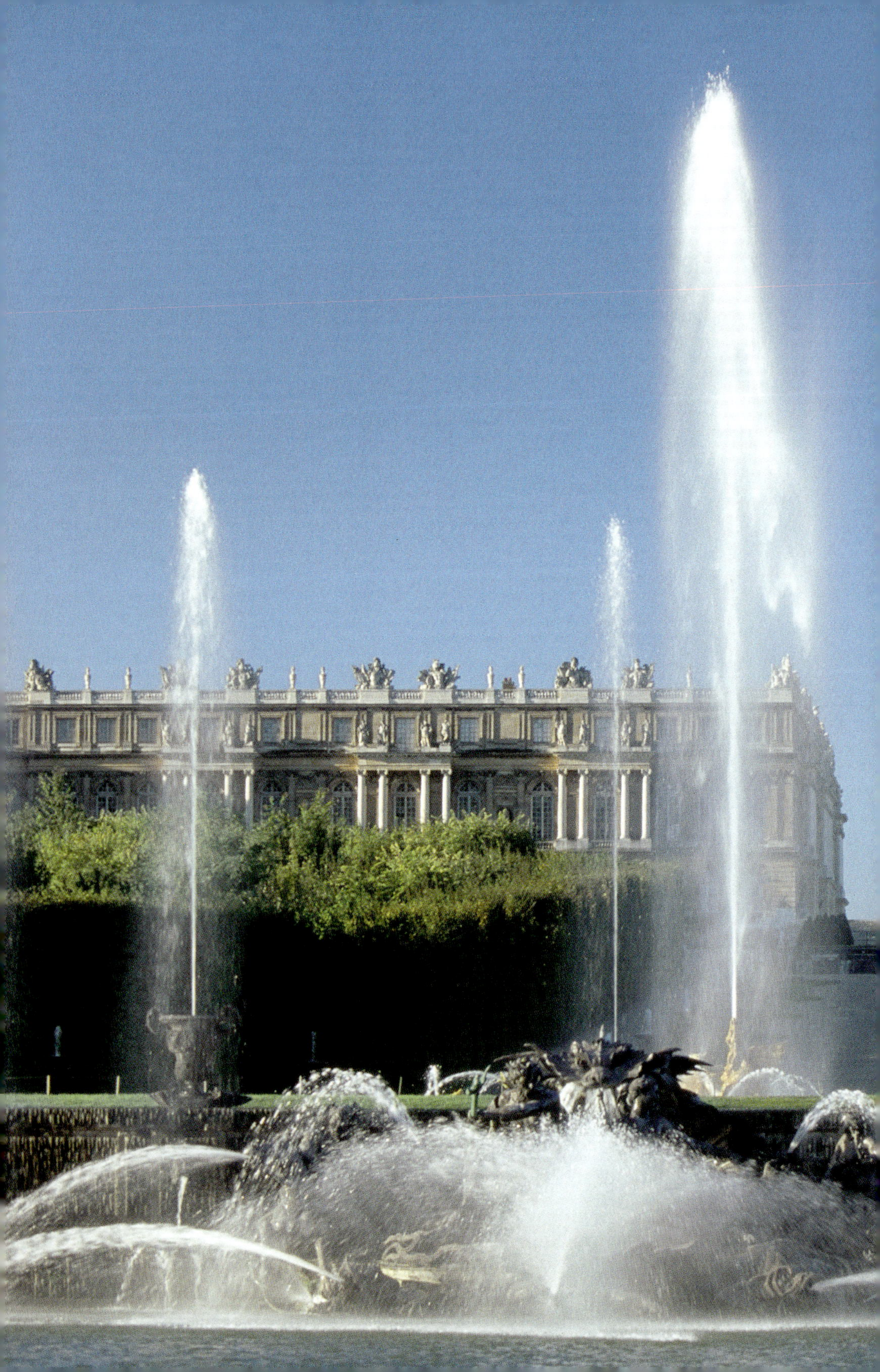

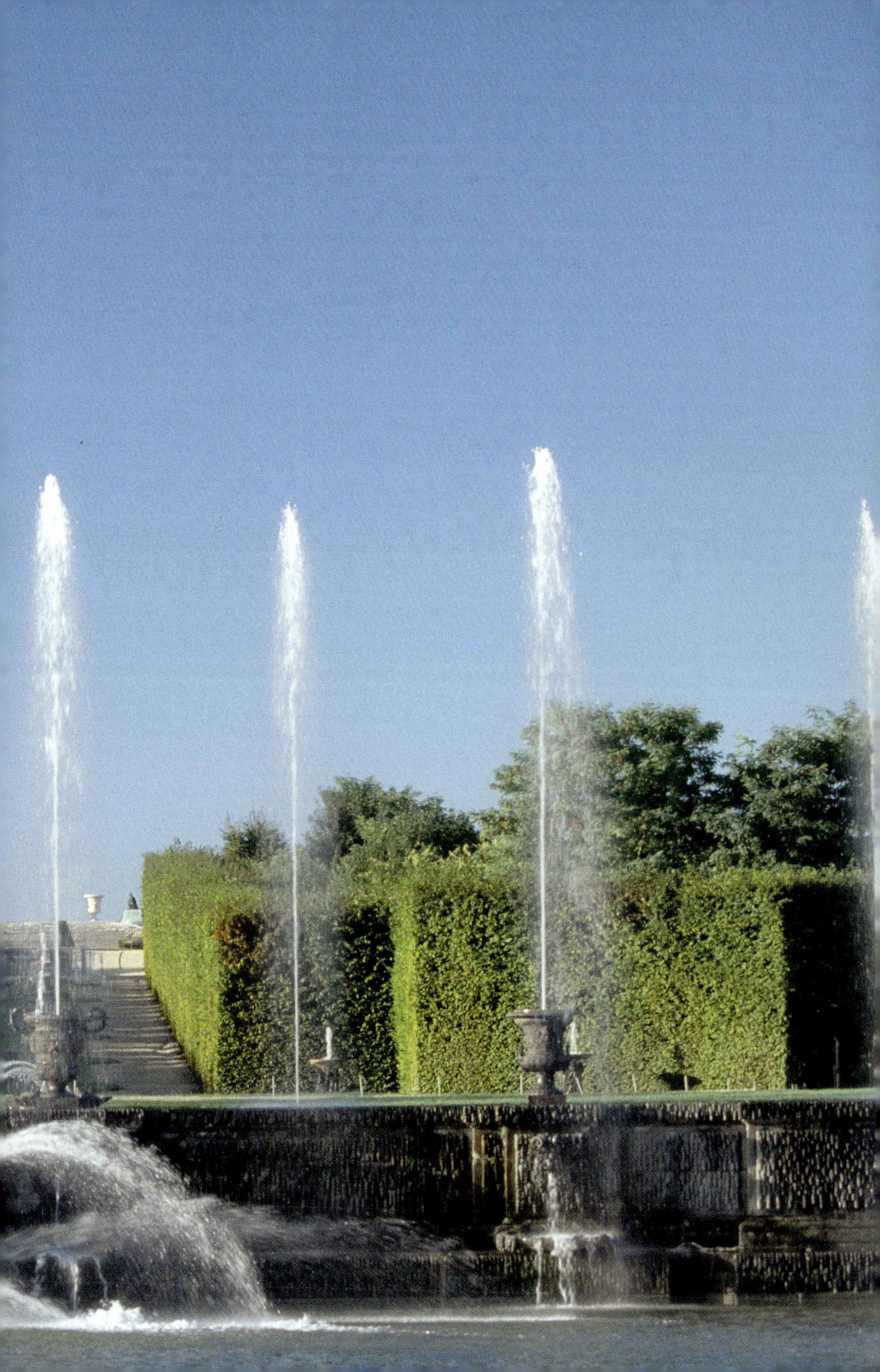

THE WATERS OF VERSAILLES

Located on a marshy plateau, Versailles has only one watercourse: a small stream, the rill of Gally, which has its source in the bottom of the park to the north of the Grand Canal, then flows westwards, and runs into the Mauldre at Beynes. To the north-east of the château, the Clagny Pond (filled in under Louis XV) constituted a naturel reservoir that for a time supplied all the water necessary for the first hydraulic effects. But this resource was soon insufficient to meet the constantly increasing needs of the garden. The water first had to be collected by drainage or pumping, conveyed by means of trenches or pipes, and stored in reservoirs from which it could finally be sent, using gravitation, to the fountains that it was supposed to supply. The collection and storage capacities were never sufficient to operate the fountains permanently.

As the Clagny Pond could no longer meet the ever-increasing demand of the hydraulic network, in 1675, the Trappes and Bois-d'Arcy plateau began to supply water, conveying it to two artificial ponds that supplied a reservoir dug at Satory. In 1680 was developed to the south-east of the network of so-called lower ponds, draining the Saclay plateau (the Saclay, Trou Salé, Orsigny, Prés-Clos and Villiers ponds) whose waters had – to reach Versailles – to cross the Bièvre valley at Buc, first via a siphon then via a large aqueduct completed in 1686. A few years later, in 1683, the network of so-called upper ponds, extending from the south-west to Rambouillet and ending at the Trappes Pond (the La Tour, Hollande, Saint-Hubert, Mesnil-Saint-Denis and Coignières ponds), was activated.

In parallel with the activation of this large network, the pumping of the waters of the Seine was envisaged from 1678. The river flowed about 10 kilometres north of Versailles but the difference

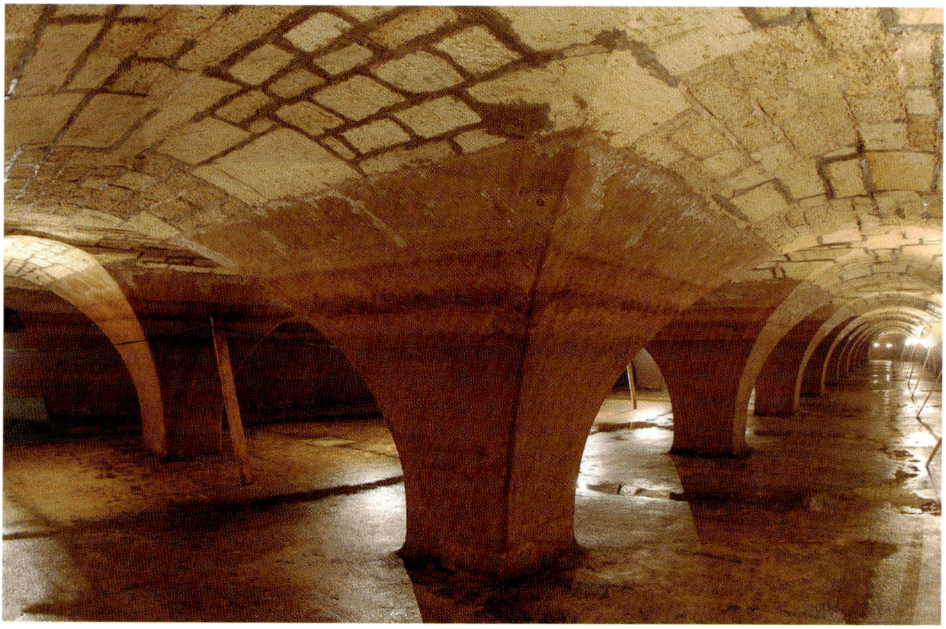

One of the two underground reservoirs, Water Parterre.

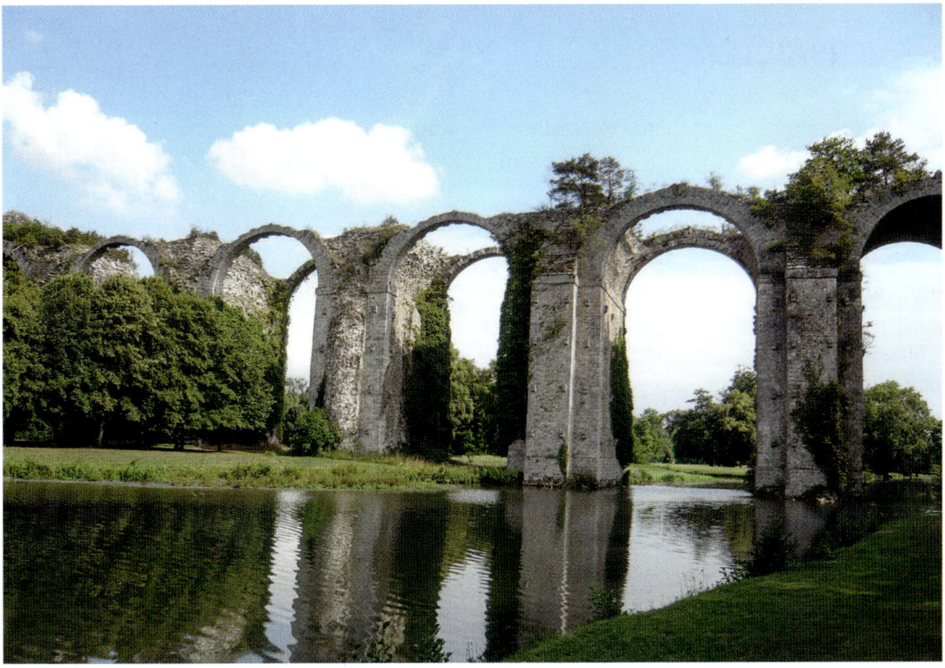

Ruin of the Maintenon aqueduct above the Eure valley.

in level between the two was nearly 150 metres. To get the water to travel that distance required serious technology, which only a team made up of the Liège entrepreneur Arnold de Ville and the brothers Paulus and Rennequin Sualem, also from the Liège region, was capable of mastering. Between 1681 and 1684, they built the imposing *machine de Marly* to pump the water of the Seine and raise it to the top of the hill overlooking it, where it was collected by an aqueduct charged with conveying it to Versailles. Despite these Herculean efforts, the output of the machine was insufficient and served in the main to supply the gardens of the Château de Marly.

From 1685, as a response to the somewhat disappointing results of the *machine de Marly*, it was a question of supplying the network of upper ponds in a way other than by the draining of the plateaus on which it was laid out and to increase the flow constantly, thanks to the harnessing of some of the waters of the Eure upstream from Chartres. Channelled, the waters had to be conveyed 80 kilometres to join the La Tour Pond, near Rambouillet. Carried out under the supervision of the Marquis de Louvois, minister for war and superintendent of the King's Buildings, the works meant that the Eure valley had to be crossed at Maintenon by means of an imposing aqueduct. The works were colossal and employed thousands of men, especially soldiers. In 1688 the War of the Grand Alliance put an end to the undertaking, which remained unfinished.

To store the water coming to Versailles, several reservoirs were built successively. First was the reservoir locate on top of the Grotto of Tethys (1666), which was soon joined by the three so-called "clay" reservoirs, moved to the end of the North Wing when it began being built in 1684. The works to harness water from the Bièvre valley from 1668

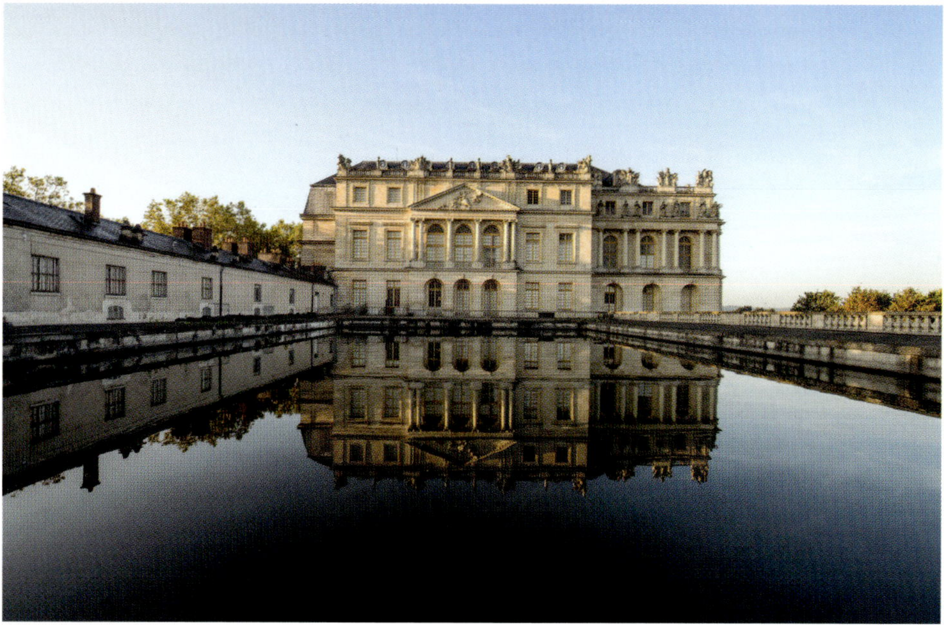

The reservoirs at the end of the North Wing and Royal Opera façade.

imposed the construction of the Satory and Martinière reservoirs. In 1672 three large underground reservoirs were built under the Water Garden (two of them remain today). The two large reservoirs at Trappes and Bois-d'Arcy date from 1677. In 1684 the putting into service of the Buc aqueduct, which allowed the Bièvre to be crossed, resulted in the creation of the Gobert reservoirs, in the Parc-aux-Cerfs quarter, south-east of the château. Finally, the putting into service of the *machine de Marly* and the arrival of the waters of the Seine at Versailles led to the creation of the Butte de Montbauron reservoirs between the Avenue de Paris and the Avenue de Saint-Cloud. The concern with constantly improving water said to be "good to drink" – as opposed to the *eaux blanches* reserved for fountains and basins – led to, in 1763–64, the construction of reservoir on the Butte de Picardie (it is now a parking lot, but its former shape can still be made out). At Trianon, the large Trefoil Basin also acts as a reservoir to supply the water effects, including those of the English Garden (streams and waterfalls). The estate of Versailles is thus surrounded by significant reserves of water that, however, are emptied much more quickly than they are filled, which explains the parsimony with which they are used.

Today, although the complex and fragile system installed during the Ancien Régime has undergone numerous amputations, a certain number of reservoirs are still in service and supplying the fountains: Montbauron (approximately 50,000 cubic metres), the North Wing reservoir (5,000 cubic metres), subterranean reservoirs (4,000 cubic metres), Jambettes (6,000 cubic metres) and the Trefoil Basin (12,000 cubic metres). If we add the Grand Canal and the Lake of the Swiss Guards which could also be considered reservoirs, the ensemble currently allows more than 650,000 cubic metres of water to be stored.

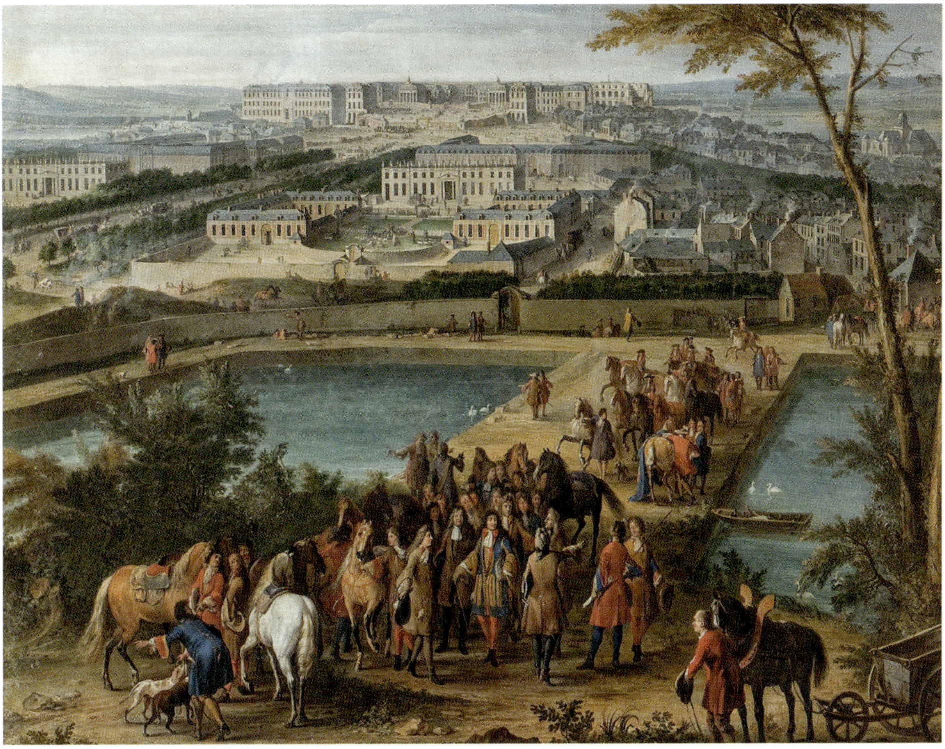

Jean-Baptiste Martin the Elder, *Louis XIV Visits the Montbauron Reservoirs in 1685 (detail).*

The Grandes Eaux

The Grandes Eaux is a show whose success has been unfailing since the seventeenth century. It allows visitors to see all the fountains come to life and penetrate the groves which could only be seen the rest of the time from the railings protecting them. It is recommended for visitors to first see the south groves up to the canal and then to return to the château via the north groves to reach the Neptune Basin, whose waters only play at the end.

Louis XIV himself had written *Une Manière de montrer les jardins de Versailles,* whose aim was the be able to visit the entire garden in such a way as no fountain, grove or vantage point is missed. Very laconic, the text is not really a guide but rather a memento drawn up by the king for his officers charged with showing important guests around the gardens. Republished on a regular basis since the late nineteenth century, these royal instructions remain current, despite the disappearance of certain groves.

Following pages:
Pierre-Denis Martin, *View of the* Machine de Marly *and the Château de Louveciennes*, 1722.

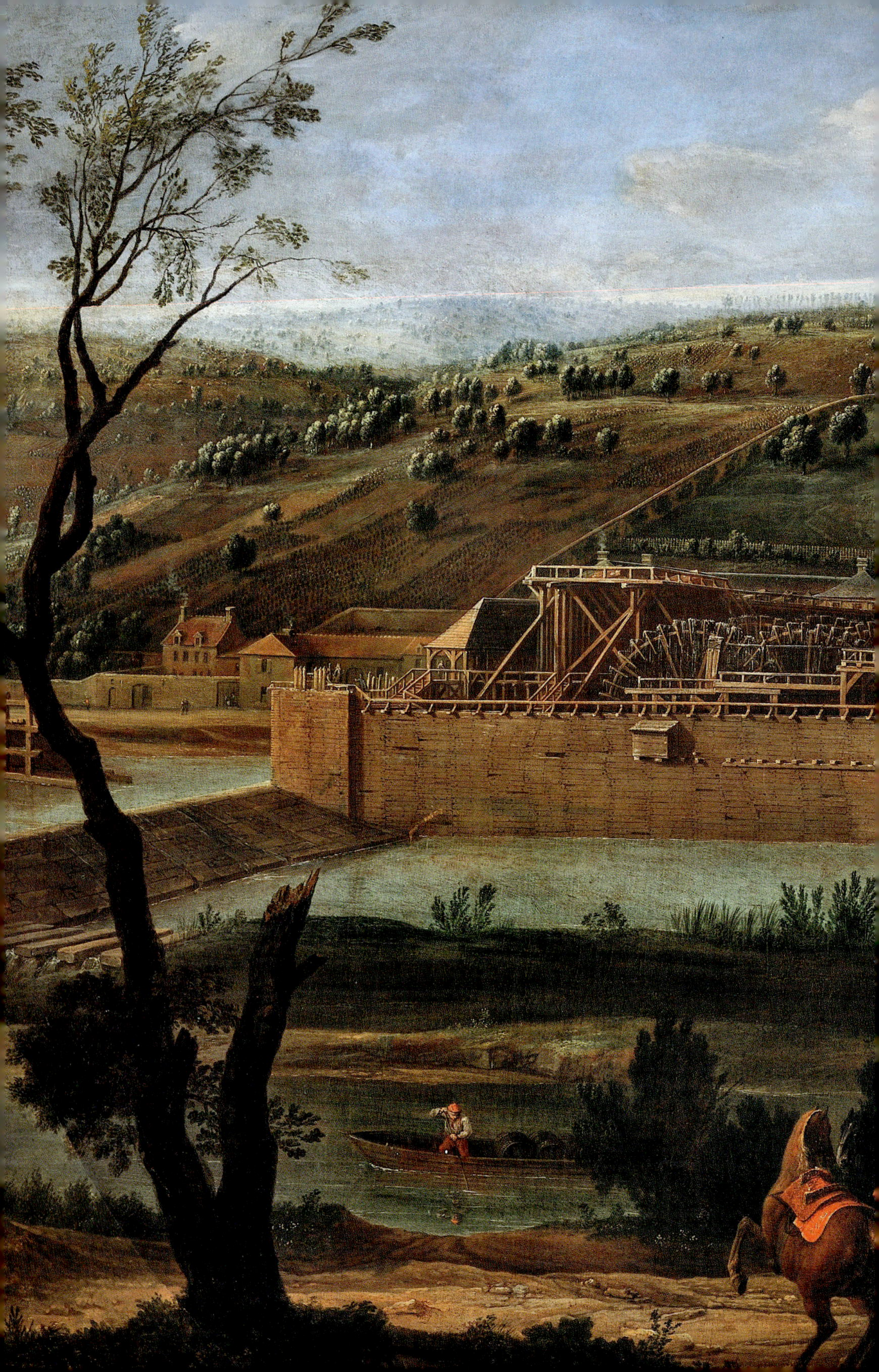

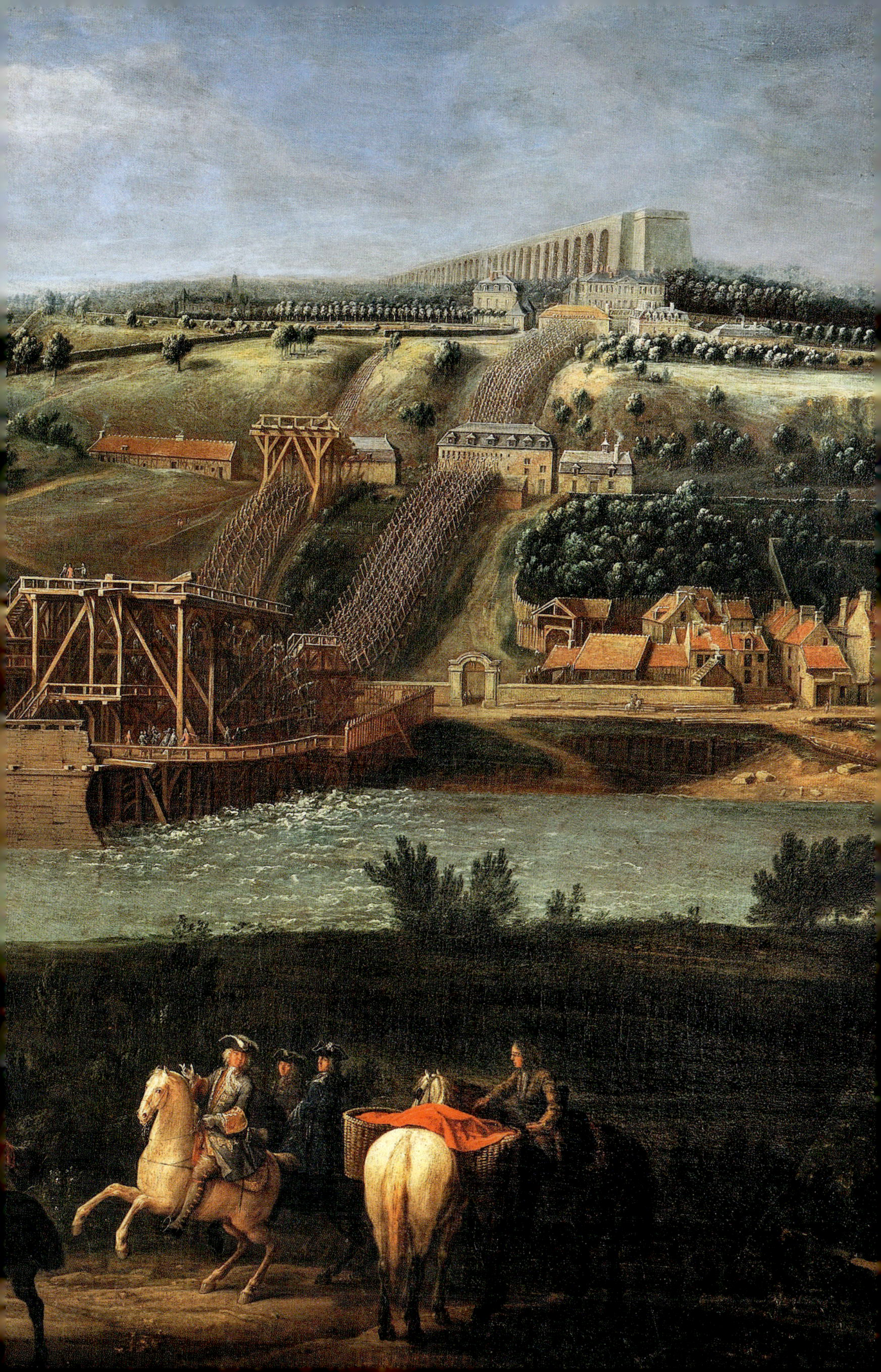

THE TRIANON ESTATE

Aerial view of the French Garden and the Grand Trianon.

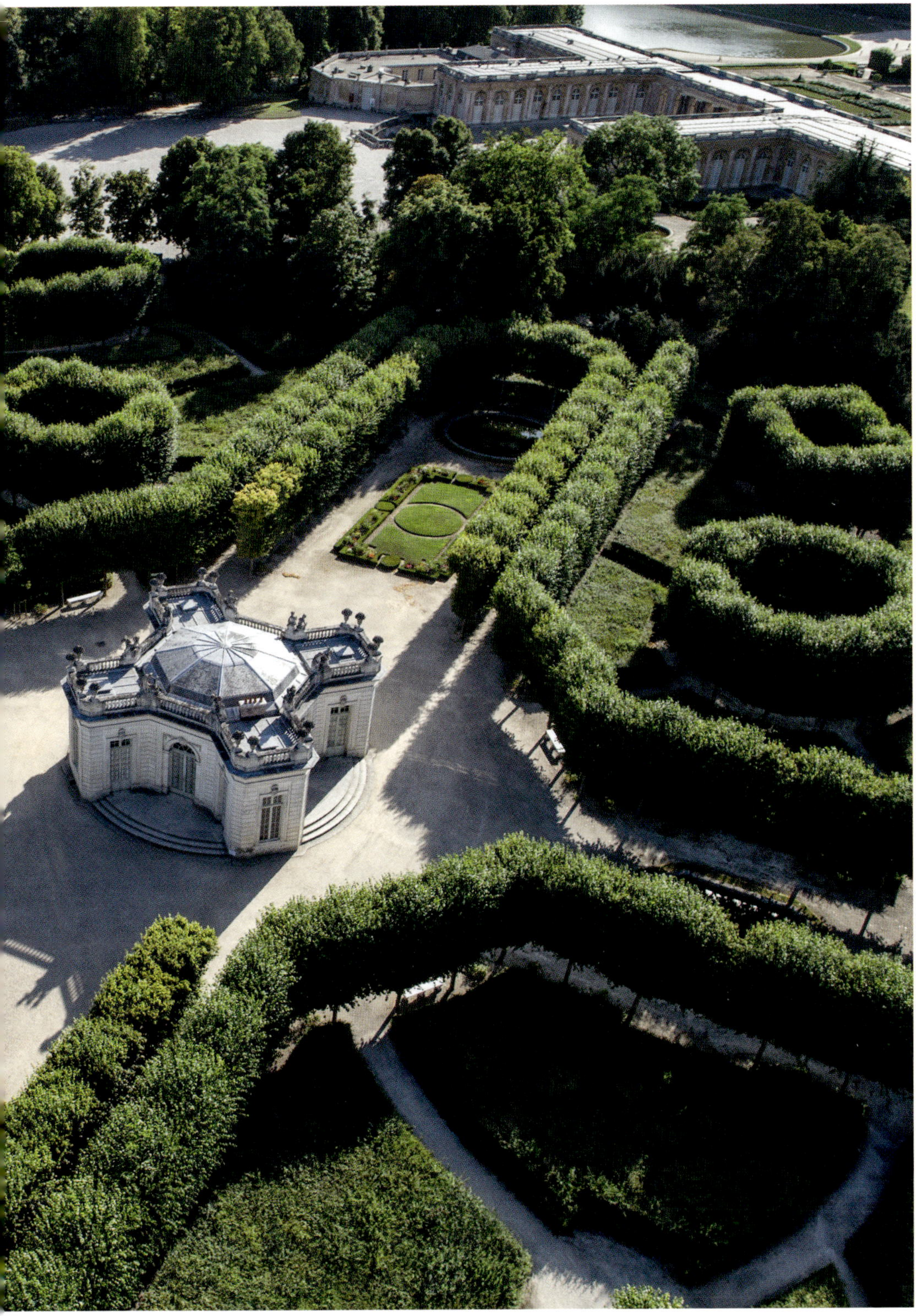

THE GRAND TRIANON

The visitor, after having seen the château and the gardens of Versailles, often casts a weary and hurried eye over those of the Grand Trianon, wanting to finish touring the two châteaus and get to the Queen's Hamlet. To do so would be to deprive oneself of discovering one of the most admirable places on the estate. The Grand Trianon was born of the taste of Louis XIV for architecture and gardens, and of his fondness for these places, which, like Marly, allowed him to spend some time with a small entourage without sacrificing the imposing court ceremonial that he himself had perfected.

In 1668 the king, who wanted to extend the domain of Versailles to the north-west, acquired a modest village named Trianon, dependent on the Abbaye de Sainte-Geneviève de Paris and which touched the limits of the garden. After the village was acquired then razed to the ground, a first garden adorned with trellises was laid out for strolling. Two years later, a small château was built there after plans by Louis Le Vau. Its exterior decoration of blue and white faience tiles earned it the nickname Porcelain Trianon. Made up of several small pavilions arranged on either side of a rectangular central building, it stood amid gardens designed by one of Le Nôtre's nephews, Michel Le Bouteux. The key features of their current plan already figured in it: by following an east-west axis, a parterre de broderie in front of the chateau, endowed with two small circular basins, a lower parterre reached by a staircase, bordered by vaulted trellises to the north and south, and decorated with an octagonal central fountain, then a wooded area crossed by alleys leading to a final basin surrounded by a grassy *vertugadin*, the so-called Flat-Bottom Basin.

A place for strolling and getting away from it all, the Porcelain Trianon soon fell out of fashion and Louis XIV decided to knock down his small château and have a new, larger one build in its place, in order to, as the Marquis de Sourches observed, "be able to host *fêtes* and entertainments there sometimes". The buildings were razed to the ground in July 1687 and as early as January 1688, the king could dine for the first time in his new Château de Trianon. The pink Languedoc marble facing of the façades earned it the nickname "Marble Trianon". The architecture of the new palace, built to plans by Jules Hardouin-Mansart and Robert de Cotte, also bore the king's personal mark. He had the idea for the peristyle between the courtyard and the garden, traditionally allocated to the larger *corps de logis*. This gallery treated as a colonnade links the two wings but also plays the role of loggia from which may be viewed the entirety of the principal vista as well as the rest of the building. The architecture of the Marble Trianon, with its single-story elevation, is similar to that of an orangery and its articulation with the surrounding gardens is essential. Charged with making a few modifications to the gardens, Le Nôtre only slightly changed Le Bouteux's plan. He redesigned the Flat-Bottom Basin, created a Springs Grove in the angle formed by the gallery and the Trianon-sous-Bois wing, laid out the King's Garden, and modified a few fountains. After his death, Jules Hardouin-Mansart took over the modifications. He got rid of the vaulted trellises of the lower parterre, the last vestige of the original Trianon, and planned new extensions of the garden to the north and north-west. He thus created a vast network of alleys and *salles vertes* with varied designs, which were evocative of horticultural urban planning. Designed for strolling, practically devoid of water features, the new garden was characterised by the simplicity of its lines and the inventiveness of its shapes and

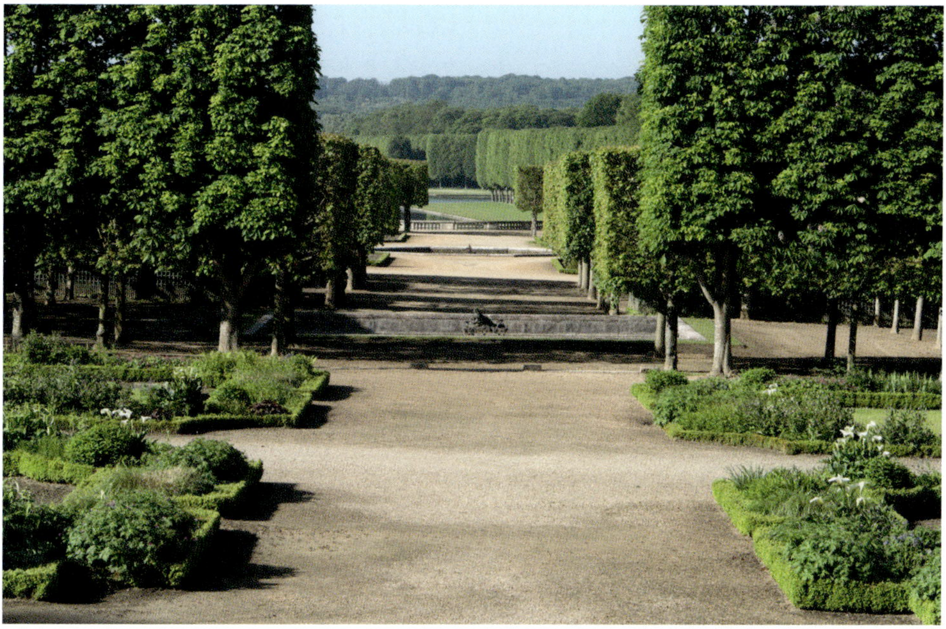

The north-south axis of the Grand Trianon gardens, taken from the Amphitheatre.

volumes. Hardouin-Mansart did, however, build the Water Buffet, a reminder of the original cascades desired by Le Nôtre and destroyed in 1700.

Louis XIV still showed great fondness for Trianon, which he considered one of his greatest successes. His contemporaries reported that he was always repairing it, watching over the details of everything, from the removal of the frames that, from 1688 to 1701, closed the peristyle on the courtyard side only, to the colour of the garden benches which he ordered to be painted green and whose mouldings to be gilt in 1700. It was at Trianon that he had his last stroll, on 11 August 1715, three weeks before his death.

After the king's death, the Grand Trianon continued to be carefully maintained. Louis XV was particularly fond of it and developed new gardens which resulted in the construction of the Petit Trianon. However, in the nineteenth century, the original design of the *salles vertes* gradually disappeared, taken over by a garden returning to the forest state: the trellises of the alleys were removed, the contours became blurred, and the plan itself became increasingly difficult to read. The storms of the late twentieth century led to the overall replanting of the Trianon gardens. Little by little, the plans took on their original forms, some *salles vertes* were reconstituted, allowing the visitor to catch a glimpse of the originality and the splendour of the garden when it will be entirely restored.

Following pages:
The peristyle of the Grand Trianon and the upper parterre.

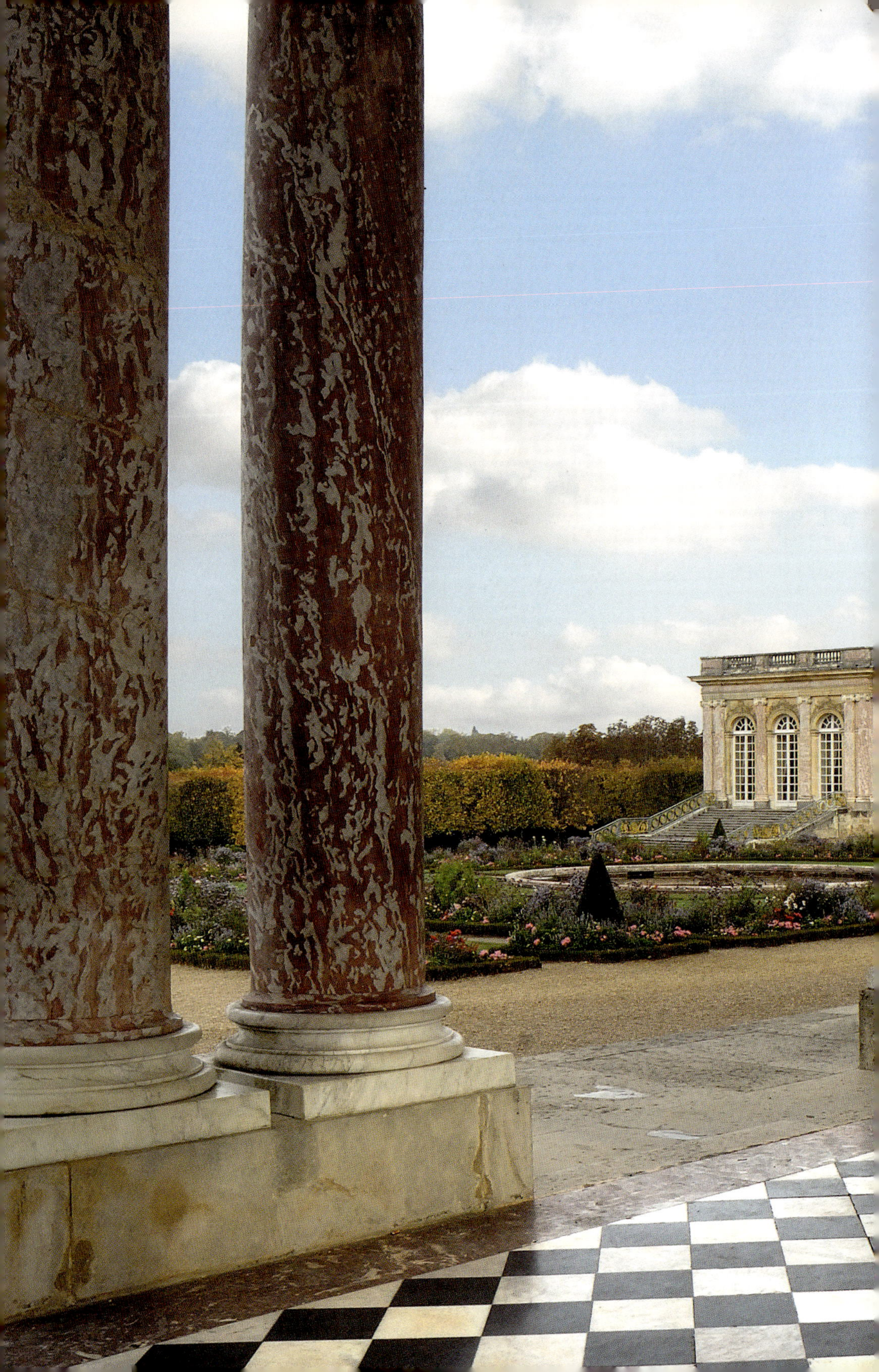

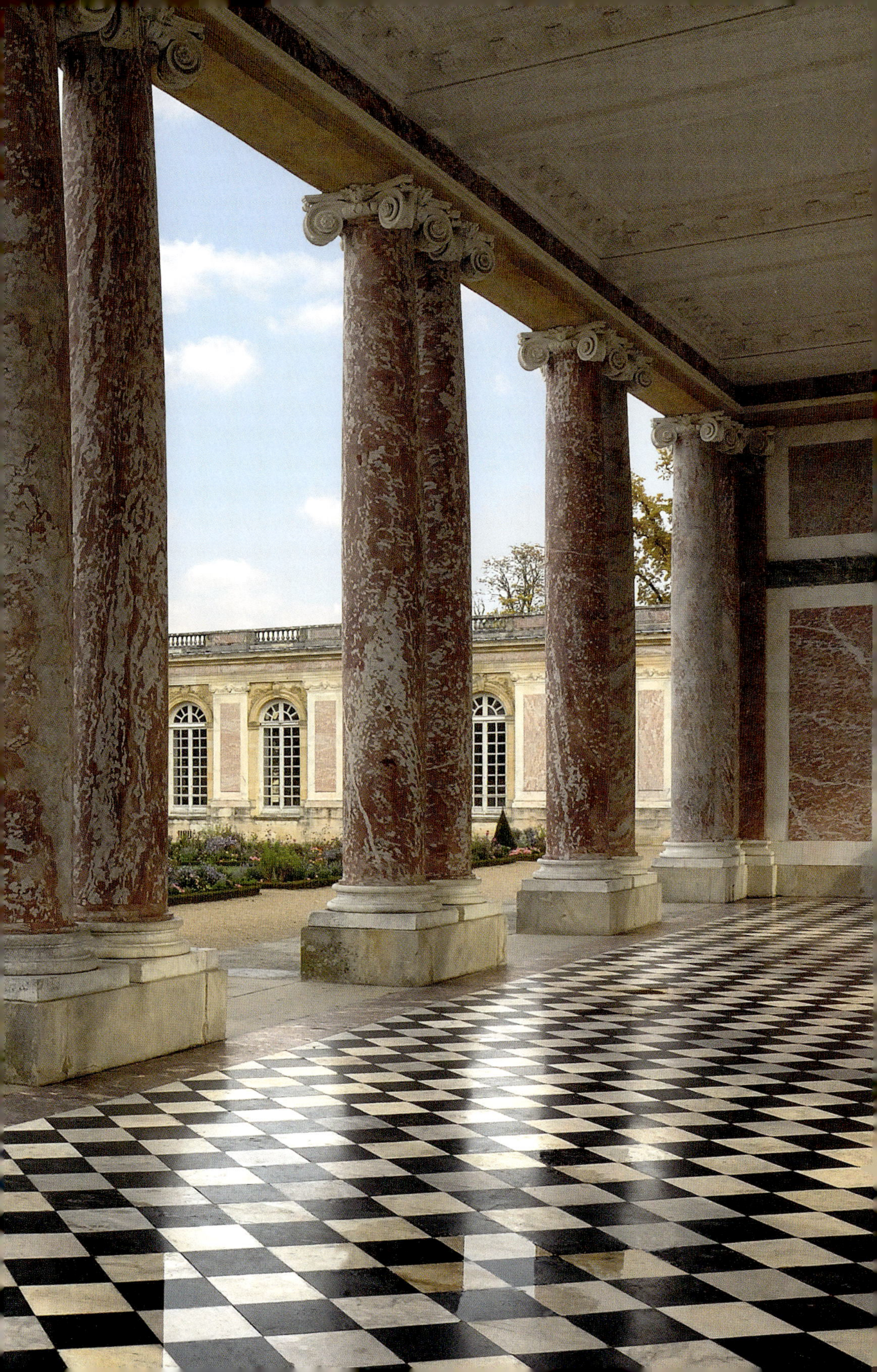

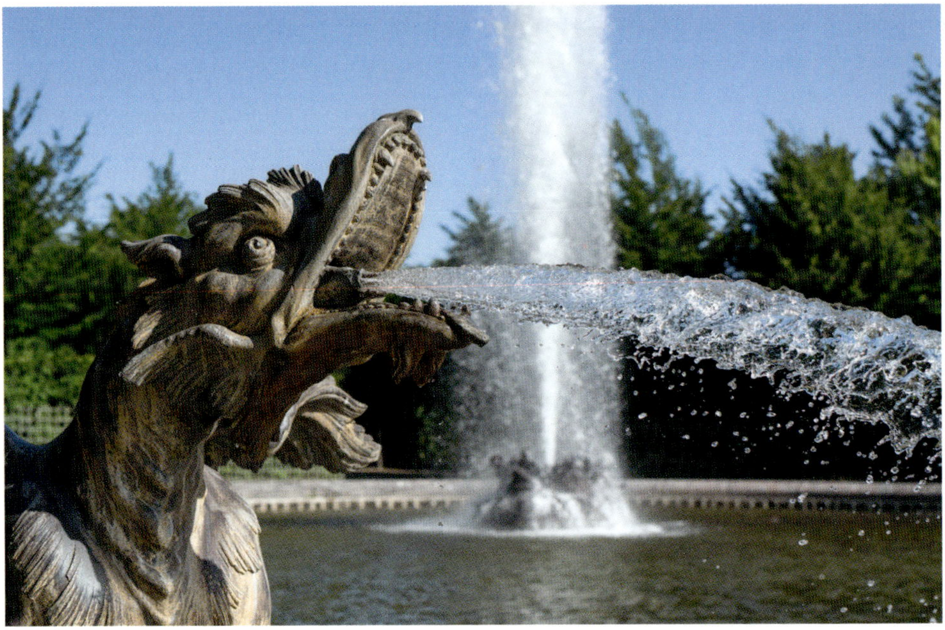

The Flat-Bottom Basin (detail).

The Flat-Bottom parterres and basin

Louis XIV took great pride in the parterres of Trianon and the thousands of flowers they were covered with in the spring and summer. Growing the flowers was facilitated by the nurseries installed nearby; the flowers were placed directly in their pots, which enabled not only the rapid replacement of damaged plants, but also spectacular complete changes that the king appreciated.

The parterres are now laid out according to the plan designed by Michel Le Bouteux for the original garden of the Porcelain Trianon. It is from the peristyle where all the components can best be seen. In the foreground, the upper parterre is circumscribed by the palace, protected to the north by the wing housing the "Cotelles Gallery". This first parterre is made up of two compartments of grass cut-outs bordered with flowerbeds organised around a circular basin. After 1705 the two basins were given four cherubs, grouped two by two, from the Saturn Basin.

A staircase of eight steps in the main axis leads to the much larger lower parterre. Four compartments of grass bordered by flowerbeds surrounding an octagonal basin placed in the centre of the parterre, in the middle of which is the copy, made in the nineteenth century, of a small satyr playing with grapes from the Bacchus Basin. Near this basin is the intersection of the two principal axes of the garden: the east-west axis, which goes from the château to the Flat-Bottom Basin and the north-south axis linking the amphitheatre to the Grand Canal. To the south, a terrace allows to be admired all the transversal arm of the canal at the end of which, over 1 kilometre away, are the huge steps that lead to the Menagerie. This viewpoint dominates the Horseshoe Basin from where visitors descend via two slopes.

A covered area, planted with limes and traversed by a central alley, provides the transition to the Flat-Bottom Basin.

The Flat-Bottom Basin is inscribed in a vast *boulingrin* overhung by the curtain of trees of the Great Park. Modified several times, it took its definitive form in 1703. Its unusual plan vaguely recalls the shape of a keyhole. The half-moon upper basin flows in a sheet into the lower basin, whose outline creates an accelerated perspective effect that give the illusion of a body of water that is longer than it really is. After 1705, two cherubs from the Flora Basin were placed in the middle of the upper basin; they were remade during the nineteenth century, as were the two groups of children with shells in the lower basin. Made by Jean Hardy, two lead dragons frame the water nappe. The four pedestals of the *boulingrin*, now bare, had been meant to support four ewer vases by Claude Poirier. As the vases had disappeared, they were replaced in the nineteenth century by new lead models, placed in 1937 in the grounds of the Mairie de Châteauneuf-sur-Loire, where they still may be found.

The Round Basin

After leaving the Flat-Bottom Basin, visitors quickly reach the Round Basin located in the line of the Gardens Room. Like most of the Trianon basins, the Round Basin benefitted from the modifications made by Mansart in many of the groves and basins of Versailles and was adorned, in 1706, with a group made up of two tritons and a cherub holding a horn of plenty. This ensemble by Gaspard Marsy came from the Grove of Fame (the present Domes Grove).

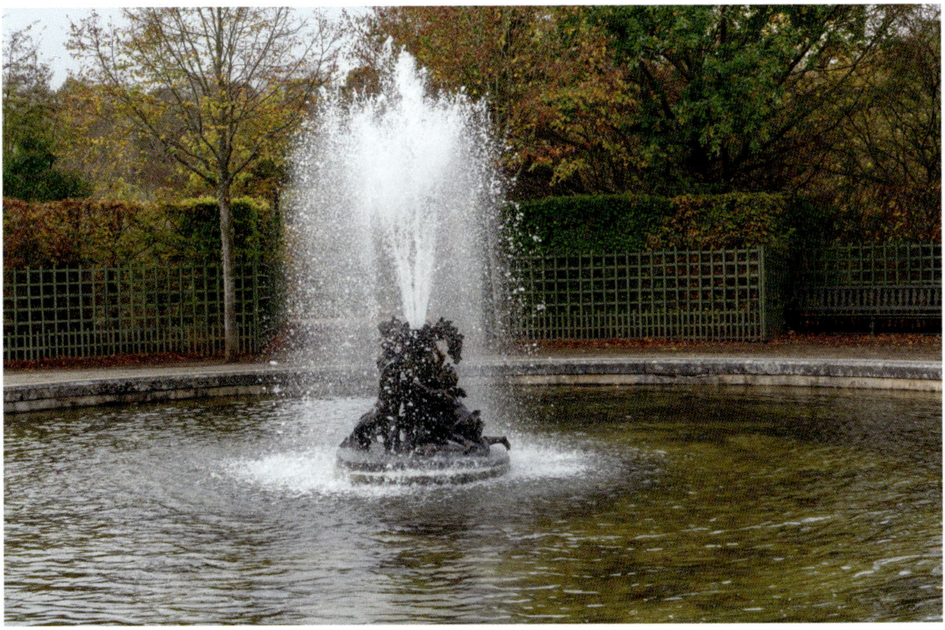

The Round Basin.

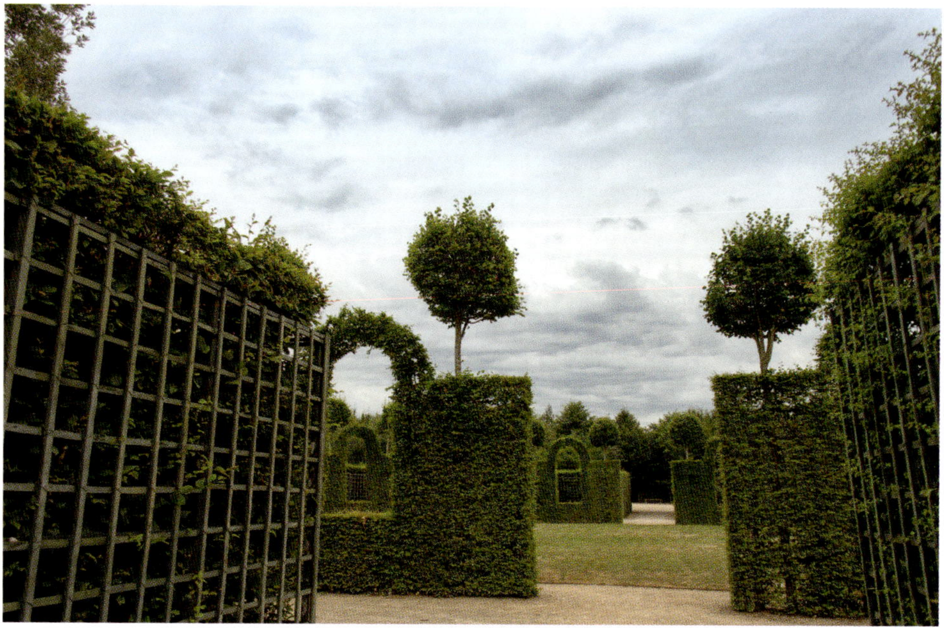

The Triangular Grove.

The Triangular Grove

West of the Water Buffet the Triangular Grove is a perfect example of the style that Jules Hardouin-Mansart had imposed in the Trianon gardens. Playing on the volumes and the designs, he accorded a very assertive architectural role to plants and structured the space into a succession of *salles de verdures* or *salles vertes* in various formats, to which rectilinear alleys lead. This geometric aspect is particularly present in the Triangular Grove, reconstructed ex nihilo in 2004, where a double hornbeam hedge circles a parterre of grass adorned with vases. The strictly clipped inner hedge evokes a botanical cloister inviting the visitor to take a stroll.

The Amphitheatre and the Chestnut Garden

Not far from the Trianon-sous-Bois Wing, the Amphitheatre constitutes the north end of the transversal axis of the parterres whose vantage point on the Grand Canal and the Horseshoe Basin below mark the south. Preceded by the Bassin du Carré d'Eau, with a small satyr playing with a panther in its centre, which came from the Bacchus Basin (twentieth-century copy), it features a succession of lawn cut-outs bordered by flowerbeds rising in steps to a semicircular hornbeam hedge at the foot of which is the Nymphs Basin. These lead sculptures, the work of Jean Hardy, had been originally created for the gardens of Marly. They were installed

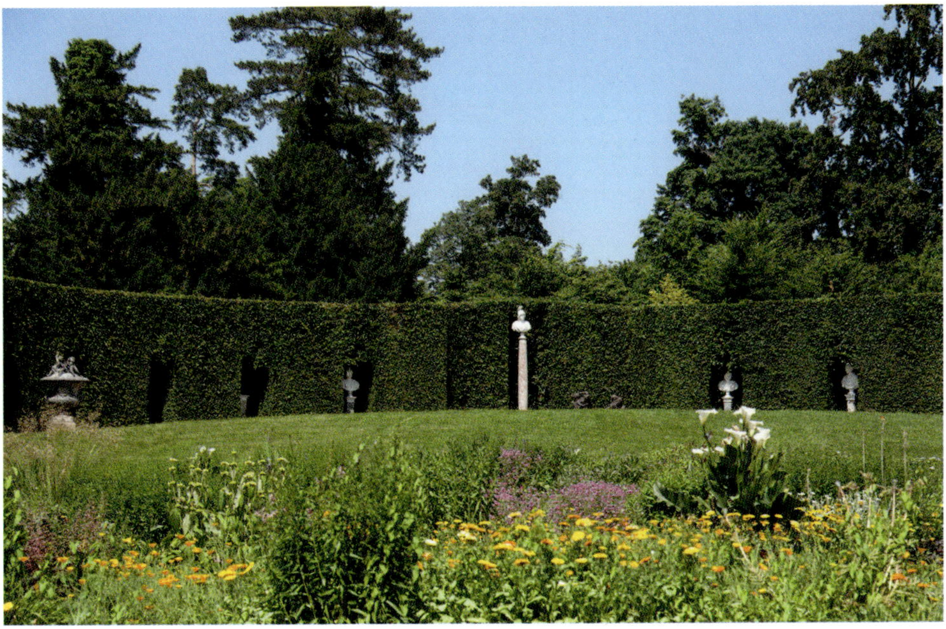

The Amphitheatre or Ancients Grove.

at Trianon in around 1707. Not far from the basin are two remarkably refined imposing lead vases topped with groups of children. All around, classical busts or busts inspired by antiquity are set in the arches of greenery, dominated by the bust of Alexander the Great placed on a Languedoc marble column.

When the visitor comes down from the Amphitheatre the elegant simplicity of the Chestnut Garden opens on the right. It comprises a succession of three *salles vertes* whose two ends are both endowed with a circular basin adorned with a group of cherubs from the Flora Basin.

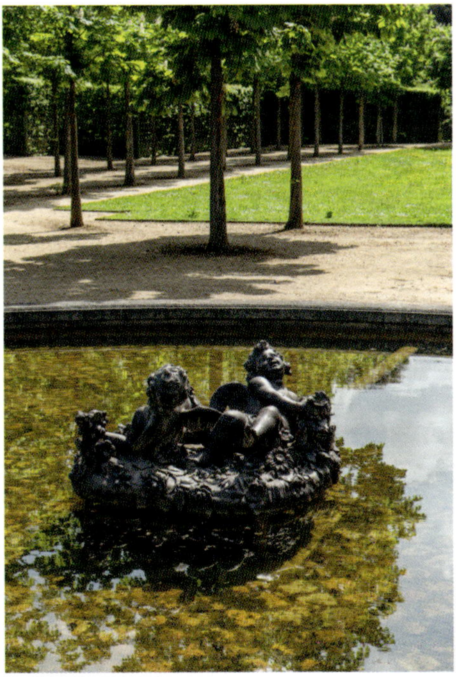

One of the basins of the Chestnut Garden.

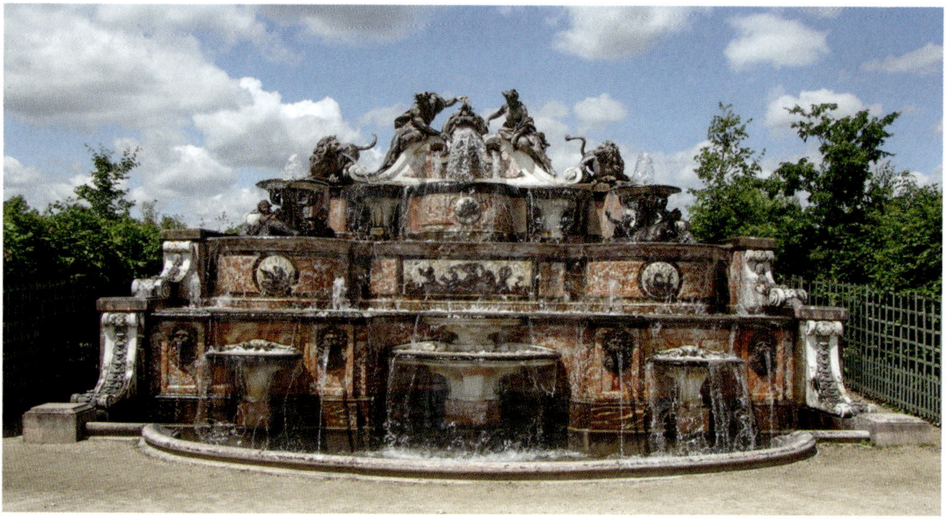

The Water Buffet.

The Water Buffet

As soon as it was completed, the Water Buffet was considered a masterpiece of equilibrium, and descriptions of the Trianon gardens did not omit to praise it. It also marked the appearance of statuary in the Trianon gardens.

Designed by Jules Hardouin-Mansart, it was completed in 1703. From 1699, when Jules Hardouin-Mansart became superintendent of the King's Buildings, Louis XIV envisaged the removal of the cascades that adorned the gardens of the Porcelain Trianon. This modification was part of larger plan to extend the gardens and marks the desire to break aesthetically with the original garden. However, and unexpectedly, the king wanted to add to the redesigned garden a *buffet d'eau* the fashion for which dated thirty years ago and of which the gardens of Versailles had fine examples at the Marsh Grove and the Triumphal Arch Grove. In 1701 the sculptors Hardy and Lespingola delivered a model of the *buffet d'eau* which pleased the king. Works began the following year. The marbles were installed by the marblers Pierre Lisqui, Claude Tarlé, Jérôme Derbais and Nicolas Desaigres: Languedoc red, Carrara white, and violet Campan and Breccia. The gilt lead sculptures were divided among the sculptors Mazière, Garnier, Lemoyne, Hardy, Lapierre and Le Lorrain. Corneille Van Clève was charged with the uppermost group representing two aquatic deities: a river and a naiad flanking an urn. At the level below, two groups of two tritons each support a basin decorated with flowers and crayfish. The lower stair features a large lead bas-relief representing the triumph of Amphitrite and two medallions decorated with waterfowl. Below, three Carrara marble basins adorned with icicles are flanked by four lead mascarons. As was his habit for all that concerned the Trianon, Louis XIV paid attention to the tiniest details. In May 1702, he intervened to have the Carrara marble that was supposed to serve as a backdrop to the lead bas-reliefs replaced by violet Breccia marble whose colour he thought contrasted less sharply. The same month, he asked that the two dragons commissioned in 1701 to flank the sides of the Water Buffet be replaced by lions. In June, the king had the central group modified again, asking that the sea monster figure that framed the two deities be replaced by the urn that we see today. He also gave the order for all the lead to be gilt.

In 1719 a nearly identical copy of the Water Buffet was complete for the Duca di Parma and the gardens of his Colorno residence. Known as the Fontana del Trianon, it is now in Parma, on the island of Peschiera, in the Parco Ducale.

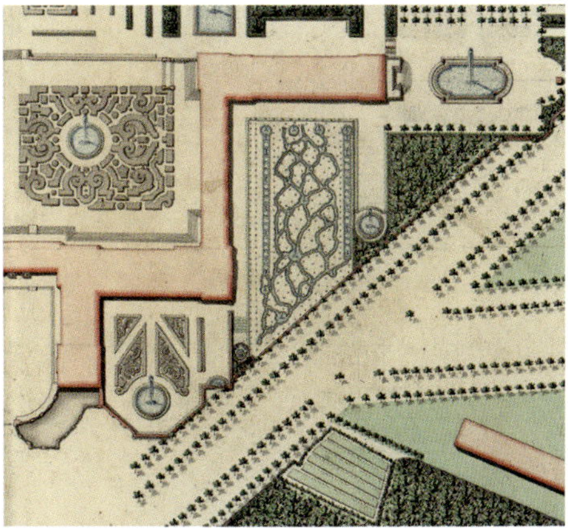

Detail of a plan of the Grand Trianon gardens in the eighteenth century. The former Springs Garden may be made out thanks to its irregular layout and many streams.

The former Garden of Springs and the King's Garden

In front of the steps of the Trianon-sous-Bois Wing, the centre of the rectangular basin is home to another group made up of a small satyr playing with a panther, also from the Bacchus Basin. The vast lawn nearby, lined with buildings on two sides, marks the location of the former Garden of Springs designed by Le Nôtre, which was considered one of the Trianon marvels. Madame Palatine, duchesse d'Orléans and Louis XIV's sister-in-law, described it well: "a small grove that was so dense that at high noon the sun did not penetrate it. Coming out of the ground there are over fifty springs, which produce streams that are barely a foot wide and that, consequently, one can step over them all." It disappeared in the late eighteenth century.

A little farther, in the middle of a wooded area, the fountain Cupid on a Dolphin by Gaspard Marsy, is a vestige of the former Water Theatre Grove.

The King's Garden surrounded by a high wall and sheltered by two of the wings of the château, comprises a parterre de broderie around a basin in which a group of cherubs by Tuby from the Ancients Gallery was placed in 1704. This space, surrounded by walls, is a novelty: no other royal residence possessed a garden of this type, reserved exclusively for the king, who could enter it directly from the French windows of his apartments. Napoleon had the north garden wall torn down and laid out the path that, via a bridge, led to the Petit Trianon. As for the door opening on to the Parade Ground its porch, originally false, was not really opened until 1892.

Following pages:
The King's Garden, Grand Trianon.

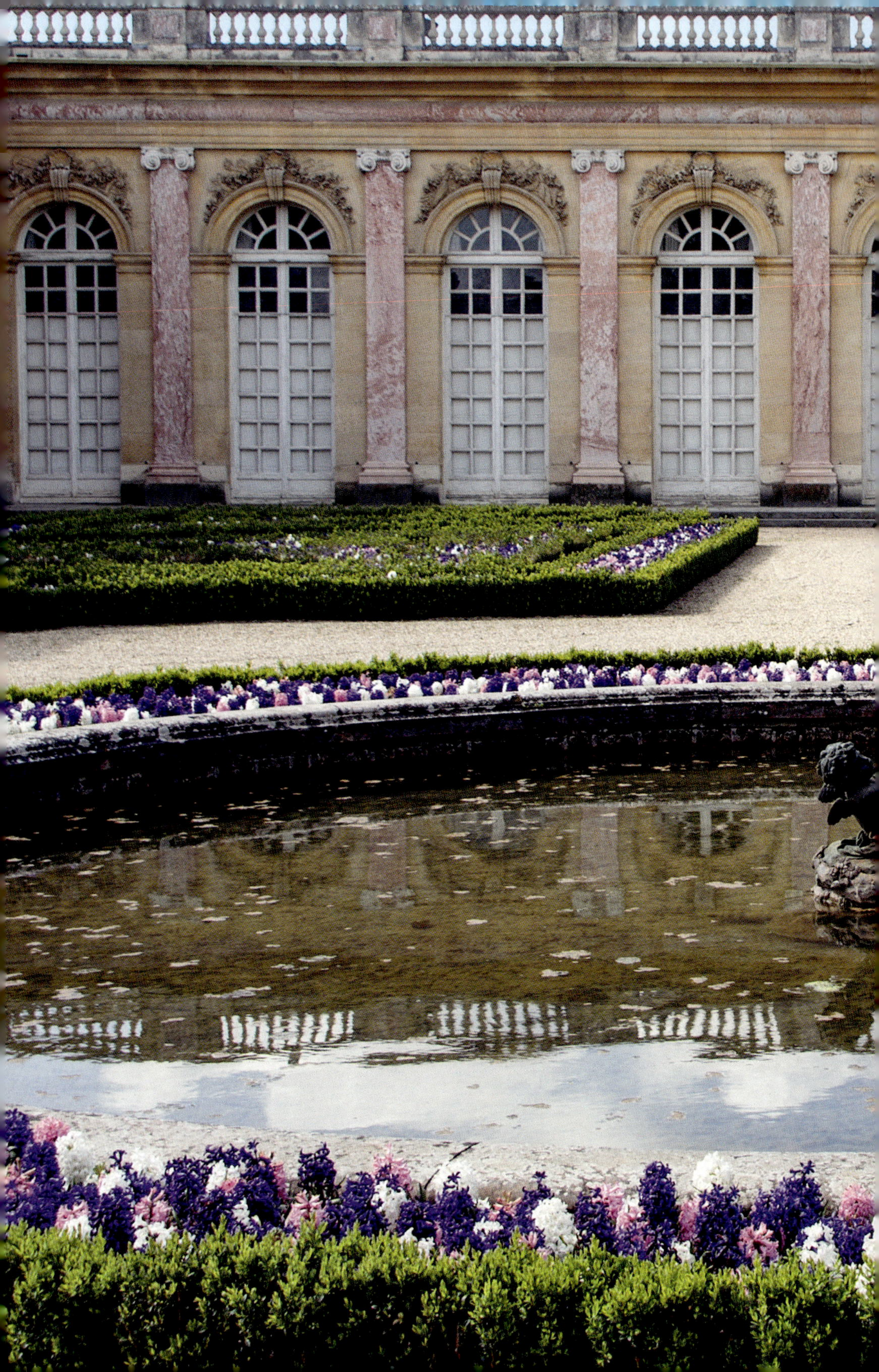

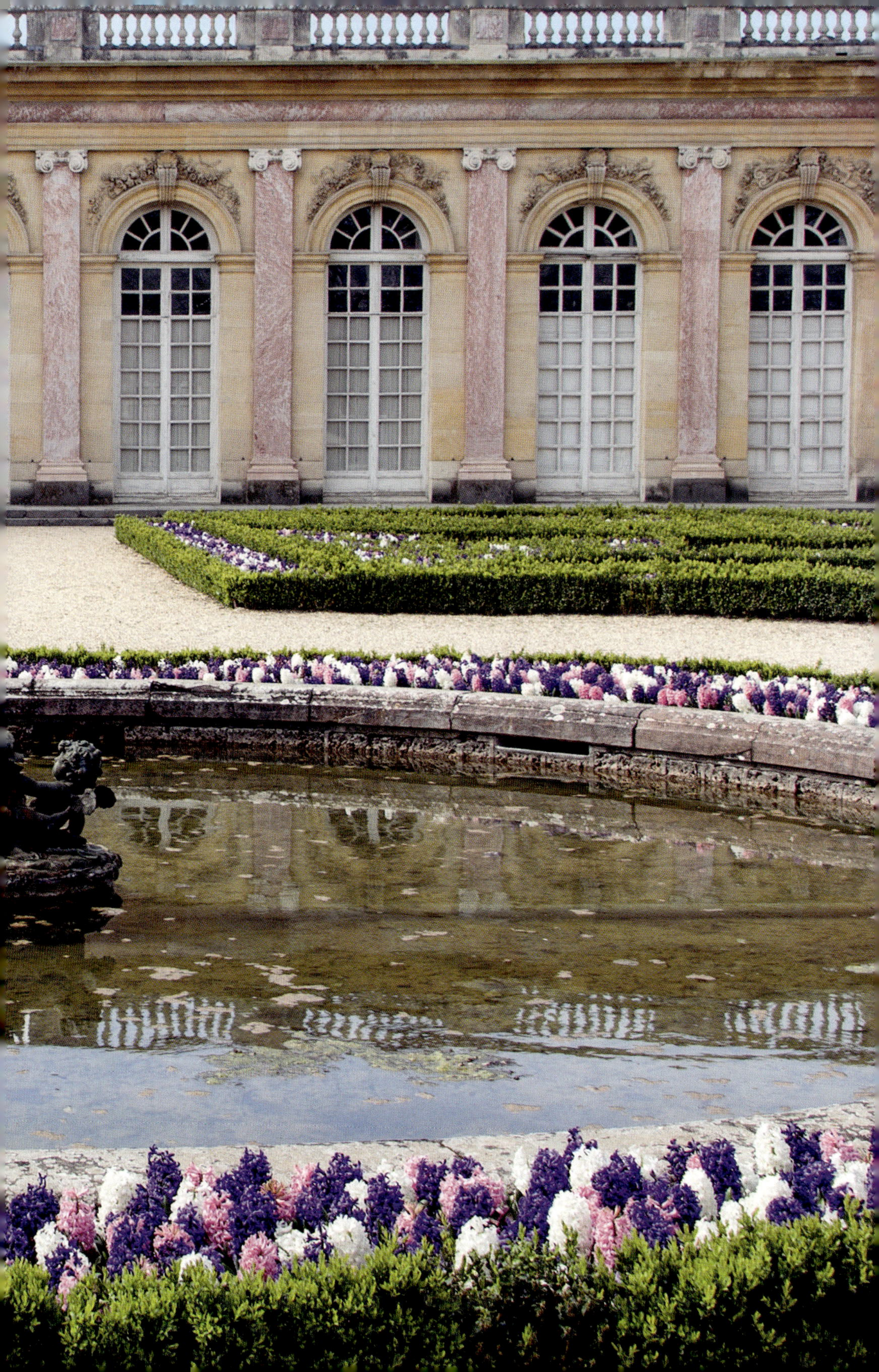

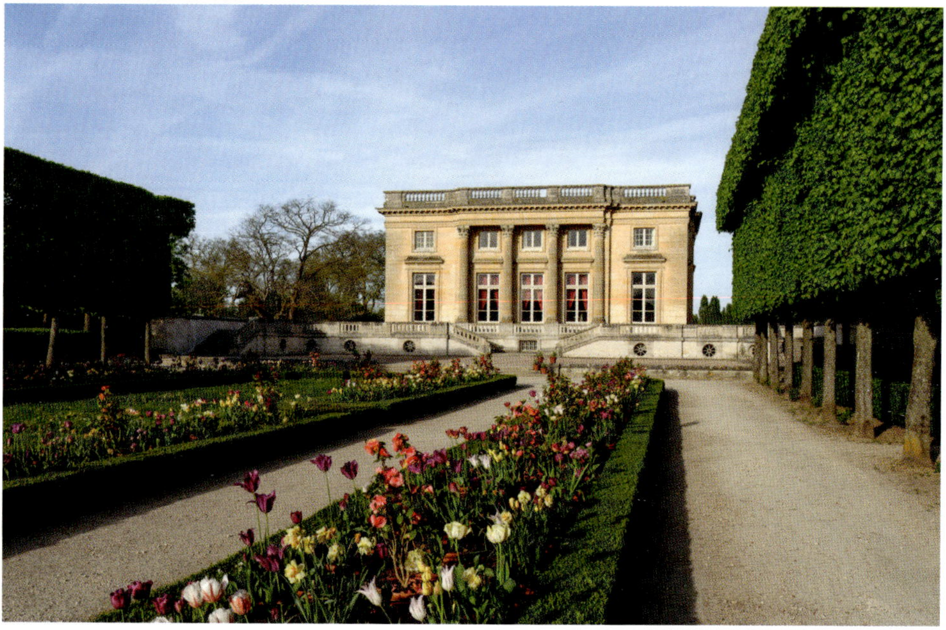

The French Garden and the west façade of the Petit Trianon.

THE PETIT TRIANON

When visitors leave the Grand Trianon gardens through the King's Garden, they cross a small bridge that leads to the Petit Trianon. The bridge over a sunken path, whose construction was ordered by Napoleon, who wanted convenient communication between the two châteaus. It leads to the west end of Louis XV's French Garden.

Louis XV was always partial to Trianon. Keen on gardening and botany, he focused on, from 1749, the landscaping of the terrains located to the east of the Marble Trianon Over the years, these creations took on major importance. Between 1749 and 1753, the present French Garden and its accompanying buildings were built: the Menagerie (1749), the French Pavilion (1750), the Aviary (1751) and the Cool Room (1753). At the same time as these constructions, the king had laid out a fruit garden, endowed with hothouses in which were grown pineapples and coffee plants, as well as a floral garden featuring an orangery and numerous flowerbeds. Every year, the gardens were further developed, becoming the theatre for experiments in acclimation and research of all kinds. Beginning in 1757, Louis XV had the first plans drawn up for a new botanical garden; it was meant to receive a collection of plants from around the world and would expand until the end of the king' reign. The king welcomed renowned botanists who, alongside Bernard de Jussieu, laid the foundations for this new science. Louis XV soon decided to build a new château at the very heart of this unique ensemble: the Petit Trianon, completed in 1769.

At the king's death in 1774, the Trianon garden was considered one of the most beautiful and richest botanical gardens in Europe. While Marie-Antoinette drastically changed the installations of Louis XV when she began to lay out her own gardens, she did not entirely banish the botanist tradition from the place. The acclimation of new exotic plants is still one of the activities of Trianon. During the Revolution, what remained of the plants of Trianon was transferred to the new Jardin des Plantes in Paris.

The French Garden

This was the only part of the gardens of Louis XV spared by Marie-Antoinette. It extends in front of the west façade of the Petit Trianon following a path punctuated by grassy parterres and ornamental lakes. On the sides, a double row of limes creates covered alleys that communicate with a succession of small *salles vertes* delimited by clipped arbours. Four basins (two round ones to the east and west, two square ones to the north and south), adorned with lead groups of children by Jules-Antoine Rousseau, decorate the parterres. The parterres, made up of cut-out areas of grass, are bordered by beds that are still flowered today employing the method used at Trianon since the seventeenth century: grown in neighbouring nurseries, the flowers are placed there in pots buried in mulch and changed regularly with the seasons.

The French Pavilion

The order from Louis XV to develop the Trianon gardens rapidly led the king to commission from Jacques-Ange Gabriel a pleasure building, placed among the new parterres and designed to communicate with them. Begun in the spring of 1749, the construction of the "New Menagerie Pavilion" was finished in the autumn of 1750. Gabriel had designed a plan combining a vast rotunda flanked by four small wings. The ensemble, crowned by a balustrade concealing the rooftops, particularly pleased the king who enjoyed taking visitors around it.

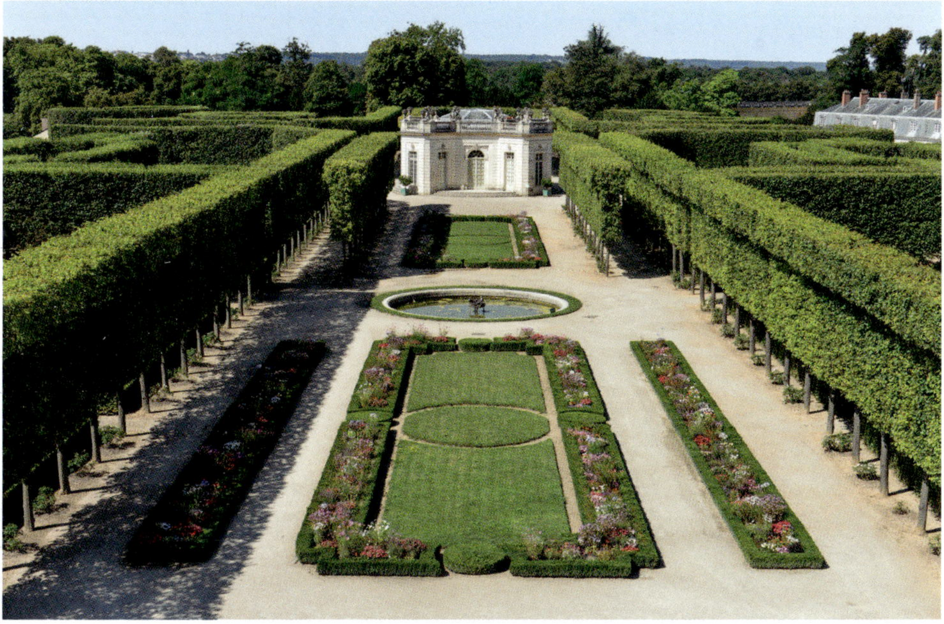

View of the French Garden and Pavilion from the attic of the Petit Trianon.

Trees in the Petit Trianon

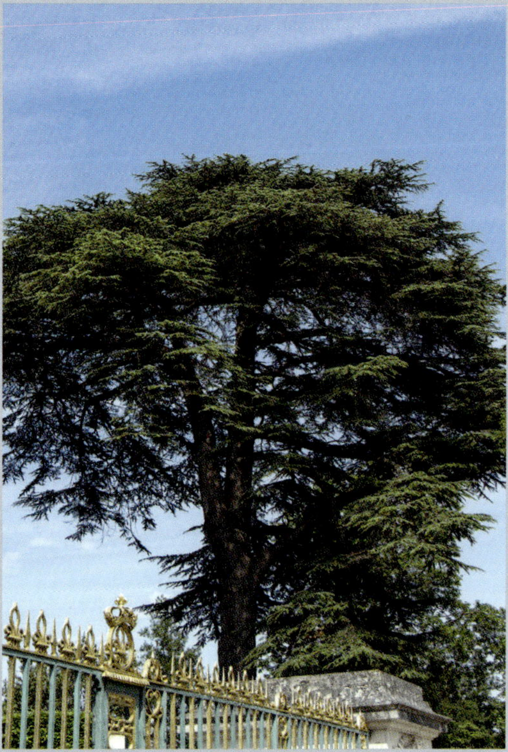

Cedar of Lebanon
Cedrus libani

In 1764 Antoine Richard, the son of the gardener to the king in Trianon, brought back from England a cedar of Lebanon that was planted at the end of the botanical collection in the family of conifers.

In 1795 and 1805, the tree was spotted near the Porte Verte entrance railings, where it measured 18 metres tall.

In 1832 Henri-Antoine Jacques (1782–1866), formerly in charge of the Trianon nurseries during the Empire, wrote: "it is remarkable only for the place it occupied in the old school; its height is only 60 to 72 feet [18–21 metres]".

In 1876 *L'Inventaire des cultures de Trianon* indicated that the tree was 30 metres tall and was planted during the reign of Louis XV.

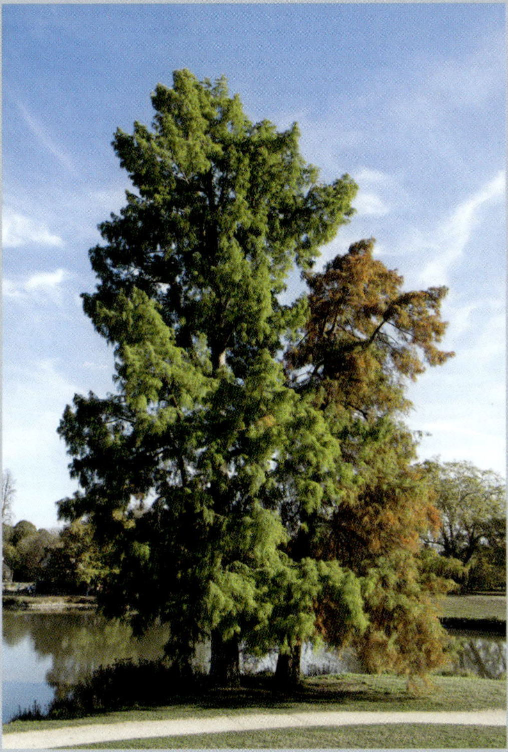

Bald Cypress
Taxodium distichum

Native to Florida and Louisiana, this deciduous conifer was introduced in England in 1637.

John Williams, in his English nursery located in Sèvres, categorised it as a "precious tree" in 1788.

From 1857, the Versailles guidebooks invited the visitor to go see in the Hamlet on the shore of the lake the bald cypress and its roots, hollow outgrowth around the trunk or pneumatophores, which bring oxygen to the roots, which lack air in the marshy soils in which they grow. Notices indicating the name of the species were placed on most of the trees in the garden.

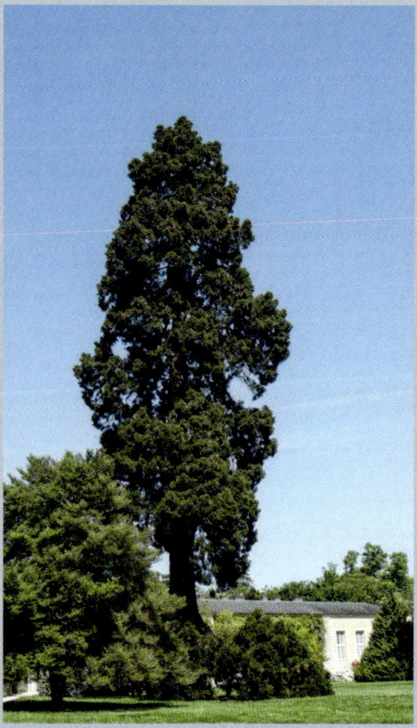

Giant Sequoia
Sequoiadendron giganteum

Discovered in California in 1841, the tree's seeds reached England in 1853. Planted by Alexandre Charpentier (1796–1883), head gardener of the two Trianons, the tree then known as *Wellingtonia gigantea* was only a few inches high in 1857. Its foliage comprises slightly prickly imbricated scales.

In 1876 it rose 8 metres high in the flower garden, also known as the Jardin Fleuriste or Jardin Charpentier. After the creation in 1922 of the Jardin de Jussieu in Chèvreloup (now known as the Arboretum de Versailles-Chèvreloup), this part of the Petit Trianon garden took the name Jardin de Jussieu.

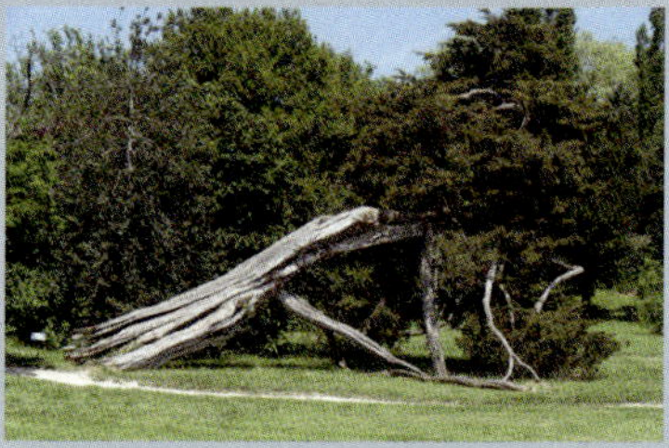

Red Cedar
Juniperus virginiana

Native to North America, this conifer with scale-like leaves, round branches, and blue fleshy fruit, was present in England from 1664. At the end of 1777, Richard Mique asked for two red cedars from the royal nurseries for the new Jardin de la Reine in Trianon.

The revolutionary inventory compiled in 1795 cited several red cedars in this part of the garden.

The Versailles/Trianon nurseries grew 1,051 plants from two stools in 1819, and 1,410 in 1847.

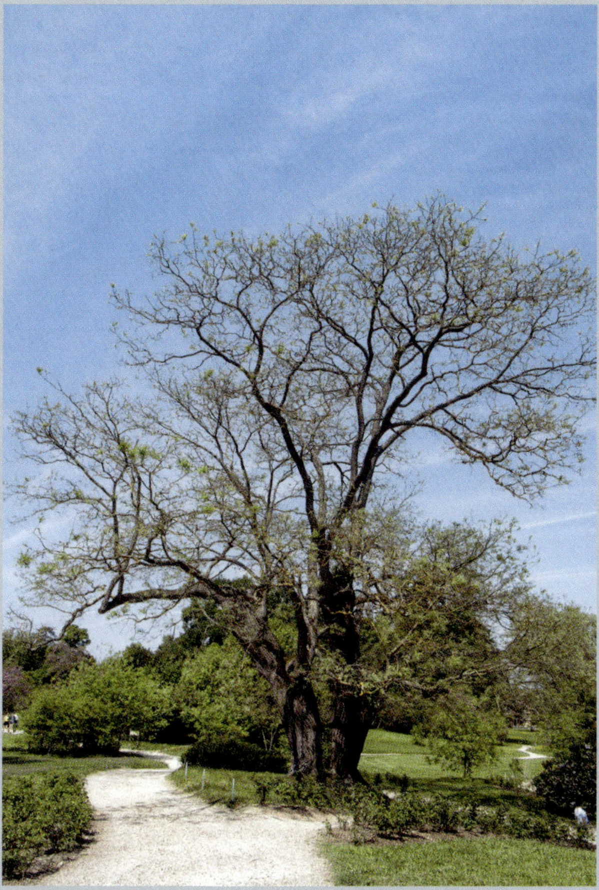

Japanese Pagoda Tree
Styphnolobium japonicum

In 1747 Father d'Incarville, a Jesuit missionary in China, sent seeds from an *Arbor sinarum incognita* (unknown Chinese tree) to Bernard de Jussieu in Paris from Beijing. They were distributed in France then in England, from where Antoine Richard brought back stock in 1764. It was planted in the botanical garden of Louis XV overlooking the east façade of the château. It was only after its first blooming in France, in the summer of 1779, that the tree was connected to the species *Sophora japonica* described by Linné in 1767. The tree that can now be seen at Trianon, grown from seeds or marcots, had been planted on a knoll in front of the Queen's Apartment in April 1783.

By having planted a tree from China beside the *jeu de bague chinois*, Marie-Antoinette gave an oriental touch to this part of the garden overlooking the north façade of the Petit Trianon.

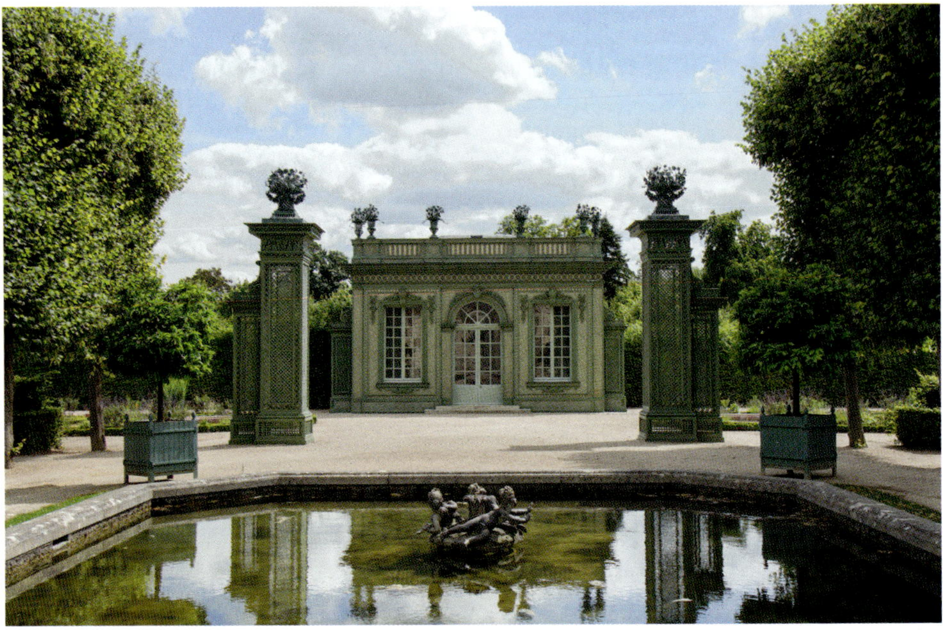

The Cool Room.

One day, he even remarked to the Duc de Croÿ "that it was in this style that he . . . should build". The interior layout is simple: a central salon, an antechamber, a boudoir, a water closet coupled with a small room for the preparation of coffee and a warming room. The groups of children by Jules-Antoine Rousseau placed on the cornice each symbolise a season or an element. The sculpted decoration of the façades recalls the four seasons: summer to the south, winter to the north, spring to the east, and fall to the west. After the death of Louis XV, Marie-Antoinette used the pavilion, in front of which she occasionally had tents or wooden shelters raised for concerts or balls.

The Cool Room

Opposite the French Pavilion to the south, two trelliswork pilasters signal the Cool Room, another building designed to adorn the new gardens of Louis XV. Completed in 1752 after plans by Gabriel, it served the king as a dining room in the summer. Covered with trelliswork, the pavilion was part of an ensemble of arcades, also made of trelliswork, which formed a genuine rectangular *cloître de verdure*, whose entrance, opposite the edifice, was marked by two pilasters. In the centre, two parterres de broderie adorned the oval basins that Louis XV wanted filled with goldfish. Fragile, this charming ensemble was half in ruins when Napoleon gave the order to have it razed to the ground. The pavilion was destroyed in 1810. In 1813 the trelliswork was taken down and the basins filled, covered with a grassy parterre. In 1980 a new edifice was rebuilt on the foundations of the old one. Thirty years later, in 2010, new works restored the parterres and basins (found during the excavations), as well as the very elaborate trelliswork of the pavilion. This first stage is meant to be followed by the complete reconstitution of the trelliswork galleries, simply evoked for the time being by the two entrance pilasters.

The location of the *jeu de bague* and the theatre gallery

Near the north-east corner of the Petit Trianon, edged by yew hedges, a circle of lawn with a tulip tree planted in its centre recalls the *jeu de bague* that Marie-Antoinette had installed on this site in 1776. A precursor of the merry-go-round, it had been designed in the Chinese style and featured eight seats: four dragons and four peacocks in the shape of baskets moving around a central axis; it was topped with a vast Chinese-style parasol. It was operated by two men posted in a ditch under the floor of the merry-go-round. Nearby a trelliswork gallery leads to the entrance of the theatre, inaugurated in 1780.

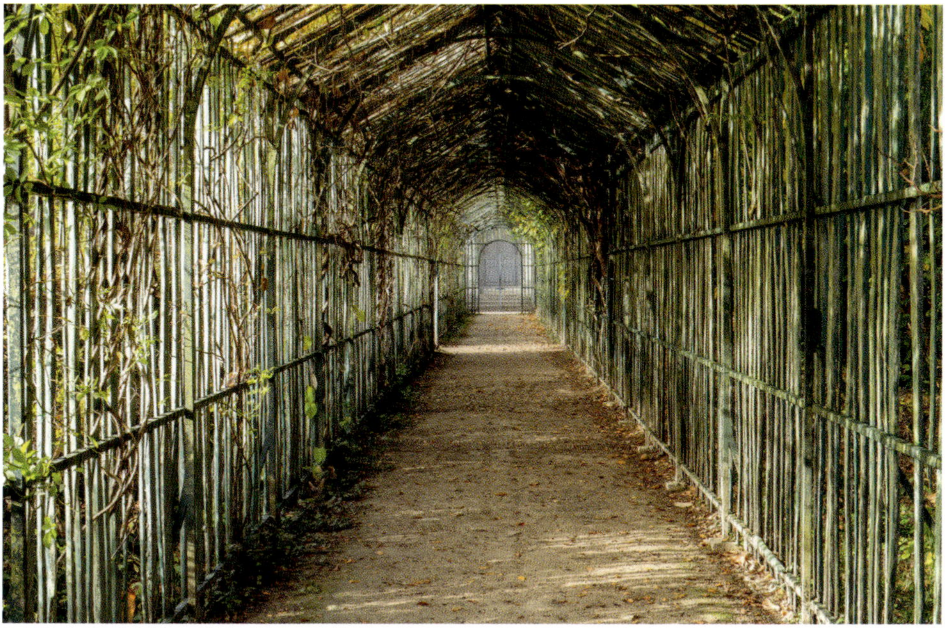

The gallery leading to the Queen's Theatre.

The English Garden

When Marie-Antoinette took possession of the Petit Trianon in the summer of 1774, she quickly decided to transform it to her liking. While the château underwent no major changes, the gardens were profoundly modified, entirely getting rid of the layouts of Louis XV. The queen wanted to create a modern garden, in the natural style of gardens à l'anglaise, also known as "Anglo-Chinese" or "picturesque". She rejected the first projects submitted to her because she thought they were too complicated and busy. In the meantime, she had the opportunity to see a certain number of famous gardens around Paris and in Paris, where she notably visited the garden of a renowned amateur, the Comte de Caraman. Charmed by the count's taste, which corresponded to her own, she charged him with designing a plan for Trianon. Caraman's proposition immediately pleased Marie-Antoinette and the works were soon started.
The result left the Duc de Croÿ, who knew the place well, stupefied: "I thought I must be mad or dreaming, to find in the place of the large hothouse, which was the most sophisticated and expensive in Europe, rather high mountains, a large rock, and a river. Never before have 2 acres of land so changed shape, nor cost so much money!"

There are two different ways to access the English Garden. Visitors can enter it from the French Garden by walking around the Petit Trianon, or they can use a door opening directly on to the main courtyard of the château. The second way is the most spectacular because visitors pass suddenly from the mineral world of the courtyard to the vast landscape until then concealed by the wall, which serves here as a theatre curtain. It is, moreover, definitely a theatre because, despite its apparent naturalness, the entire garden has been skilfully laid out. Winding alleys, river, rocks and other reliefs, woods or open terrains: everything was designed to make each viewpoint a genuine horticultural painting in which the follies chosen by the queen naturally have their place. Having entrusted the embellishment of her gardens to the architect Richard Mique, Marie-Antoinette asked him to adorn them with a few edifices now considered masterpieces of equilibrium and elegance, which the Prince de Ligne dubbed the "peak of perfection, taste and refinement".

The Temple of Love

To the east of the Petit Trianon, nearly underneath the façade that, during the reign of Louis XV, overlooked the vegetable garden, flows an artificial river whose meanders lead to the lake. It begins in the middle of the meadows from which the Temple of Love appears in the distance. In 1777 Mique started working on the places for the edifice. On 5 May, he presented the queen with a wood, plaster and wax model made according to his instructions by the sculptor Joseph Deschamps. Unusually, Marie-Antoinette immediately accepted the project with no restrictions. Mique had adopted the design of the monopteros temples, such as that of Vesta in Rome or that of Tivoli, themselves heirs to the Greek tholoi. The edifice, built on an island in the river planted with paradise apple trees and snowball roses, stands on a base of seven steps. Twelve Corinthian columns support a surbased cupola in Conflans stone, covered in lead painted to look like stone. The interior of the cupola is treated in coffers sculpted with roses, surrounding

The Temple of Love.

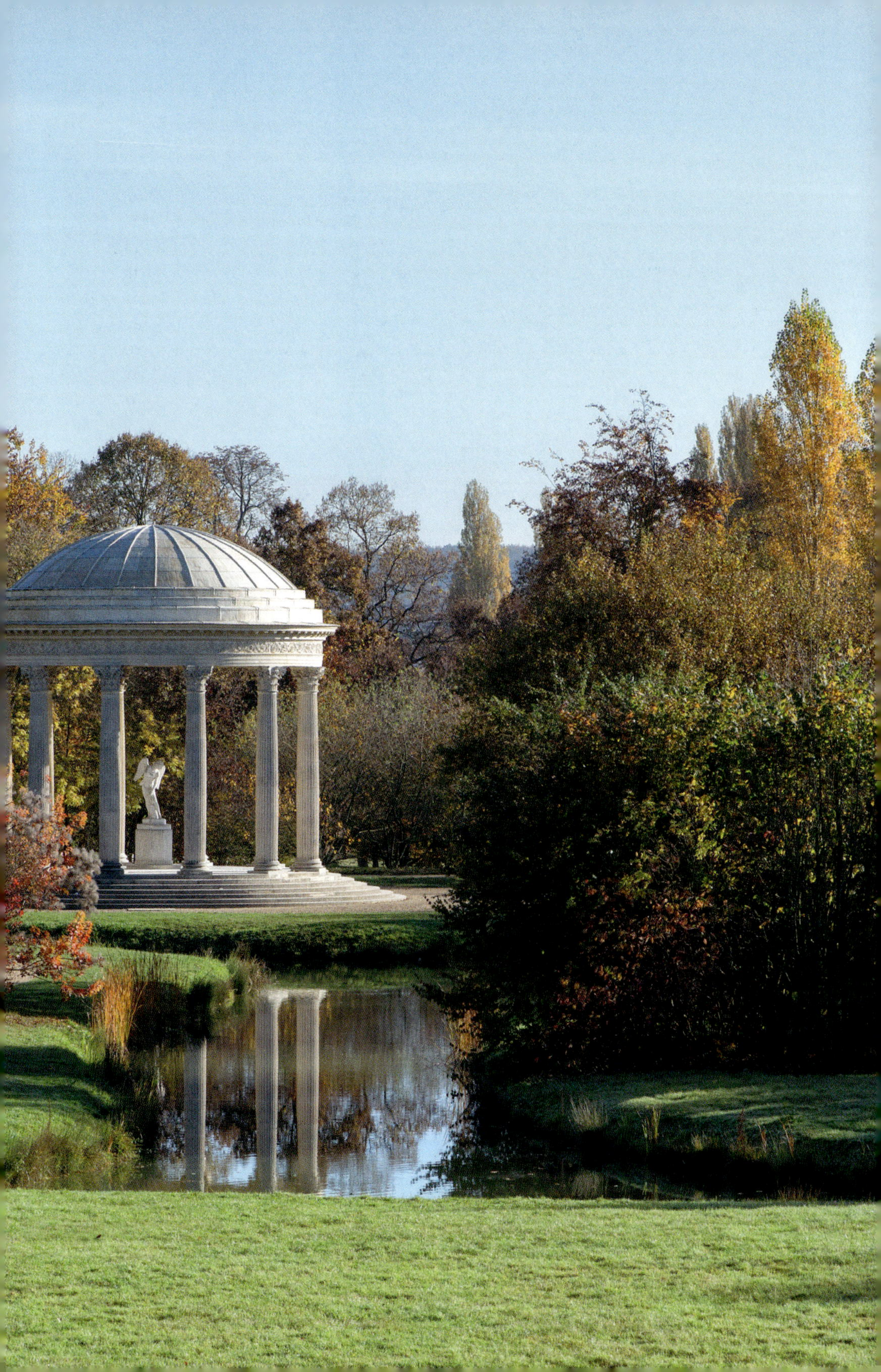

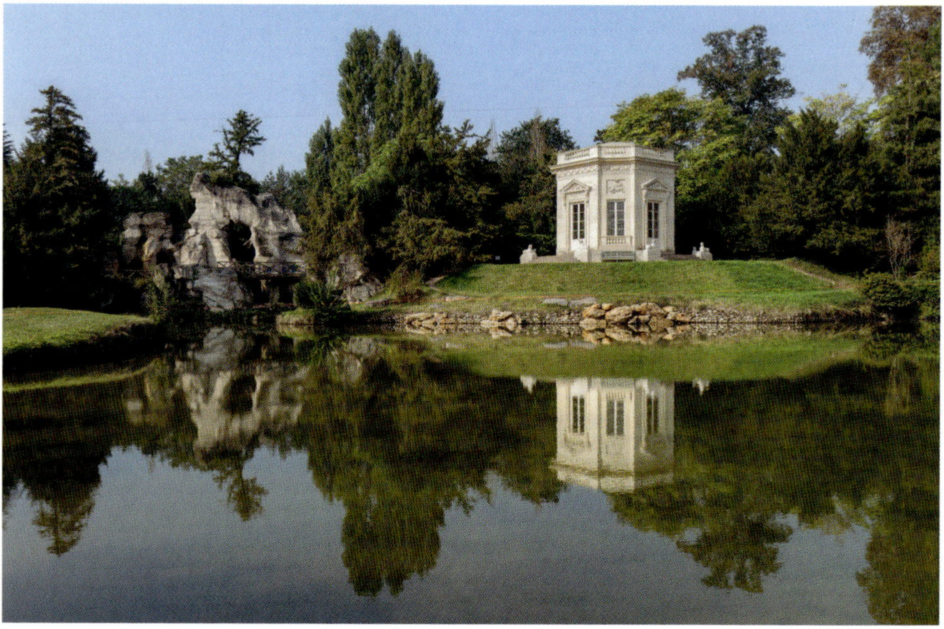

The Rock and the Belvedere.

a central trophy of nearly 2 metres in diameter comprising quivers, arrows, and flaming firebrands tied together by intertwined ribbons and decorated with roses and olive branches, made by Deschamps. The entablature is made up of an architrave whose soffit is decorated with roses, an arabesque frieze – both inside and out – and a composite cornice. The floor of the temple, the work of the marble cutter Le Prince, comprises veined white marble and red Languedoc marble. Construction was completed in July 1778.

To adorn the centre of the temple, the queen refused the group proposed by Deschamps and had installed a copy of Bouchardon's statue *Cupid Cutting His Bow from the Club of Hercules* (1750), originally intended for the Hercules Room and relegated to the Château de Choisy in 1752. Marie-Antoinette had the work sent to the Louvre so that it could be copied by the sculptor Louis-Philippe Mouchy. Mouchy's copy left the Trianon during the Revolution, spent some time in Saint-Cloud, then was replaced in its original setting in 1816. The restoration of the Temple of Love was completed in 2006.

The Rock and the Belvedere

By walking along the river from the Temple of Love after having encountered a small cascade, a stone bridge, and left behind to his left the small hill containing a *salle verte*, the visitor reached the lake that marks the end of the stream. The bank offers a view of the ensemble formed by the Rock, the rustic bridge and the Belvedere, which dominates the lake. This view, moreover, had often won over painters and draftsmen, such as Claude-Louis Châtelet, two of whose paintings showing this landscape are kept in Versailles, exhibited in the attic of the Petit Trianon.

At the queen's request, Mique created and enormous artificial rock to overhang the lake. It was meant to evoke a wilder nature and a sacrifice to the taste for the picturesque. The works, begun in

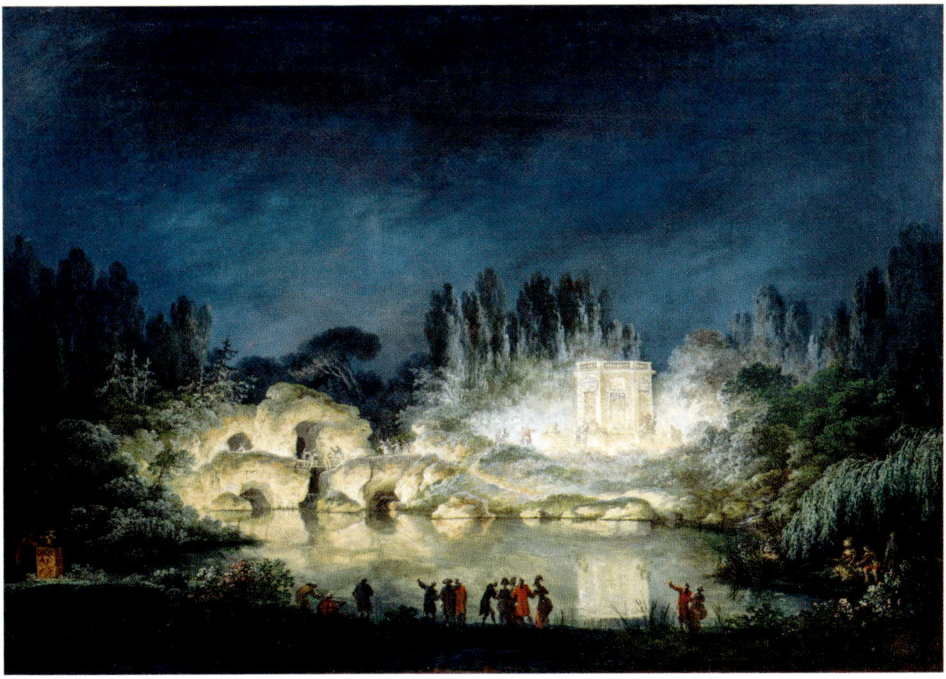

Claude-Louis Châtelet, *Illumination of the Rock and the Belvedere in 1781.*

1779, dragged on. Demanding, Marie-Antoinette rejected fourteen models of the project before she was satisfied. The Rock was completed in 1782. Surrounded by large trees, it has a rugged design and is pierced with two arches. The back of the highest looks over a small reservoir of water, which supplies a cascade falling into the lake; the other is a passage that allows visitors to take a path leading to the neighbouring Jussieu Pavilion. The breakwaters of the base support a rustic bridge providing access to the Belvedere Hill. When the water is turned on, a cascade flows from the top of the rock, veiling the great arch with a curtain to great effect.

Another masterpiece by Richard Mique, the Belvedere dominates a vast landscape, bordered to the south by the Petit Trianon. Its construction began in March 1778 and ended in May 1781. As for the other follies, Mique submitted several successive models for the queen's approval. Built on a stone base to which four staircases flanked with female sphinxes give access, the edifice is octagonal in shape and contains a circular salon open to the outside by four windows and four French windows. The sculpted decoration is the work of Joseph Deschamps. Each door is topped by a triangular pediment whose decoration has been inspired by hunting and gardening: a dog chasing a waterfowl, a trophy of game, a trophy of gardening tools and a crown of roses. Above each window, a bas-relief evokes one of the four seasons. The entablature frieze is decorated with a lead garland with a floral motif, attached to the stone and painted. A balustrade crowns the edifice, concealing a surbased cupola also painted to look like stone. The interior features a lavish stucco decoration highlighted with oil paintings with floral motifs and a floor with a polychrome marble paving.

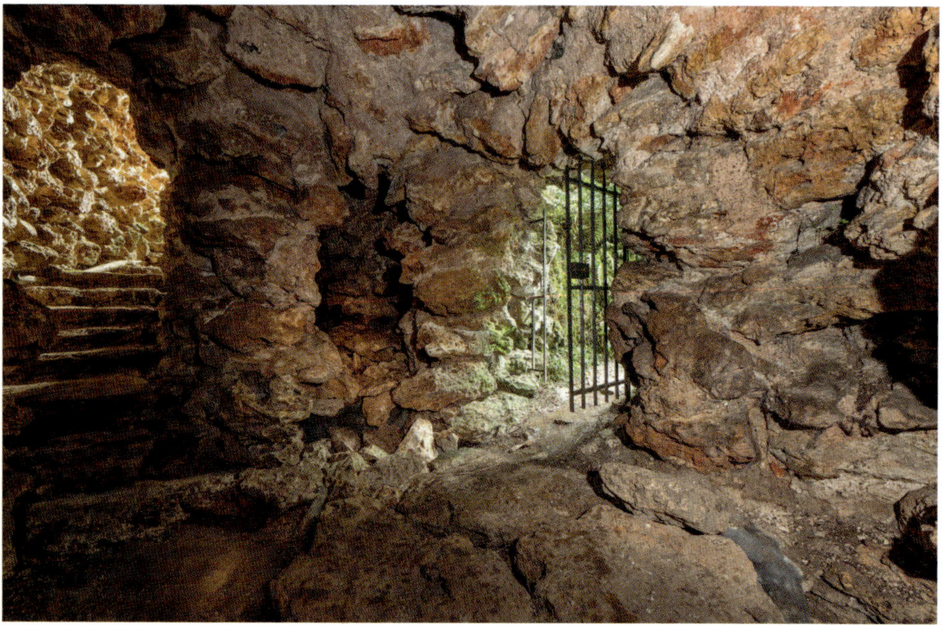

The interior of the Grotto.

The Grotto and the Snail Mountain

In the eighteenth century, the grotto was one of the most popular elements in Anglo-Chinese gardens. Marie-Antoinette, who had had the opportunity to visit several versions in various gardens of the Paris region, commissioned one for Trianon and chose to have it laid out not far from the rock on which the Belvedere was built. Work on the grotto was completed in 1782, at the same time as the neighbouring Snail Mountain. The contemporaries who visited the folly were unanimous in praising its style and picturesqueness. The Prince de Ligne spoke of a "perfect grotto, well-located and very natural". When going down the path from the Belvedere, visitors discover on the left the entrance to a small valley at the bottom of which flows a stream. The footpath, which runs along the stream, makes a curve to the left and allows to appear a heap of rock from which the water seems to spring. A door, originally a wooden trellis and now an iron gate, allows visitors to enter the grotto itself. The space is dimly lit by a few openings made in the crevices of the wall. A bench (covered at the time with green plush imitating moss), which looked like it was carved out of the rocky mass, offer visitors an opportunity to rest. In a recess, a cavity lets flow a cascade whose waters then traverse the grotto to supply the stream. Finally, at the back, a staircase leads to another iron gate door that opens directly above the ensemble, on the Snail Mountain side. The queen would pay dearly for this innocent feature. Rumours flew about how it was used and, in 1789, a crowd of onlookers hurried to see what was just a picturesque element, like the many that could be found elsewhere. Highly damaged over the years, the ensemble, which had become nearly illegible in the twentieth century, was given a restoration completed in 2006: the interior artificial waterfall was recreated, and the entire valley was landscaped. Dominated by a hundred-year-old yew, the upper exit of the grotto allows the visitor to reach the Snail Mountain whose helicoidal layout, a faint echo of the labyrinths of the previous centuries, leads to a small belvedere.

The Hamlet

In 1783 Marie-Antoinette asked Richard Mique to extend her garden to the north and to build a genuine village there around a new lake. Works began in the summer of 1783 and were completed in 1786. The fashion for country homes meant to comprise a picturesque decoration in a garden arose in the second half of the eighteenth century. From 1754, Claude-Henri Watelet, a rich financier, artist, and man of letters, introduced the style at his Colombes property, the Moulin-Joly. In 1774 the Prince de Condé had a hamlet built in the Anglo-Chinese garden at Chantilly. Four years later, Mesdames, the daughters of Louis XV, had one build on their Bellevue estate. Marie-Antoinette, who knew each of these hamlets as she had visited them, thus naturally wanted her own at Trianon. As was her wont, she evaluated the projects that Mique (advised by Hubert Robert) submitted in the form of very realistic models. She could thus judge not only the overall implantation but also the architecture and aspect of each of the constructions. The thatched cottages, whose style is not clearly identifiable (a blend of varied rural architecture) but which features an undeniable unity, are arranged around the eastern shore of the large lake, like a genuine decor in the form of an arc of a circle whose ideal viewpoint is located on the other side of the lake, a meadow in which flow small artificial streams.

The Hamlet is divided into three distinct sectors. The first, located to the

Following pages:
View of the Hamlet from the Cascatelles Meadow. On the left, the model dairy and the Marlborough Tower. On the right, the queen's house.

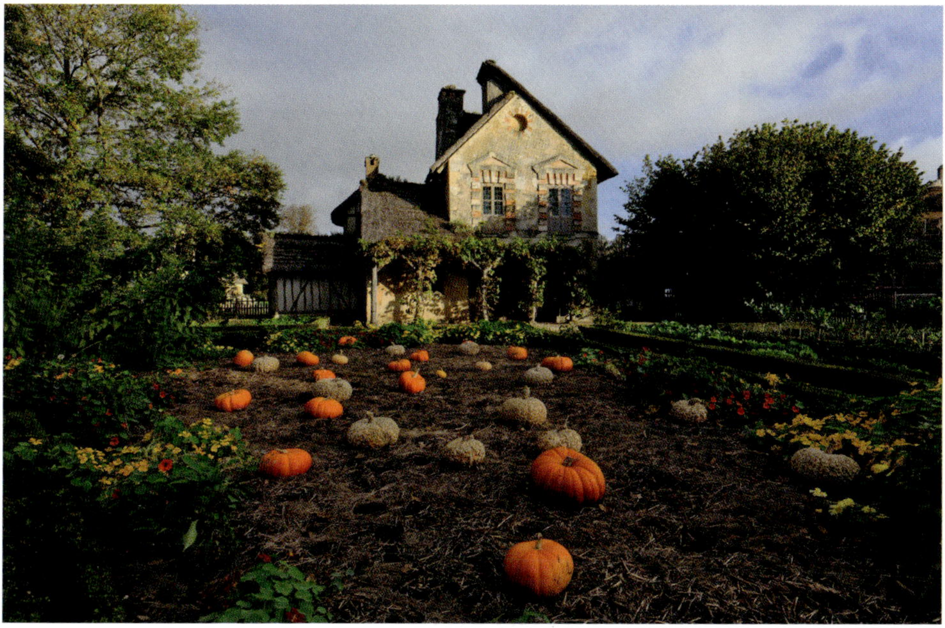

The guard's house, Queen's Hamlet.

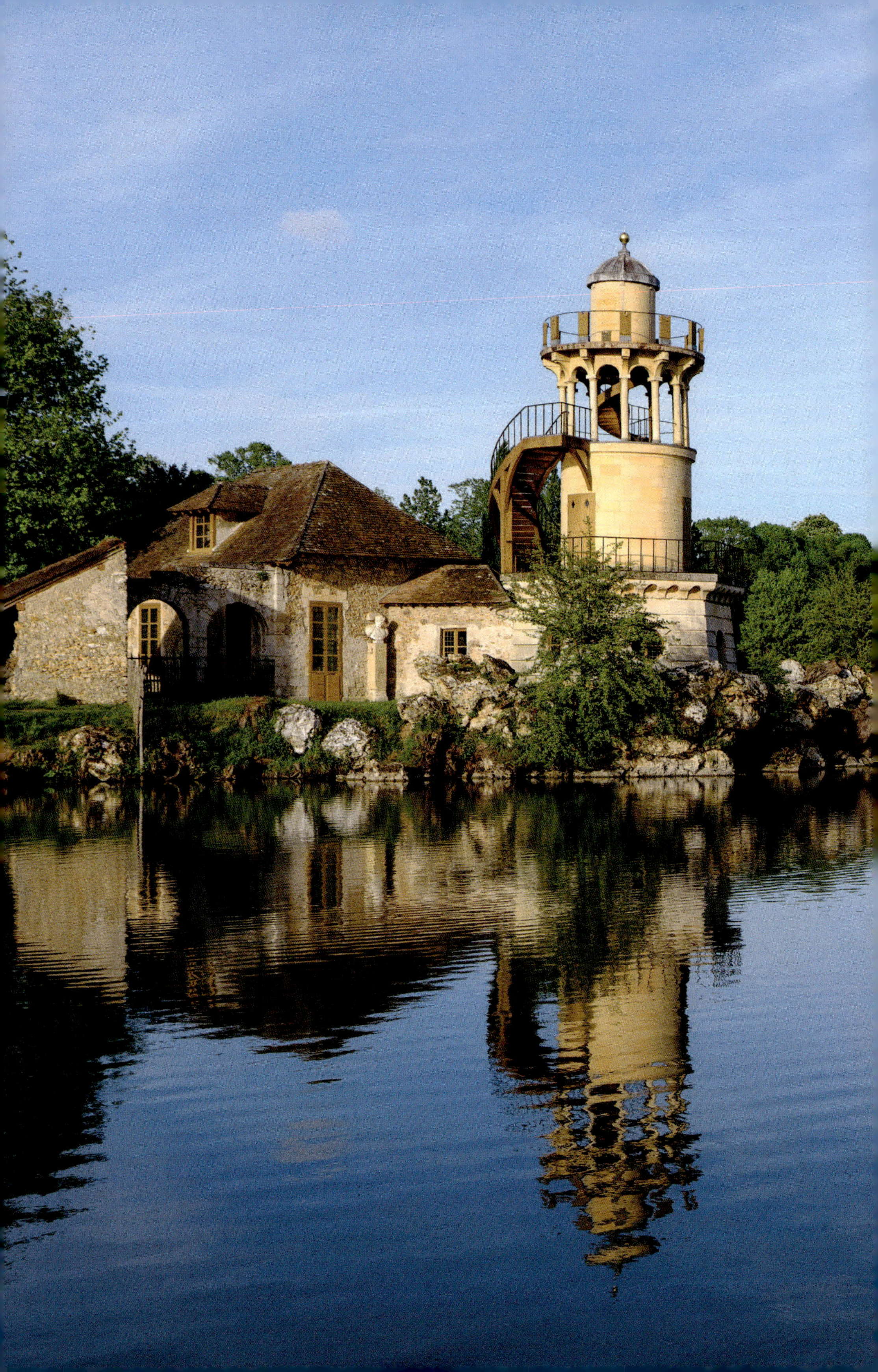

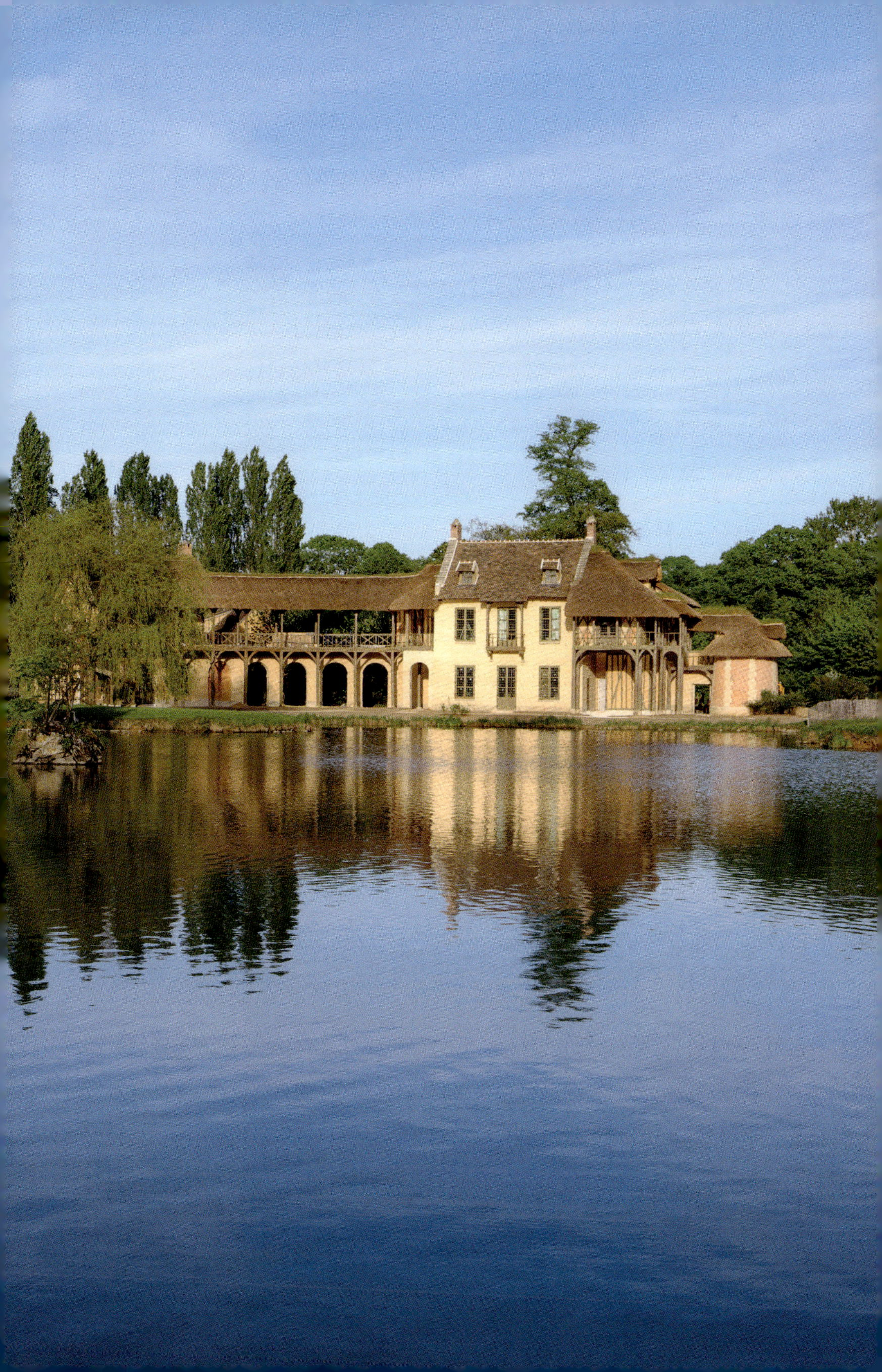

south of the stone bridge that spans the river, comprised buildings intended for pleasure: the mill (whose wheel is only a decorative element), the boudoir, the queen's house, the billiard room and the stove room. These buildings concealed interiors which were carefully decorated and often richly furnished, where the queen could host the society guests she invited to Trianon. On the other side of the bridge are the buildings used for agricultural purposes: the barn, the working dairy, the model dairy, the fishery and the guard's house. The tower overlooking the lake was named the Marlborough Tower – in reference to a popular song of the day "Marlbrough s'en va-t-en guerre" – is reminiscent of the Gabrielle Tower, which the Marquis de Girardin had built on his Ermenonville estate. Finally, located much further back, is the farm, a going concern until the eve of the Revolution, comprising stable, pigsty, sheepfold, and henhouse. It was run by a Touraine farmer, Valy Bussard.

Contrary to the deeply entrenched tradition that the queen and her entourage "played at being farmers" in this bucolic setting complete with sheep trussed up in ribbons, Marie-Antoinette above all used her hamlet as a place to stroll and receive guests. The fact that the Hamlet was a working farm, a point upon which the queen insisted, meant that it also played an educational role for the royal children. That is what made Trianon original in relation to other leisure hamlets, such as that at Chantilly, exclusively destined for the pleasures of the Prince de Condé and his guests. At Trianon, there are no "surprise" thatch cottages whose interiors feature luxurious decoration behind cob walls, even though, for the furniture of her house, the queen placed certain remarkable pieces such as the small desk by Riesener, veneered with purpleheart and sycamore, and adorned with gilded bronze (acquired by the Musée National des Châteaux de Versailles et de Trianon in 2011, this desk is now on display in the château in the Queen's Inner Rooms). During the Revolution, the Hamlet survived after a fashion. Like most edifices of this type, the constructions, which were not built to last, aged badly, damaged by bad weather. Napoleon had them fully restored between 1810 and 1812, tearing down the most badly damaged buildings, such as the barn and the working dairy. A second restoration campaign saved the Hamlet from inevitable ruin in the 1930s, thanks to John Rockefeller's donation. In the late twentieth century, part of the Hamlet was restored once again. Some of the houses were even restored to their original configuration, notably the mill. The farm, which had more or less disappeared in the nineteenth century, was entirely rebuilt in 2006. In 2018 the queen's house was completely restored. Now open to visitors, it has been refurnished in a state corresponding to that of the period of Empress Marie-Louise, the second wife of Napoleon I.

The Jussieu Garden

A little way from the English Garden, behind the "Snail Mountain", stretch the lawns of the so-called "Jardin de Jussieu", in memory of the eighteenth-century botanist who helped Louis XV organise the Trianon gardens. To the north, an orangery, built in around 1780, and to the south, a pavilion built in 1751 to house, by order of the king, the gardener Claude Richard, whom the king appointed to oversee the Trianon gardens. His son Antoine later occupied the same functions and notably, in 1795, managed to prevent the parcelling out of the entire estate, thus saving it.

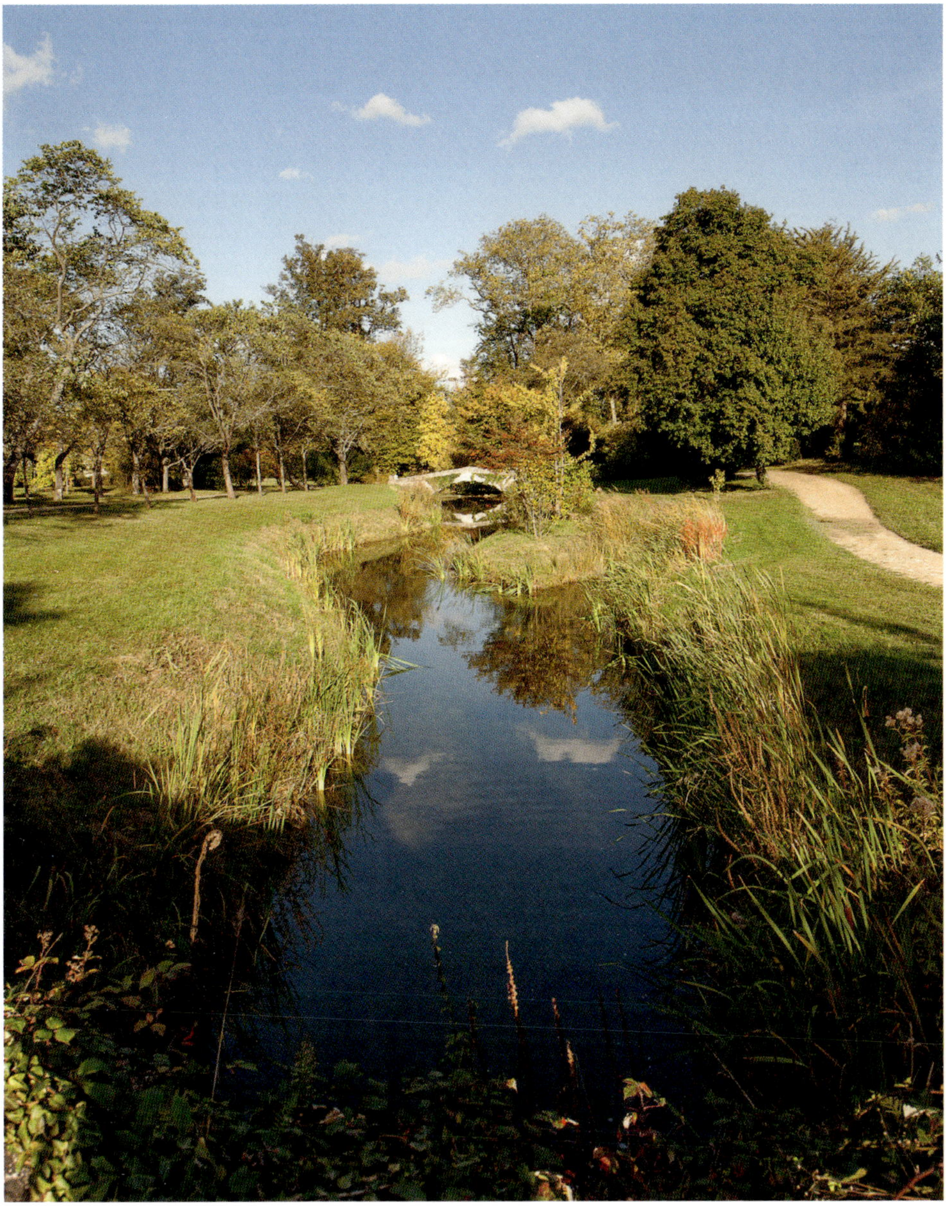

The river, English Garden, Trianon.

MARLY

In 1676 Louis XIV acquired the estate of Marly located north of Versailles. He intended to build a leisure house there where he could, as at Trianon, stay from time to time in the company of a small, select entourage. Construction of the château began in 1679, under the supervision of Jules Hardouin-Mansart and Robert de Cotte. The king first stayed there in 1686. A place to relax and be entertained, Marly gradually became the king's favourite residence; towards the end of his life, spent more time there than at Versailles.

For the king and his guests, Mansart had designed a central pavilion, square in plan, and twelve small pavilions arranged in two lines along the central axis of the gardens. These pavilions benefited from the king's attentions and, after the innumerable changes that he had made to it, were considered the finest of the royal residences, Versailles included. The water, thanks to the machine set up on the Seine, flowed there abundantly and allowed for often spectacular effects, such as the Grand Jet, rising nearly 40 metres, which was a real technical feat (in Versailles, the Dragon Basin can rise nearly 28 metres). The pronounced relief of the small valley in which the estate was located also favoured the creation of expanses of water and cascades. The most imposing was the famous Rivière, laid out from 1696 along the steep slope behind the château: it measured nearly 300 metres long and was made up of fifty-two tiers covered with marble. Very expensive to maintain, it was removed by Louis XV and replaced by the current Tapis-Vert.

In the eighteenth century, Marly was still visited by the king and the royal family but the gardens experienced a certain decline. As a cost-saving measure, certain groves were simplified or removed. The statuary was in part transferred to the Tuileries, like the two equestrian groups by Antoine Coysevox, *The King's Fame* and *Mercury Mounted on Pegasus*, which adorned the Watering Place at the bottom of the garden. They were replaced in 1745 by the two groups of *The Horses of Marly* by Guillaume Coustou, themselves transferred to Paris in 1794 and installed on the Place de la Concorde, at the entrance to the Champs-Élysées.

During the Revolution, the estate was sold as a property of the state and gradually split up. The twelve pavilions were destroyed in 1808. In 1811, wanting to protect what remained from disaster, Napoleon purchased Marly, but the château was so dilapidated he could not save it. The royal pavilion was finally demolished in 1816. Throughout the nineteenth century, the abandoned park progressively returned to its natural state. In 1879 the estate was allocated to the presidency of France for presidential hunts.

It was not until the interwar period that the first works attempted to restore the garden's legibility. Basing themselves on abundant archival documents (plans and drawings), major earthworks were undertaken to restructure the landscape. The site of the royal pavilion was materialised on the ground while certain basins were refilled with water. After the war, a program of installation of replicas of the original statues (most of which are now in the Louvre) was launched. In 1982 the creation of the Musée-Promenade de Marly-le-Roi-Louveciennes at the entrance to the Royal Railings led to renewed interest in the estate. In the early twenty-first century, the Watering Place was completely restored (2006). In 1987 it had already received the replicas of Coustou's horses, erected on the original site of the groups. In 2009 the presidency of France abandoned Marly and entrusted its management to Versailles.

While the garden is only a shadow of what it was in the time of Louis XIV, the visitor can nevertheless appreciate, thanks to the patient restoration work, the originality and beauty of the site. Coming from the Royal Railings, visitors take a steep alley, lined with imposing retaining walls, that lead to the location of the royal pavilion. From the platform, the view extends, to the north, over the great perspective, punctuated by the vast Basin de la Grande Pièce d'Eau and ending in the terrace overlooking the Watering Place. Here and there, in the middle of the lawns, edges indicate the locations of former basins: the rectangular Pièce des Gerbes, located between the Grande Pièce and the royal pavilion, and, nearby, the small circular basins of the former groves known as the "Appartements Verts". Above the Watering Place, the regularity of the difference in level clearly indicates the former triangular Bassin des Nappes and its water staircase, flanked by two small round basins. The double rows of trees framing the perspective mark the location of the small pavilions that were connected by trelliswork galleries. To the south of the royal pavilion, the Bassin du Grand Jet precedes a restitution of the Demi-Lune des Vents which marked the lowest point of the Rivière or Grande Cascade, whose site the Tapis-Vert now occupies. On the right, a diagonal alley leads to the site of the former Bacchus Grove, one of the rare ones to remain legible.

When leaving the estate, visitors should not forget to admire the Watering Place, which marked the end of the garden, from the exterior. Completed in 1698, it has two levels whose retaining walls feature rocaille decoration. It is topped by a wrought-iron balustrade adorned with fleurs-de-lis, framed by massive pilasters that support copies of Coustou's horses.

Pierre-Denis Martin, *Overall View of the Château and Gardens of Marly*, c. 1724.

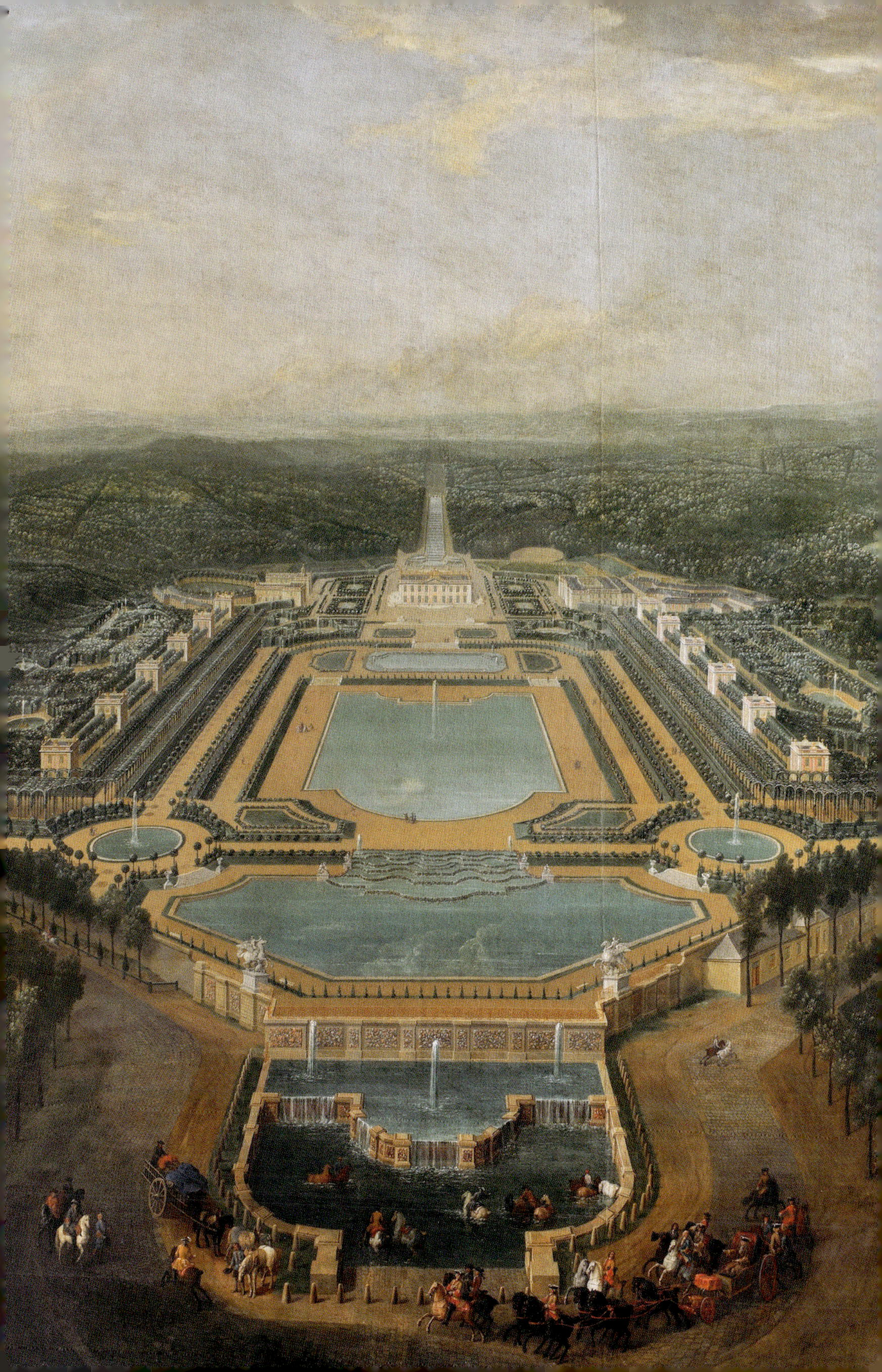

Bibliography

This deliberately brief bibliography only contains accessible references that will enable a curious reader to venture into the bountiful literature on Versailles.

A few old but indispensable references may be easily consulted online, notably on Gallica, the digital library of the Bibliothèque Nationale de France, including:

BARBET, LOUIS-ALEXANDRE. *Les Grandes Eaux de Versailles – Installations mécaniques et étangs artificiels, description des fontaines et de leurs origins.* Paris: Dunod et Pinat, 1907.

DESJARDINS, GUSTAVE. *Le Petit-Trianon – Histoire et description.* Versailles: L. Bernard, 1885.

NOLHAC, PIERRE DE. *Les Jardins de Versailles.* Paris: Goupil & Cie, Manzi, Joyant & Cie successeurs, 1906.

A complete and abundantly illustrated history of the gardens is available in:

LABLAUDE, PIERRE-ANDRÉ. *Les Jardins de Versailles.* Paris: Scala, 1995.

PINCAS, STÉPHANE. *Versailles, un jardin à la française.* Paris: La Martinière, 1995.

For the work of André Le Nôtre and Jules Hardouin-Mansart, often cited in this guide, readers may consult:

HAZLEHURST, FRANKLIN HAMILTON. *Des jardins d'illusion – Le génie d'André Le Nostre.* Paris: Somogy, 2005.

GADY, ALEXANDRE, ed. *Jules Hardouin-Mansart, 1646-1708.* Paris: Maison des sciences de l'homme, 2010.

The sculptures of Versailles and particularly the statues of the gardens in the following authoritative volume:

MARAL, ALEXANDRE. *Le Versailles de Louis XIV – Un palais pour la sculpture.* Dijon: Faton, 2014.

By way of a complement, the sculptures of the gardens are listed in their entirety and noted on a useful plan:

MARAL, ALEXANDRE. *Parcours mythologique dans les jardins de Versailles.* Paris: RMN–Grand Palais, Versailles: château de Versailles, 2019.

On water at Versailles:

LOBGEOIS, PASCAL, AND JACQUES DE GIVRY. *Versailles – Les Grandes Eaux.* Les Loges-en-Josas: JDG Publications, 2001.

About the Château de Marly:

MABILLE, GÉRARD, LOUIS BÉNECH AND STÉPHANE CASTELLUCCIO. *Vues des jardins de Marly – Le roi jardinier.* Montreuil: Gourcuff Gradenigo, 2011.

MAROTEAUX, VINCENT. *Marly – L'autre palais du Soleil.* Geneva: Vögele, 2002.

Readers may also consult the Centre de Recherche du Château de Versailles bibliographical database, which lists articles and makes older ones available online: www.chateauversailles-recherche-ressources.fr

Finally, readers may learn more about botany at Versailles thanks to:

Base Hortus, Centre de Recherche du Château de Versailles: this database brings together all the sources on plants in the great European gardens of the modern period. http://www.chateauversailles-recherche-ressources.fr/jlbweb/jlbWeb

JAUBERT, HIPPOLYTE-FRANÇOIS. INVENTAIRE DES CULTURES DE TRIANON. Paris: Imprimerie nationale, 1876.

VINCENT, JEAN. *Versailles – Les arbres du parc.* Paris: Éditions du Cosmos, 1960.

Credits

© Bibliothèque municipale de Versailles : p. 101
© Château de Versailles / DRIVE.PRODUCTIONS : p. 20-21 ;
© Château de Versailles / ToucanWings : p. 91
© Château de Versailles (dist. RMN-Grand Palais) / Christophe Fouin : p. 10, 15, 16, 34, 36, 48, 53, 55, 60, 70 haut, 74, 87, 97, 99 bas, 111, 114, 116 ; © Château de Versailles (dist. RMN-Grand Palais) / Thomas Garnier avec Skydrone : p. 13;
© Château de Versailles (dist. RMN-Grand Palais) /Thomas Garnier : p. 14, 18, 19, 24-25, 28, 30 haut, 32-33, 40-41, 42, 50-51, 57, 61, 62, 65 haut, 67, 70 bas, 76, 78, 79, 80, 81, 86, 93, 96, 104, 105, 110, 113, 117, 118-119;
© Château de Versailles (dist. RMN-Grand Palais) /Jean-Marc Manaï : p. 56, 66, 75, 84, 88-89, 94-95, 125 ;
© Château de Versailles (dist. RMN-Grand Palais) /Christian Milet : p. 30 bas, 31, 43, 72-73, 100, 121 ;
© Château de Versailles (dist. RMN-Grand Palais) /Didier Saulnier : p. 29, 38, 39, 44, 45, 46, 47, 49, 68-69, 98, 99 haut, 102-103, 106-109 ;
© Château de Versailles / Droits Réservés : p. 59 ;
© RMN-Grand Palais (Château de Versailles) / Daniel Arnaudet : p. 115 ;
© RMN-Grand Palais (Château de Versailles) / Gerard Blot : p. 58, 77;
© RMN-Grand Palais (Château de Versailles) / Hervé Lewandowski : p. 65 bas
© RMN-Grand Palais (Château de Versailles) / Franck Raux : p. 27 haut et bas
© Collection Jean-Baptiste Leroux / Château de Versailles (dist. RMN-Grand Palais) / Jean-Baptiste Leroux : p. 17, 35, 63, 82-83
© Versailles, Musée Lambinet / Christophe Fouin : p. 54
© Creative Commons BY- SA 3.0 : p. 85

Établissement Public du Château, du Musée et du Domaine National de Versailles

Publishing Department
Jean-Vincent Bacquart
Anne Carasso and Cécile Bouchayer
assisted by Marie Paret
With the collaboration of Géraldine Bidault, Christophe Fouin, Thomas Garnier, Christian Milet and Didier Saulnier

Réunion des Musées Nationaux – Grand Palais

Director of publishing: Sophie Laporte
Head of publications: Muriel Rausch
Editorial coordinator: Sophie Zagradsky
assisted by Clothilde Bollard-Duval
Translator: Chrisoula Petridis
Picture researcher: Consuelo Crulci-Perrois
Graphic designer: Agnès Rousseau
Layout: Catherine Enault, Hervé Delemotte
Production manager: Philippe Gournay
Photoengraving: Fotimprim, Paris

Printed by Ingoprint, Barcelona, Spain, in June 2019.

ISBN: 978-2-7118-7164-3
GK197164
Dépôt légal: June 2019